THE BOOK OF
BITTERNE

From Roman Town To City Suburb

BITTERNE LOCAL HISTORY SOCIETY

HALSGROVE

Title page: *Bitterne in 1972, viewed from the east.*

British Library Cataloguing-in-Publication Data.
A CIP record for this title is available from the British Library.

ISBN 978 1 84114 635 5

HALSGROVE

Halsgrove House
Ryelands Industrial Estate, Bagley Road,
Wellington, Somerset, TA21 9PZ
Tel: 01823 653777
Fax: 01823 216796
email: sales@halsgrove.com
website: www.halsgrove.com

Printed and bound in Great Britain by CPI Antony Rowe Ltd, Chippenham, Wiltshire

Foreword

It is delightful to transport oneself into the spirit of the past, to see how a wise man has thought before us, and to what a glorious height we have at last reached.

Johann Wolfgang von Goethe

You have in your hands a panoply of goodies from Southampton's most enterprising historical society; rounded portraits of people and places with very little left out.

So comprehensive is it that I expressed the view that there was no need for any further books on Bitterne. Society chairman Ian Abrahams put me right: 'You should see the amount of material we had to leave out!' Bitterne's memory well is obviously a bottomless one.

This *Book of Bitterne* is something for natives of the suburb as well as 'incomers', who will enjoy taking their dogs for walks over the pleasantly hilly landscape (Midanbury's Dell Road is positively alpine).

Names like Muddy Bottom and Donkey Common resonate still from my happy childhood east of the Itchen. Despite the building excesses, much of 'old Bitterne' still remains and the editorial team have ensured that little is forgotten.

John Edgar Mann

The wedding entourage of Mr H.C. White and Miss W. Osman outside Lorne House, Chapel Street, 31 July 1907. Left to right, standing: Mary White, Emma Marks, Revd Vincett Cook, Herbert White, Winnie Osman, George Gould, David Osman, Mrs Vincett Cook, Tom Stokes; sitting: Maria White, May White, Lily Gould, Gertie Osman, Rose Waterman, Lizzie Stokes, Dolly Gould, Susie Waterman, Ethie ?.

Broomfield and Gatehouse's van, decorated for Dunlop Tyre Week, 1960

The end of an era: the closing down sale of Ted Broomfield and Bert Gatehouse's cycle repairers in Commercial Street, August 1988 after 28 years.

Contents

Acknowledgments

Many people have contributed towards this book by helping us in our aim to reflect a broad spectrum of history and life in Bitterne. The editorial team would especially like to thank all the authors who have made their research or their memories available to us for inclusion; some were kind enough to record these and have since passed on, so acknowledgment is offered to their kin. Although we have endeavoured to ensure that all the information given is correct, memories can play tricks, so we apologise if any inaccuracies have crept in.

Unless otherwise attributed, the illustrations are from the BLHS's own archive. Thanks go to members and friends who have loaned them, and also to the Hampshire Record Office, Southampton City Council, West End Local History Society and *Southern Daily Echo*. The Ordnance Survey maps are reproduced with kind permission of Ordnance Survey.

Finally, Alan Leonard deserves hearty thanks for proofreading the manuscript and for his constructive advice.

The editorial team beside the water trough, erected in 1905 by public subscription, to refresh horses after the climb up Lances Hill. Left to right: Keith Marsh, Joy Bowyer, Ian Abrahams, Deirdre Abraham, Denis Abraham, Pete Crawford.

Editorial Team

Ian Abrahams

Ian's ancestry is deeply rooted in Bitterne, his family having lived here over 120 years, and during that time they have played a major role in village life. His great-grandfather 'Honest' John Brown was a Parish Councillor a century ago, and his grandmother celebrated over 70 years as a member of the Congregational (now United Reformed) Church. Ian's family have always been staunch supporters of this church, and Ian's wedding to Sarah Cardy (another old Bitterne name) was the last held in the church before it was demolished for the bypass. Growing up in the 1960s, Ian attended the Bitterne schools followed by Merry Oak School and even at this age was conscious of the vast changes that were taking place. He had been collecting items of local interest for some time before opening Bitterne's first museum in 1977 in the front room of the Manse, the house he rented in Dean Road. As a youthful driving force behind the creation of the BLHS in 1981, he was elected Chairman at its inception, and still holds this position. Despite the time and attention he devotes to the society, he continues the family tradition of being a leading figure in the UR Church, is involved with various societies such as the Austin A35 Owners' Club, and still finds time to work for the Solent MIND Project at Mayfield Nursery.

Joy Bowyer

Joy has lived in Bitterne since the age of one, with gaps for three spells of wartime evacuation, college and a year teaching in Spokane, Washington State as an 'exchange alien'. She lived in Peartree Gardens until the bypass and rebuilding of the schools caused demolition of the family home – apart from a brick-lined air-raid shelter furnished with piano candlesticks, which is under the school playground awaiting archaeologists of the future) – moving to a new one just outside the parish boundary. She moved back to the parish six years ago and can see the top of the spire of Bitterne Church from her front bedroom window. Joy is a lifelong member of the Parish Church, being the first female churchwarden, among many other church responsibilities and involvements. As a member of the BLHS and helpfully being computer literate, she got involved with this fascinating project – and her typing speed increased as the articles came flooding in!

Keith Marsh

Keith moved to Glenfield Avenue, Bitterne, with his parents in 1955 at the tender age of seven months, and attended Glenfield and Beechwood schools before progressing to Bitterne Park Comprehensive. A member of the Bitterne Cubs, Scouts then Ventures, he later served as Air Scout Leader, and participated in the local gang show, Roverang (which daughters Vickie and Suzie now enjoy). He was a member of Bitterne Covenanters and enjoyed several Easter cruises on the Broads. At age 16 he joined Ordnance Survey as a draughtsman (a now redundant occupation) and after a spell in charge of the Information Department, he now manages an online map data ordering service. Having met Julie through Scouting, they married in 1979 and live in Harefield. Keith was BLHS treasurer for 11 years, has guided walks around Bitterne, and gives talks on the history of Harefield. Having researched and written several books and local papers, an aspiration is to write his family's history.

Denis and Deirdre Abraham

Denis was born in Whites Road and left when he was ten years old. He returned to live in the Glenfield area with wife Deirdre and young son Frank, soon followed by Jim, John and Peter. Denis's interest in history is engendered by a family legend and in researching this Denis and Deirdre became interested in the history of their families, centred on Botley, Curdridge and Bishop's Waltham. This led to research in the area where they have lived for over 40 years. Denis is also interested in classical music (having been surrounded by musicians since childhood) and is enthusiastic about cricket (in the summer he is frequently found at The Rose Bowl). Deirdre loves handicrafts especially lace-making, which she demonstrates at Botley Manor Farm and at Bursledon Brickworks open days.

Pete Crawford

Although Pete does not live in Bitterne now, he was born in a nursing home there, in the care of Nurse Lamb and attended Itchen College when it was a grammar school. He is interested in local history and is a member of BLHS. During the compilation of this book he has mostly been surrounded by a pile of reference books and albums, tirelessly searching for some elusive piece of information or photograph.

A Timeline of Major and Local Events

Celtic Britain	c.1500BC	Date of the palstaves found on Peartree Green
Roman invasion of Britain	AD43	Vespasian established Clausentum
Roman Empire in decline	c.446	Clausentum abandoned
Edward the Confessor on the throne	1045	Land at Stanham granted to Winchester Cathedral
King Henry II on the throne	1171	'Byterne' mentioned in the Register of Pontissara
Louis of France captured on Crusade	1250	King Henry III's first stay at Bitterne Manor
King Henry III captured at Lewes	1264	The Archbishop of Canterbury stayed at the manor house
King Edward I's conquest of Wales	1284	The manor of Bitterne formed
Queen Elizabeth I on the throne	1575	First use of the spelling 'Bitterne'
King Charles I beheaded	1649	Bitterne Manor seized by the Commonwealth and sold
Restoration of King Charles II	1660	Bitterne Manor restored to the See of Winchester
Tory government in England	1710	Itchen Navigation Canal opens with a new bridge at Woodmill
First cricket club (Hambledon) formed	1760	Farm workers' cottages built at Bittern-in-Mousehole
Revolution in France	1790	Bitterne Grove built
Income tax first introduced	1799	Northam Bridge and the roads to Botley and Bursledon opened
Union of GB and Ireland	1800	The duel on Netley Common; Bitterne's population: 100
Slave trading made illegal in England	1806	Founding of Methodism in Bitterne
Napoleon's retreat from Moscow	1812	The Act of Enclosure for Bitterne
First running of the Grand National	1836	Post Office opened in Alma Road
Rubber vulcanisation developed	1839	Red Lion opened
End to transportation of criminals	1853	Bitterne parish formed and parish church consecrated
Indian mutiny	1857	Miss Usborne paid for the first infants' school to be built
East India Company wound up	1858	Hampshire Constabulary open a police station in Bitterne
London Underground opened	1863	Congregational Chapel erected
Cholera swept through London	1866	The Southampton & Netley Railway opened
Natural History Museum opened	1881	The Martin Hall built as a temperance working men's club
Boys' Brigade founded	1883	The Free Cobden Bridge opened
Zip fastener invented	1891	Lankester & Crook's The County Stores opened
Tower Bridge opened	1894	Bitterne became a civil parish with a council
Accession of King Edward VII	1901	Bitterne drainage system begun
First England v France rugby match	1905	Horse trough provided at the top of Lances Hill
First Selfridge's opened	1909	The 17th Southampton (Bitterne) Scout Troop formed
RMS Titanic sank with loss of 1,513	1912	The High Street 'flinted' by the Northam Bridge Company
Partition of Ireland	1920	Bitterne, Sholing and Woolston incorporated into Southampton
Wembley Stadium built	1923	Tram line to Bitterne Park extended down Bullar Road
Imperial Airways formed	1924	Many road names changed to remove duplication
Penicillin discovered	1928	Bert Hinkler's epic flight from England to Australia
Wall Street crash	1929	Freeing of the tolls on Northam Bridge and Lances Hill
Invention of first practical radar	1934	The Bitterne Park clock tower was relocated from Above Bar
King Edward VIII reigned and abdicated	1936	The Ritz cinema opened
Second World War started	1939	The Walrus crash on Lances Hill; Cobbett Road Library opened
Nationalisation of the railways	1948	Tram route along Bullar Road closed
Petrol rationing ended	1950	The animal pound last used; Harefield council estate started
Wartime rationing ends	1954	Harefield and Thornhill incorporated into Southampton
Ruth Ellis was last woman hung	1955	Sub-control bunker opened
The first Christmas message on TV	1957	Jacob's Coaches started in Shales Road; first Roverang Show
First succesful kidney transplant	1960	RC Church opened
Russians put first man into space	1961	The Ritz cinema closed
President Kennedy assassinated	1963	Eastern (now Bitterne) Library opened
Sir Winston Churchill died	1965	Sainbury's opens a shop in Bitterne; new police station opened
British troops sent to Northern Ireland	1969	Wesleyan Methodist chapel demolished
VAT introduced	1973	A Bend in the River first published for the Parish Church festival
Hot summer caused water shortage	1976	Eric Thompson on That's Life; Saints bring FA Cup to Bitterne
First London Marathon	1981	Bitterne Local History Society formed
Argentina invaded Falkland Islands	1982	Leisure centre opened; Congregational chapel demolished
IRA bombed Tory conference	1984	Maybray-King Way opened
Live Aid pop concert	1985	Health centre opened
Hurricane hit southern England	1987	The Lion returned to Bitterne
IRA bomb exploded in London	1993	BLHS's Heritage Centre opened; the Bitterne Hoppa inaugurated
The National Lottery introduced	1994	Chessel Bay designated a Local Nature Reserve
The euro introduced in 12 countries	2002	Woolston Millennium Garden opened; trees planted in Bitterne
Thousands died in Asian tsunami	2004	Diapers' cottage demolished; Gospel Chapel closed
Government considering toll-roads	2006	BLHS's silver jubilee

Chapter One

Clausentum

The earliest historical evidence of occupation in the area now known as Bitterne is a hoard of palstaves (decorated axe heads) dating from c.1500BC found on Peartree Green in 1894. The discovery of Belgic tribal graves confirms occupation by the Belgae (people of German and Gaulish origin) whose main defended settlement was at Winchester with a hill-fort in what is now Telegraph Wood, West End. Tumuli (burial mounds dating from 4,000BC to AD600) were found near Moorgreen Hospital and on Netley Common, and late Iron Age (c.400BC) settlements protected by earthworks have been discovered on lower ground, indicating the possibility that the ditch and bank at Bitterne Manor are pre-Roman: late Bronze Age implements (an axe, a fragment of spearhead, a cremation urn and a brooch) together with evidence of an Iron Age circular hut, support this theory. Near Cobden Bridge a sword and axe heads have also been found.

In 58BC Julius Caesar led the Romans to conquer Gaul (France, Belgium and parts of the adjacent modern countries); in 55BC, and again a year later, he led expeditions to Britain, leaving part of Southeast England in a state of nominal subjection. However the Romans were under threat at that time, so it was not until AD43 that, under Aulus Plautius, the Romans completed their invasion of Britain. Historians have identified the various independent tribes and kingdoms existing about 20BC as the Catuvellauni north of the Thames, the Atrebates in the Southeast and the Durotriges in Dorset. In the years before the full invasion there was considerable trade between these tribes (particularly the Atrebates) and the continent. British nobles wanted luxury goods from the Mediterranean, such as fine glass, pottery, wine and jewellery, and in return exported wheat, cattle, hides, hunting dogs, slaves, gold and silver (as recorded by Greek historian and geographer Strabo, between c.64BC and post-AD23). The Catuvellauni tried expanding their kingdom across the whole of the Southeast, driving out the Atrebates' leader Verica, who appealed to the Roman emperor for help. Thus the decision of Claudius to conquer the island was made partly to counter the Catuvellauni aggression in addition to his personal ambition. In AD43 an expeditionary force of four Roman legions, comprising about 6,000 men, together with a similar number of auxilia (auxiliary troops in cavalry and infantry regiments raised from the warlike tribes within the empire) and commanded by Aulus Plautius, landed near Richborough in Kent after an initial delay caused by the troops' unwillingness to cross the sea, which they regarded as the boundary of the human world! The Catuvellauni were defeated and retreated into Wales, whilst other tribes submitted. Having crossed the River Thames, the Roman army waited two months before Emperor Claudius arrived from Rome (with his elephants) to lead the final major attack on Colchester. To subdue the remainder of the country smaller expeditionary forces were formed consisting of single or part legions, with their auxilia.

Romans were last seen in Bitterne in 1989 when Justine Young and Elton Gray from Itchen College took part in the revived Bitterne Carnival.

The best documented campaign is that of Legion II under its legate Vespasian, who set out from Chichester proceeding westwards, taking the Isle of Wight and conquering the hill-forts and towns of Dorset in a series of 30 battles, before advancing into Devon. Vespasian made the former Belgic town at Winchester the regional capital, renaming it Venta Belgarum, and it is likely that the town built at Bitterne Manor was his supply base, the sheltered position on a bend in the River Itchen with double tides making it an ideal port. The remains of timber quays have been found, which suggest that it was a major port capable of accommodating ocean-going vessels.

The only Roman reference to the name Clausentum occurs in *The Antonine Itinerary*, a book which gives details of all the routes in the empire with distances between places; a late-second-century road atlas! This lists Clausentum as being the first station on Itinerary VII, the road from Noviomagus Regnorum (Chichester) to Londinium (London), describing it as being XX (i.e. 20) miles from Noviomagus Regnorum and X (i.e. 10) miles from the next station, Venta Belgarum; a Roman mile equals 1.086 statute miles. Although it is now generally accepted that Clausentum was the Roman town at Bitterne Manor, the name might have referred to the Roman site at Wickham, which also roughly matches these distances. An Ordnance Survey map of Bitterne Manor surveyed in 1866–74 states 'Roman Station supposed to be Clausentum'.

The road east to Noviomagus Regnorum has been excavated on Netley and Fremantle Commons, a tablet being set up on the latter marking its position.

This plaque in Peartree Avenue shows the crossing point of the Roman road to Chichester.

The road north to Venta Belgarum is now thought to have been via a ferry across the River Itchen to St Denys; the myth of a ford may come from from investigations by Dr John Speed in 1770 referring to a very old person giving evidence on oath in a trial c.1730 that within his lifetime the river had been fordable. Although the river may be fordable given certain tidal conditions, there can be a 16ft tidal range. Remains of massive oak piles, carbon-dated to AD210, have been found at Bitterne Manor and near Colliers Close, St Denys. With much of the stone used in building Venta Belgarum being quarried on the Isle of Wight, it is most likely that this would have been unloaded on the west bank rather than at Clausentum (and then having to transport it across the river). The name Clausentum is believed to be derived from the Latin *clausus* (shut up) and *intus* (inside).

In 1607 William Camden associated Clausentum with Southampton in his *Britannia*, the first comprehensive topographical survey of England, but it was Dr Speed who first identified Clausentum with Bitterne Manor. However, the credit for doing so generally goes to Revd Richard Warner who in 1792 published *An Attempt to Ascertain the Situation of the Ancient Clausentum*. In *Historical Perspectives of Southampton* Burgess and Fairclough suggest that in AD150 Clausentum covered the area between the river and a fosse (a Roman moat), constructed across the promontory from close to the Chafen Road/Vespasian Road junction south to Kemps Quay. It has been suggested that the river flowed through this fosse at high tide and that the stream from Glenfield made the area marshy, increasing the town's security. There is also evidence that water from this stream was piped into the town. A harbour existed where Northam Bridge now stands, and it is thought that a suburb developed on the other side of the river across the ferry; certainly Roman relics have been found in St Denys.

Following the conquest of Wales in AD78, the advance into northern Scotland and the building of Hadrian's Wall (c.AD122–130), troops were removed from southern Britain and self-governing civitates (administrative areas based mainly on the indigenous tribes) were formed. For a while Britain became a separate empire when Carausius, having been refused recognition as co-emperor when in command of the fleet of war galleys protecting the coast against Saxon pirates, led a rebellion c.AD286/7. He proclaimed himself Emperor of the Britons, being protected by his naval power and a system of Saxon Shore forts he created. Coins bearing his head have been found at Clausentum, as have coins of Claudius, Nero, Vespasian, Sabina, Antonius, Commodus, Lucilla, and other emperors. Roman rule was re-imposed when Emperor Constantius I invaded in AD296.

Clausentum c.AD150.   *(L.A. BURGESS & H.S. FAIRCLOTH, SO'TON CITY COUNCIL)*

Life at this port was probably typical of any small Romano-British town; streets of gravel or stone, timber-framed houses with walls of wattle and daub under red-tiled or stone-slated roofs. Floors may have been gravel, cement or mosaic-paved, the wealthier homes having glazed windows and painted walls. Public buildings, such as the baths, temples and markets, would have been of stone, possibly decorated with marble brought from the Mediterranean.

The fourth century was a period of great prosperity in towns and countryside alike, and Britain seemed a safe refuge for wealthy continentals, yet its defence was controlled from Rome. In AD407 Constantine III was declared emperor by the army and removed troops to Gaul, leaving insufficient numbers to protect Britain against the Picts and Saxons. Appeals were made to the legitimate emperor, Honorius, but he could not provide sufficient help and instead authorised towns to provide their own defence. By c.AD450 Clausentum was enduring attacks by Jutes and Saxons, so to counter these a wall, earth bank and second fosse were constructed. Traces of the fosse are just discernable on the bend of the main road where, according to legend, the ghost of a Roman soldier patrols at night (though he seems to walk on his knees as the ground level has been raised over the years).

This second fosse reduced the town's area to about eight acres, small for a town but indicating its importance as a port for Venta Belgarum, whilst between the fosses was an area of approximately 20 acres. Sir Henry Englefield investigated the Roman remains during rebuilding work on the manor house and the establishment of a kitchen garden in 1804/5:

The Roman wall itself is singular in its construction... Its thickness is about nine feet and its materials flint, faced very roughly with small square stones, and a bonding course of large flat bricks running through its

interior part; but it is extraordinary that it has no foundation whatever, but is literally set down on the surface of the ground... A large bank of earth is thrown up against it on the inner side, and... it seems as if, at a distance of about nine feet within the outer wall, another wall of about two feet thick has been erected, seemingly as a sort of strengthening to the rampart of earth.

At each end of the wall was a round tower of solid masonry, the northern one being 18ft in diameter, and a third semi-circular tower 24ft in diameter projected from the wall towards the middle. This was probably the gateway; large foundation-stones, presumably the base, have recently been rediscovered. A similar wall, without the earth bank, protected the coastline, a 69ft stretch having been excavated in 1937/8 when a structure known as the water gate, which had been incorporated into the cellars of the manor house, was investigated, but this is thought to date from the twelfth century.

Roman artefacts found in the area of Bitterne Manor include two Roman pigs of lead, inscribed with the name of the Emperor Vepasian, discovered in 1918 where Clausentum Quay now stands. In the 1920s much of the site of Clausentum, including a fosse, was built over, but subsequent subsidence resulting in underpinning yielded a number of Roman pots, wine flagons and Samian plates. The 1937/8 excavations produced a badly corroded Valens coin (dating from AD364–79), a few scraps of wall plaster, marble mouldings, a large quantity of late-period New Forest pottery, an iron arrowhead and various items of bronze jewellery. Recently bones were found by a company digging near the manor house, and a householder in Hawkeswood Road found Roman building remains whilst digging his front garden, leading to a company applying for planning permission for a site opposite, being required to conduct an archaeological survey; this

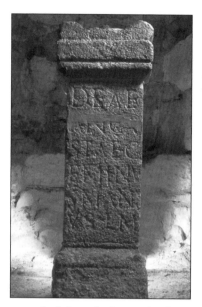

A Roman altar dedicated to the goddess Ancaster, recovered from Bitterne Manor c.1805.

(JOE LOW, SO'TON CITY MUSEUMS)

From Roman Times to 1799

The name 'Byterne' is derived from two Old English elements, 'byht' which means 'bend' (referring to the shape of the River Itchen or to the hill ridge to the east) and 'aern' meaning 'house' (possibly a storehouse). Clausentum itself seems to have disappeared by the fifth century, although A. Temple Patterson, in his *History of Southampton*, suggested that the fortified area may have been used as a refuge by the Saxon inhabitants of Hamwic across the river, and that it may have been one of the burghs (fortified places) of the kingdom of Wessex listed in the Burghal Hidage, an early tenth-century document.

In 1045 King Edward the Confessor gave land at Stanham to the monastery of St Peter and St Paul (Winchester Cathedral) and several historians consider Stanham to be Bitterne Manor. It is thought that a manor house existed here at the time of the Norman Conquest, so this may explain Bitterne's omission from King William I's survey of 1086, the Domesday Book. The survey mentions the manor church of Stanham (now known to have been St Mary's on the site of Hamwic) and the manor of South Stoneham (that Stanham became) did straddle the River Itchen. The present manor house is medieval in origin, being built of stone quarried at Binstead, Isle of Wight, at a quarry that also supplied the Tower of London and Winchester Cathedral.

revealed foundations of a large wooden storehouse or granary, typical of the Roman temporary buildings erected during their campaigns. About 150 skeletons uncovered are probably early Norman as Roman law dictated that only infants could be buried within a town's walls.

Perhaps the greatest finds have been an altar stone inscribed *DEAE ANCASTAE GEMINVS MANI VSLM* which translates as 'To the goddess Ancasta, Geminus Mani willingly and deservedly fulfils his vow' (Ancasta being a deity otherwise unknown throughout the Roman Empire) and seven milestones, or honorific pillars, inscribed to record the various road resurfacing operations undertaken during the second and third centuries, as on a pillar dated c.AD180-217: 'In the eighteenth year of the emperor's rule, the roads, rendered unusable through old age and in a ruinous state, were restored.'

The first known reference to Byterne was made in the Bishop of Winchester's register in the late-eleventh century. It tells of Blacheman Aurifaber, a monk in the service of Bishop Wakelin who was employed to copy books and manuscripts. He was found guilty of fraudulently writing 'Chichester' instead of 'Porchester' in a King's charter he was copying, of stealing a book of

The south front of the Manor House in 1910, showing the parapet wall and porch added in the nineteenth century.

(SO'TON CITY ARCHIVES)

Above: *T. Milne's map of 1791, eight years before Northam Bridge opened up the area for development.*

Left: *Sydney Cottage by Freemantle Common, c.1870. From 1864 to 1876 it was the home of Professor Edmund Parkes, then working at the Army Medical School at Netley.* (WELLCOME LIBRARY, LONDON)

Below left: *The view from Chessel House in 1840 shows why the high ground at Bitterne became popular for gentry folks' houses.*
(HANTS RECORD OFFICE, 15M84/P1 FO42)

Below: *The first Northam Bridge, constructed entirely of timber, opened in 1799. Bitterne Grove is on the hill to the right.*

StyheAthelwold, and of numerous other crimes. Six months and three days later his neck was wrung 'by an evil spirit' and he died on the shore at Byterne.

In the Register of Pontissara, dated 6 August 1171, King Henry II confirmed the grant made by Bishop Henry de Blois of the return of lands unjustly taken, to various monks and churches. This included returning the chapel of Hamtun and the tenement of Byterne to the monks of the church at Stanham. Around the end of the twelfth century, Bishop Godfrey de Lucy established mills at Alresford and legend has it that he made the River Itchen navigable between Alresford and the sea in order to carry his goods. Certainly Bitterne was the bishop's wine depot from where it was distributed as required, as was salt, which was made in large pans in the river estuary.

The Bishops of Winchester lived at the manor house when in the area. Bishop Peter des Roches stayed whilst visiting King John at Southampton Castle, and King Henry III stayed there in 1250, 1252 and 1253, whilst checking on the progress of the construction of Netley Abbey.

The manor of Stanham (South Stoneham) covered much of present-day Southampton, and the area east of the river formed the nucleus of the manor of Bitterne, granted by King Edward I to the Bishops of Winchester in 1284. Later that year permission was granted for men of the bishop's manor of Bitterne to be answerable to his hundred court at Waltham, instead of Sweynston as previously.

In 1319 Bishop Sandale's register records that a canon from St Denys Priory, together with four other men, was convicted of poaching at the rabbit warren at the bishop's manor at Bitterne.

By the end of the fourteenth century medieval customs had begun to wane, including the feudal system introduced by the Saxons and adapted by the Normans. This was hastened by the Black Death, the plague of 1348/50, during which one third of the country's population died, resulting in an acute labour shortage. Landowners were forced to pay wages, and eventually many decided to let land to tenant farmers as this offered a more secure financial return. The Bishop of Winchester let the manor at Bitterne to a tenant who lived in the manor house and farmed about 200 acres nearby. Other manorial land, such as along the Glen valley, was divided among tenants who held between ten and 35 acres each. Cottages were built and eventually the hamlet of Bittern-in-Mousehole came into being.

Wool was England's prime export at this time, a trade that contributed to Southampton's prosperity, and there is little doubt that sheep farming would have been predominant in the area. Sheep may also have grazed the heathland to the east, where Bitterne, Thornhill and Sholing are now. The area between Southampton and Portsmouth was a wilderness then, similar to the New Forest of today: heath and gorse interspersed with woods, with farmland and the occasional isolated hamlet in the valleys. This remoteness is illustrated by a reference in the South Stoneham church registers to Henry Dorset and his daughter Mary, interred in one grave on Sunday 28 December 1684; they were found dead on the track between Itchen Ferry and Wildern, following a bitter easterly wind and snow the previous Tuesday.

From Norman times a ferry boat, licensed by the Bishop of Winchester, had operated across the River Itchen at Itchen. Until the eighteenth century the lowest point at which the River Itchen was bridged was Mansbridge. The local inhabitants (including those at Bitterne) had to keep the bridge in good repair until the mid-fourteenth century, when the Abbot of Netley was prevailed upon to maintain it, the abbey being considered the main user.

At Michaelmas 1520 Bishop Fox let the manor house, together with pasture called 'Bytterne Parke', to John Tanner (otherwise Mason) of Weston for 31 years, for the annual rent of £13.13s.4d., agreeing to keep the house, walls, gates, ditches, etc., in good repair. It is likely that the manor ceased to be a residence of the bishop's at this time.

From 1284 until 1551 the Manor of Bitterne remained in the possession of the See of Winchester, but then Bishop John Poynet surrendered it and other manors to the Crown in exchange for other property in Hampshire. Three months later the Manor of Bitterne, together with other lands, was granted to William, Earl of Wiltshire and Lord High Treasurer, but it was returned to the See of Winchester in 1553, during the reign of Queen Mary. Seized by the Commonwealth under Cromwell, it was sold in 1649 to John Barkstead, Esq. for £1,716.6s.8d., but in 1660 was again restored to the See where it remained until 1869, when it was vested to the Church Commissioners.

John Leland (c.1506–52) was a graduate of Christ's College, Cambridge, and in 1530 was appointed keeper of the king's library. Under a royal commission he travelled the country, making notes on the topography, and these notes were transcribed by the Revd G.W. Minns c.1910, though he retained Leland's quaint spellings. Of Bitterne he recorded:

And on the right hand on the est ripe lyith almost agayn in Bythern, sumtyme a castelle longing to the bisshopes of Winchester, whereof yet some ruines remayne: now a ferme longing to the Bisshop of Winchester. Wood Mille lyith scant a mile upward, as at the hedde of the creeke: and hither resotith Alresford Ryver augmented with dyvers brokes. The toun of Hampton is not half a mile above the mouth of this creke.

Revd Minns adds:

At Bitterne the Bishops of Winchester had an Episcopal Palace with a square embattled tower. Here, as Lords of the Manor, they held their courts, and in 1264 the Archbishop of Canterbury, Kilwardby, came on a visitation and kept Christmas. Part of the walls of the mediaeval palace are built into the present Bitterne Manor House.

In the sixteenth century Bitterne started appearing on maps: Saxton's map of 1575 spells Bitterne as it is now, but Nordon's map of 1607 uses the bird's spelling, dropping the second 'e', and this seems to have been the accepted spelling through to Harrison's map of 1788.

About 1598 Francis Mylles moved into Bitterne Manor House. At various times he was a Burgess of Southampton, Freeman of the City of Winchester, Clerk of the Privy Seal, secretary to Sir Francis Walsingham (who established and ran the Elizabethan secret service), Clerk of the Peace for Hampshire, and MP for Poole and Winchester. As Leland has confirmed, the manor house was in a state of disrepair, and Francis gained permission from the Bishop of Winchester to cart away stone from it to build a new house at Peartree. In his sixth edition of *Britannia* (published in Latin in 1607), William Camden describes Francis as an honest gentleman who showed him the old walls and trenches at Clausentum and explained that Roman coins were being dug up there. According to a lease of 1747, James Mylles, the grandson of Francis, had held the tenure of the lordship of the manor, so it is possible that Francis had been lord of the manor, and that it was held by his descendants, son James (c.1587–1638), grandson James, his son Francis (died 1717) and his son Francis (1696–1767). It probably then passed to the latter's youngest brother George, known to be living in 1769.

In the centuries that followed the Black Death the country's population doubled, although bad sanitation and the flea-carrying black rat combined to infect Southampton with the plague again in 1584, 1604 and 1665. Bitterne seems to have been unaffected, although refuge was given to friends from the town. Likewise the Civil War of the 1640s had little effect, apart from the plundering of food by troops as they passed through. The Hearth Tax Returns of 1665 give the first indication of the size of Bitterne's population. There were 15 houses and an estimated 75 inhabitants; 39 hearths were taxed, one house having six (probably the manor) and one having a dozen (Peartree House) whilst another five were untaxed.

In the mid-eighteenth century Southampton became fashionable as a spa town and bathing resort, an image enhanced by a visit in 1750 by Frederick, Prince of Wales, who found the water at Western Shore 'salubrious and invigorating'. His four sons, the eldest of whom became King George III, also visited and where royalty went, the nobility and gentry followed. Business improved, the town's hotels were renovated, and the town expanded. Local farming communities such as Bitterne benefited from the need for more produce, transported to town via the new bridge at Woodmill. It is thought that a mill has been on this site since Saxon times, but it only became a bridging point when the Itchen Navigation Canal opened in 1710. Some wealthy visitors to the spa found the area attractive enough to want to build homes, and the hill ridge across the River Itchen proved especially popular because of its views across the town and New Forest. Thus the first large houses in Bitterne came into being: Bitterne Grove, Ridgeway Castle, Townhill Park and Midanbury House. As the gentry needed servants and tradesmen to provide for them, cottages and shops were also built.

One of the most influential new residents was David Lance, who in about 1790 acquired land known as the Upper and Lower Guillames, consisting of most of the land between the river, the track from Itchen Ferry to Mansbridge (now Peartree Avenue) and Bitterne Road; the exception was a small triangle of land containing a house, workshop and garden belonging to Thomas Freemantle, a coachbuilder. Shown on maps as Freemantle's even after he had left, this is the likely source for the name of Freemantle Common. David Lance was conscious that access to his land (on which he built Chessel House in 1796) and to other properties in the area was poor, so offered encouragement to the Northam Bridge Company, a company formed largely with money from Portsmouth businessmen, with the purpose of building a toll-bridge across the River Itchen, and a toll-road from it to the new bridge beside Botley Mill. Because the new road would reduce the distance between Portsmouth and Southampton by four miles the Admiralty were keen supporters and the required Act of Parliament was passed without delay. The wooden bridge and the road was opened in 1799 with toll-huts on the bridge, on Great Lances Hill and at Hedge End. However, David Lance was not satisfied with this plan, and on 20 July 1796 he chaired a meeting at the Southampton Guildhall (then in the Bargate) to promote another road. The Bursledon Bridge Company was formed to build a toll-bridge over the River Hamble at Bursledon and a road from it to join the Northam Bridge Company's road (with their permission) at Bitterne. This road also opened in 1799, thus forming the infamous fork, and stimulating the growth of Bitterne village at the top of the hill.

Nineteenth and Twentieth Centuries

For centuries Southampton has been a port of embarkation for armies fighting overseas, and the countryside around has often provided camp sites. In 1800 troops were camped on Netley Common before embarking for Egypt, and a quarrel broke out resulting in Lt Smith challenging Ensign O'Brie (both

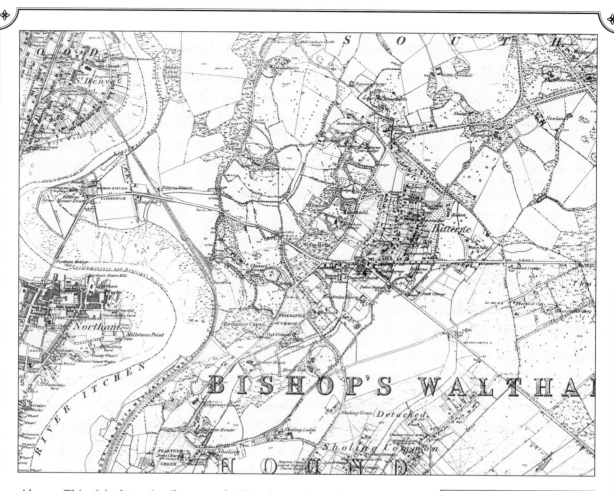

Above: *This 6-inch to 1-mile map of 1871 shows the village character of Bitterne at that time, separate from Southampton.*

(ORDNANCE SURVEY TOWN MAP OF SOUTHAMPTON)

Right: *Brownlow North (1741–1820) Bishop of Winchester, to whom land in Bitterne was alloted in 1814 to compensate for the loss of tithes. The land became the Brownlow estate.* (HANTS RECORD OFFICE, 15M84/P1 FO33)

Below: *A relic of the stagecoach and toll-roads era, this milestone on Lances Hill is the sole survivor of four that were around Bitterne.*

Below right: *Bitterne High Street c.1908, showing Minns Drapers on the left, the Wesleyan Chapel is on the corner of Pound Street, and the Red Lion on the fork with Bursledon Road.*

of the Ninth Regiment) to a duel. Smith died on the spot and is buried at Peartree Green; O'Brie was apprehended at Winchester and found guilty of manslaughter.

In 1802 the Bishop of Winchester leased Bitterne Manor, which had survived as just a farm for many years, to Henry Simpson, for restoration to a residence and during 1804/5 it was extensively altered and extended, with mock battlements built, the stonework rendered and part of the medieval tower removed; the Roman inner ditch was possibly filled in at this time. Some suggest that the manor house became an inn following the opening of Northam Bridge, but this may be an incorrect association with the Bridge Tavern just to the east and on the other side of the road.

Over a couple of centuries the enclosure of land had been taking place, and from 1740 this increased rapidly so that by 1837 most arable land was enclosed and 30 years later most commons were as well. The aim was to increase production by consolidating land into larger parcels instead of numerous of isolated strips, yet only a weak case for the enclosure of land in Bitterne could have been made as it was poor quality and, in the aftermath of the Battle of Waterloo, farm prices were dropping. The application for an Act of Enclosure was made in 1812 by the main landowners, James Dott of Bitterne Grove, the Bishop of Winchester, Ann Frances Middleton of Townhill and Edward Jewell of Midanbury. It is likely they had residential development in mind, Northam Bridge having made the area more accessible. A number of 30ft-wide carriageways were to be built including West End Road, Pound Road, Chapel Street, Brewery Road and Upper Spring Road. The glebe land on which the church, vicarage and schools were later built was allocated to the Vicar of South Stoneham (in whose ecclesiastic parish Bitterne then fell) in compensation for loss of tithes; the land that was to become the Brownlow estate was allocated to the Bishop of Winchester, Brownlow North, whilst Freemantle Common became a public common.

By the 1860s Bitterne had grown from a mere hamlet to a pleasant village with a population of about 1600, with several handsome modern mansions boasting tasteful pleasure grounds and commanding views. These included Bitterne Lodge, Heathfield, Mersham, Oak Lodge, Shales and Moorlands House. In 1866 the railway between Southampton and Netley opened with a station at the foot of Great Lances Hill; it was nearly built at the top, but that's another story. The railway made travel easier for the inhabitants whilst encouraging more gentry to establish 'seats' in the area.

On 27 June 1883 the National Liberal Land Company opened the Free Cobden Bridge, built at a cost of £11,500, a mile upstream from Northam Bridge, giving free access from Southampton to the estate it was developing at Bitterne Park. This led to the so-called Battle of Cobden Bridge when residents from the developing St Denys district crossed the bridge and 'invaded' Bitterne, supposedly after primroses (Bitterne lads suspected they were after their young ladies). The conflicts were sometimes bloody affairs, as reported in the *Southern Evening Echo* in May 1885:

The neighbourhood of the new Cobden Bridge, erected over the River Itchen at St Denys, was the scene of a riot on Sunday. Some few weeks ago, Southampton boys went over to Bitterne 'primrosing' and this seems to have annoyed the boys of the latter place who considered the 'townies' were trespassing, and drove them back into the borough. The news of this skirmish spread, and bad feeling was increased when a week later 200 roughs gave battle to a similar number from Bitterne and Woolston. On Sunday afternoon about 400 men and boys marched over Cobden Bridge to battle again with the Bitternites, only to find Superintendent Brearly and several constables armed with sticks, who gave them a warm reception and routed them.

The National Land Corporation, successor to the NLLC, commenced the development of Bitterne Manor area in 1899, having purchased the land from Lady Amy Macnaghten, the widow of Sir Steuart. Initially the entire peninsular west of the railway was to be housing, but the MacNaghten family bought back the manor and seven acres of land, so by 1905 the plans had been revised. Subsequently the plans were amended again with Clausentum Avenue (now Vespasian Road) becoming a cul-de-sac and Roman Road not being built. Mud flats to the north of Northam Bridge were reclaimed, resulting in the demise of one local landmark, Blackberry Island, which was absorbed into the mainland.

As late as 1905 Bitterne was described as 'a picturesque village two miles north-east of Southampton', and the village's reluctance to be incorporated into the County Borough of Southampton can be appreciated.

One custom that disappeared about this time was mumming: at Christmas a group of village men, disguised in costumes made from strips of paper or rag, would visit large houses and inns in the village and perform the Mummers' Play. The words, costumes and characters (who usually included St George, a Turkish knight, a doctor and Father Christmas) varied from village to village, but the story was the same: good triumphing over evil and the resurrection.

Following a cholera epidemic in 1875, Parliament passed the Public Health Act setting up a General Board of Health, and a nationwide system of rural and urban sanitary authorities to consider sanitation and drainage. At its meeting on 21 May 1895, the Bitterne Parish Council discussed a letter from the local board, but decided against providing drainage for the village as it considered the cost would be too

Above: *The Lances Hill toll, looking towards Bitterne, c.1900, with the wall of the Chessel estate on the right. The gate was moved three times as road building enabled it to be avoided. The final toll-house was 253 Bitterne Road.*

Below: *In July 1923 Southampton Corporation extended its tramway from Bitterne Park Triangle down Bullar Road. Here car 21, on an LRTL enthusiasts' special in 1942, blocks the line for car 3. Note the wartime grey upper deck, white fender and hooded headlight, and the spark shield on the overhead wire. This line closed in 1948. (MARTIN PETCH COLLECTION)*

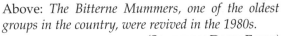

Above: *The Bitterne Mummers, one of the oldest groups in the country, were revived in the 1980s.*
(SOUTHERN DAILY ECHO)

An enthusiastic crowd listened to speeches outside the Red Lion following the freeing of the tolls at Northam Bridge and Lances Hill, 16 May 1929. The dignitaries then went on to free the Hedge End and Bursledon Bridge tolls, travelling between the gates on one of the Corporation's new six-wheeled Thornycroft HC buses, purchased for services across the Itchen.

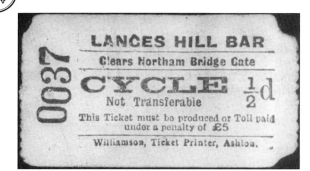

Left: *Tickets purchased at the Lances Hill toll entitled the traveller to pass across the toll-bridge at Northam as well.*

Below: *The top of Lances Hill, c.1934, with G. Auger's 'high-class tobacconist', also agents for Lyon's ice-cream bricks.*

Above: *Looking along West End Road from its junction with Lances Hill (to the left) c.1943.*

Right: *The Bitterne fork where Bursledon Road met Bitterne Road, pictured in the late 1950s. Bitterne School is on the left with the Wesleyan Chapel opposite, on the corner of Pound Street. On the opposite corner is Lloyds Bank.*

high a burden for the rates. Dr Seaton confirmed that with a death rate of only 1 per cent, drainage was unnecessary. Various schemes, such as a joint system with other villages east of the River Itchen, were considered over the next few years, and eventually Bitterne was linked with a drainage scheme for Itchen and Sholing.

Attempts by Southampton Corporation to incorporate Bitterne into the borough were discussed at various meetings of the Parish Council, and at the meeting on 9 June 1895 a resolution was passed to protest against the proposed inclusion. The Parish Council agreed to ask South Stoneham Rural District Council (in which the parish fell) for help in resisting the takeover and Mr Culme-Seymour was asked to present their objections to HM Inspectorate. The resistance was temporarily successful, Bitterne Park joining Southampton in 1895, but not Bitterne.

However the proposal was not dropped and there was a constant flow of correspondence between Southampton Borough Council and Bitterne Parish Council. At a Parish Council meeting in May 1908 a letter from the Town Clerk was read out, extolling the advantages of the incorporation, one of which was given as the extension of the tram network to Bitterne; how it proposed to get trams up Lances Hill was not stated! Defeat finally came in 1920 when Bitterne was fully incorporated into the Borough of Southampton; the consequence being the renaming of many roads in 1924 to avoid duplication. How much the village gained has always been debated, but by the mid-1930s most residents had benefited in some way. Transport links with 'the town' were improved, street lighting (championed by the Ratepayers' Association) was installed, roads and footpaths were 'made up'. Most were of gravel without clearly defined footpaths, so travel on them must have been very uncomfortable, with deep ruts in the winter and clouds of dust in dry weather; the latter was alleviated by the water carts which sprayed the roads (to the delight of small boys) to keep the dust down. Even in those days motorcars were blamed for causing a nuisance, mainly by the dust they stirred up: there were complaints about speeds in excess of 20mph on the county roads, when the limit was only 10mph.

But by far the biggest change took place on the 16 May 1929 when the tolls were freed, the Corporation having bought out the Northam Bridge Company so that the toll bars could be removed on Northam Bridge, on Lances Hill and in Hedge End. Concurrently the County Council took over the Bursledon Bridge Company, freeing that route at the same time, and allowing the unimpeded movement of traffic between Southampton and the east. One result of this was a dramatic reduction in traffic on the floating bridge, leading to a collapse of the Southampton & Itchen Bridge Company's value, enabling the Corporation to assume control of that as well.

Removing the tolls was to open Bitterne up for ultra-rapid development: country lanes, where villagers used to pick blackberries, became busy roads with shops and houses. Bitterne's shopping centre more than doubled in size, new shopping areas were created at Merry Oak, Midanbury and The Garden Suburb Centre, and housing replaced the country estates at Brownlow and Glenfield. The acute shortage of postwar homes led to the development of the remaining estates of Bitterne Lodge, Townhill Park, Harefield and Thornhill by the Council, even though the latter two were outside of Southampton until 1954.

An interesting incident of 1950 was the last use of the pound, a small fenced-off area at the southern end of Pound Street, hence the name. Stray animals were common in rural areas, when flocks and herds were driven through on the way to market, and these strays were put in the pound until claimed. One night four calves escaped from Upper Townhill Farm and were found wandering in Manor Farm Road, where they were rounded up by the police and driven to the pound for safe keeping; one wonders how long it took to cajole the animals that distance!

By now Bitterne was no longer a village, but a suburb of Southampton and to ram home the subjugation, the city planners tore out its heart by bulldozing the oldest part to make way for the bypass. True, the traffic along what is now the precinct was slow and heavy: shoppers risked life and limb to cross the road and the Bitterne fork and the crossroads at the top of Lances Hill gained reputations as bottlenecks. But lost was much of the community spirit that exists in the face of adversity. Some residents, such as Claude Diaper, fought the changes, whilst others salvaged items such as the Bitterne Lion. Ultimately the motorist won when the bypass was opened on 10 December 1984.

In 1993 the lordship of the manor of Bitterne was offered for sale by the Church Commissioners, with offers invited in the region of £7,500. No rights (fishing, hunting, hawking, mineral extraction, wrecks, holding fairs and markets, etc.) seem to have been included with the title, nor any manorial documents (which are mostly at the Hampshire Record Office). The title was bought by Arnold 'Mac' McMullen, owner of Bonaparte's Boatyard, Quayside Road, presuming that it would include rights over the mud flats. The Crown Estates (custodians of the foreshore) disputed this, but before the issue could be resolved Mac died and his wife inherited the title; it is believed she reached an agreement with the Crown Estates resulting in them obtaining the title.

Bitterne celebrated the millennium with the planting of five trees on what remains of The Sandpit, but Woolston was far more ambitious, creating a millennium garden with the theme of 'Flight and Float' in the centre of the shopping area, where it is possible to spot the inscribed BLHS brick!

The Bitterne Lion

The Lion sat on Lion Place,
Looking down with lordly grace,
For a hundred and fifty years or more,
But never once did we hear him roar.

But if you watched at dead of night,
Down he'd jump with step so light,
He'd prowl about with ne'er a sound,
Then back on his perch at dawn he'd bound.

'Tis said the Romans brought him here,
(But if that's true is never clear)
Then when they left ol' Leo remained;
Bitterne village for 'is kingdom he claimed.

And now he's gone for 'restoration'
The new precinct will be his next 'station'.

Unknown

2The unveiling ceremony performed by the Mayor, Cllr Ivy White, accompanied by the Boys' and Girls' Brigade band, 23 June 1987. (SOUTHERN DAILY ECHO)

The Lion on the parapet of Lion Place (top left). *The shops shown are Dowty's chemist, Lion Drapery Stores and Lankester & Crook.*

The Lion being lifted down, 2 November 1983. Coincidentally amongst the last occupants of the shop below were animals! This picture also shows Lankester & Crook's extension to Lion Place. (MORIEN WILLIAMS)

For nearly 150 years the Bitterne Lion looked down on the people of the village from the roof of Lion Place, a row of four houses built in the 1840s in what was then the High Street. The name was possibly derived from the proximity of the terrace to the Red Lion Inn; not the present Red Lion but an older building that stood slightly further along Bursledon Road. This inn, converted to cottages when the present pub was built c.1860, was finally demolished when the bypass was built.

Within a few years Lion Place was converted to shops, with living rooms behind and on the upper floor. The first to open was Percival Henning's grocery and drapery at Nos 3 and 4. At the time Mr Henning was the village postmaster and churchwarden of the district church of the parish of South Stoneham. Anglican services were held in the disused Baptist chapel in Chapel Road before the Parish Church was built in 1853. When Lankester & Crook, The County Supply Stores, came to Bitterne in 1891 the terrace changed considerably. No. 4 was reconstructed and two more shops of similar design were added, so putting the lion off centre. Lankester & Crook, as well as being the first 'superstore' in Bitterne, had the first Public Call Office (i.e. public telephone) in the village; in 1896 it was phone number 103 of the Southampton

A photo of Bitterne looking east, c.1970, with the alignment of the bypass, slip-roads and Peartree Gardens car park added. (SOUTHERN DAILY ECHO)

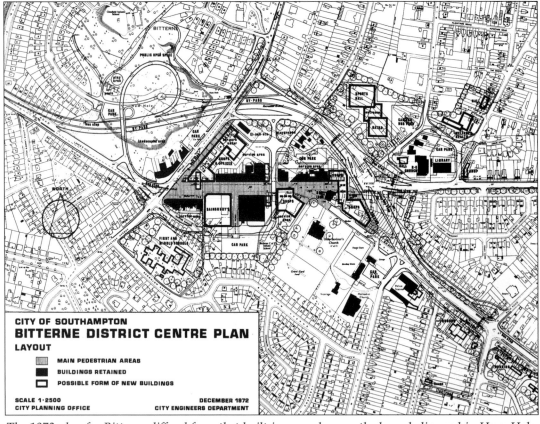

The 1972 plan for Bitterne differed from that built in several ways: the looped slip road in Hum Hole, Angel Crescent bridging the precinct, the dual carriageway extending beyond Ruby Road, and a play-ground on the remains of The Sandpit. (SO'TON CITY COUNCIL)

exchange National Telephone Company Ltd.

In 1924 many of the road names in Bitterne had to be changed to end duplication within the County Borough of Southampton, into which it had been absorbed. The Council renamed the High Street as Arcadian Road, but locals objected and the new signs were tarred and feathered in the dead of night, and had to be replaced. On the third occasion the culprits were caught and taken to the police station. They remained unknown until 1991, when the names of Mr Dowty the chemist, and Mr Bristow the manager of Lankester & Crook were revealed by Mr Dowty's daughter Veronica in a BLHS book. Mr Dowty had the presence of mind to put the tarred brush in his sock, and as no evidence could be found, no charges were brought. They won the day as the road was renamed Bitterne Road.

The Bitterne Lion was removed from the top of Lion Place by the Council's stonemasons department on 2 November 1983, prior to demolition of Lion Place for the bypass. Originally it had been offered to the BLHS, but the Council subsequently decided to restore it themselves. After an absence of four years, it was returned to Bitterne and was unveiled by the Mayor of Southampton, Cllr Ivy White, on 23 June 1987 on the spot where the freeing of the tolls ceremony had taken place 58 years earlier. The society objected to its new position directly outside the Red Lion public house as it infers a direct connection between the two, but this was overruled. However,

the society was successful in persuading the Council to put it on a plinth high enough to be out of reach of vandals! And now it is the society's emblem.

The Bypass

There's a brand new road what's coming through,
They've pulled down some shops and houses too!
Some says 'tis progress – that I doubt;
Cars and lorries is all they thinks about.

They've pulled down the Drill 'All and
the old church,
Both fine old buildings, that's what 'urts;
Godwin's is gone and Lanky's too,
Just for the new road what's coming through.

They've took 'alf of 'Um Hole, that's so bad,
I used to play there when I was a lad;
No eye for beauty they 'aven't got,
If they'd 'ad their way they'd pull down the lot!

Sometimes when I'm lonely I sits and I sigh,
And thinks of old Bitterne and days what's gone by,
And I 'spects time I'm gone and up there
looking down,
I won't know the difference 'tween Bitterne
and town!

By Bill Hulbert

Main picture: *The construction of the bypass in 1983 turned Bitterne into a huge building site. This is looking west along Bitterne Road with the back of the Red Lion on the left and the construction of the subway in progress in the foreground.*

Inset: *Looking west along the bypass in 2006. The positioning of speed cameras here is controversial to many people.*

23

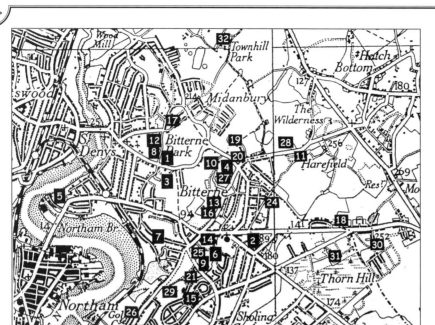

Left: *The location of some of the larger houses in the area.* (ORDNANCE SURVEY 1-INCH TO 1-MILE MAP, SHEET 141 DATED 1936)

Below: *The Ridge in 1906, a large house in West End Road previously known as Rutland Court.*

Below, oval: *Chessel Lodge on Lances Hill was one of three to the Chessel estate, and at one time was the home of the toll collector at the toll-gate. The lodge became derelict in the 1950s and a telephone exchange was later built on the site on the corner of Garfield Road.*

Above: *The view down the Itchen from Chessel House, c.1920.*

Below: *Chessel House in 1840, when sold by Lord Ashtown.* (HANTS RECORD OFFICE, 15M84/P1 FO42)

Right: *This lodge to Brownlow House stood in Peartree Avenue until c.1977 when it was demolished for the new schools to be built.*

Chapter Two

Homes for the Gentry

The desirability of the Bitterne area as a place to live in the nineteenth and early twentieth centuries is shown by the large number of gentry and middle-class folk who lived there. Many of the houses had fine views across Southampton and the water to the New Forest and the Isle of Wight. In 1850 Philip Brannon wrote : 'The magnificent view of the town, the rivers, estuary, and surrounding country obtained from this point, should be enjoyed by every visitor.' The following are some of the larger houses that have existed in the area. It is not a definitive list as many were rebuilt or renamed and size is difficult to compare! The numbers refer to the map opposite.

No	House	Existed between	Residents included (not chronologically)
1	Beechwood	c.1890–c.1967	Mrs Addiss, Mrs White
2	Bitterne Court	c.1840–1936	Mrs Bramwell, Admiral James Wigston, Daniel Brooks
3	Bitterne Grove (now St Mary's College)	c.1790–now	Richard Leversuch, James Dott, Alexander Hoyes
4	Bitterne Lodge	c.1830–c.1960	Admiral Thomas Martin JP
5	Bitterne Manor	c.1200–now	Bishops of Winchester (Henry III stayed), Valentine Fitzhugh, Col de Billinghurst, Sir Steuart MacNaghten
6	Brownlow House	1840–1878	Lt Col Bucknill, Mrs Lister
7	Chessel House	c.1796–c.1925	David Lance (Jane Austen a guest), Sir William Richardson
8	Deepdene	c.1890–now	Sir Henry Milner-White
9	Eastfield	c.1840–c.1935	Henry Aldridge
10	Glenville	c.1830–c.1938	Cmdr Culme-Seymour JP, Hon. Algernon Annesley, Henry Culme-Seymour MA, JP, Revd Coppin
11	Harefield	c.1840–1917	Hon. Sir Edward Butler, Edwin Jones, Dr Thomas
12	Hazelwood	c.1900–post-1935	Col Martin
13	Heathfield	c.1825–1982	Gen. H.P. Raymond JP, Robert Richardson FSA, Capt. G. Quinn
14	Lancehill/Tryermayne	pre-1865–now	David Lance (latterly QS shop)
15	Merry Oak	c.1800–c.1925	Hugh Kean, Geo Errington, George Ede, John Hopton-Forbes
16	Mersham	c.1830–1945	Oswald Grimston, Mr Nokes, Maj. W. Lister
17	Midanbury House	1791–c.1936	John Morse, Michael Hoy, James Barlow-Hoy MP
18	Mons	c.1912–1973	Maj. Henry Kendall MM, MSM
19	Moorlands House	c.1840–post-1935	Capt. Charles Sholto Douglas
20	Moorlands Villa/ Brydon	c.1830–post-1933	Admiral Sir Charles Elliott KGB, Mr Courtney-Wilson
21	Oak Cottage/Oak Lodge	c.1840–2007?	J.W. Barnaby, Robert Wilson, now SCC
22	Peartree House	c.1590–now	Frances Mylles MP, Capt. R. Smith, Rear Admiral Sir J. Wentworth, Gen. H. Shrapnell, John Cruikshank, now SCC
23	Peartree Lodge	c.1775–1949	Antony Munton, Capt. Thomas Bradby, Col Oswald Grimton
24	Redcot(e) (became Redcote Convent)	c.1860–c.1990	Revd Henry Usborne
25	Redlands	c.1900–now	Thomas Fisher-Hall
26	Ridgeway House/Castle	c.1792–c.1920	Thomas Lewin JP, James Ede, Mornington Cannon, Maj. Brown
27	Rutland Lodge/The Ridge	c.1835–c.1945	Augustus Henry Smith
28	Shales?Langstaff House	c.1840–1984	Sir Charles Coote, Admiral Robert Coote CB, JP, Dr Harold Brown, Col Perkins MP
29	Sydney House	c.1790–c.1945	Sir Joseph Hoare, Lady Rumbold
30	Thornhill Park	1795–1923	James Barlow Hoy MP, Henry Dumbleton, Col Frank Willan
31	Thornhill Villa/Thornfield (now Royal British Legion Club)	c.1860–now	Lt Col J.T. Bucknill
32	Townhill Park (now Gregg School)	1787–now	Nathaniel Middleton, Lord Swaythling (Queen Mary a guest), Caleb Gater

Harriet Grote:
'The Cleverest Woman in London'
Sarah Lewin

Ridgeway House was built in the mid-sixteenth century on the west side of modern Peartree Avenue just north of Peartree Green. From 1791 it was owned by Thomas Lewin who lived there with his family. A local road map of 1806 names the road from West End to Itchen as Lewin's Road. On 1 July 1792 Harriet Lewin was born at The Ridgeway, as it was then called, and she spent her childhood there. In 1820 she married George Grote, having studied hard so that she could share his intellectual interests including philosophy, German, music and politics. Their courtship had been a secretive affair and, according to *The Temple Bar* magazine, '... they were married at Bexley Church in time for the young lady to take her place at the breakfast table as if nothing had happened.'

A self-portrait of Harriet Grote (née Lewin).
(FROM A PRIVATE COLLECTION)

George was born in Kent in 1794 and following an education at grammar school and Charterhouse, he entered the family bank, Grote, Prescott & Co. He befriended a circle of radical thinkers and reformists, and developed a dislike of the monarchy and established Church. From 1826 to 1830 he was one of the promoters of the new University College, London, of which he later became president. Following the 1832 Reform Act, he became MP for the City of London, but became disillusioned and left Parliament in 1841. He left the family bank to complete a project he had started in the 1820s and for which he is most remembered: writing the 12-volume *History of Greece*, which was finally published in 1856 and still forms the nucleus of classical Greek history.

In February 1853 Harriet, who was always a diligent keeper of diaries and notebooks, started recording her reminiscences, but she stopped writing these in 1865 when she started a biography of her husband, published in 1873, two years after his death. Harriet herself was not the typical lady-of-the-house: she is said to have been a formidable early feminist, nicknamed 'the cleverest woman in London'. She died in 1878.

In 1882 Thomas Herbert Lewin (Harriet's nephew) began researching his family history, the results of which were published in 1909 as *The Lewin Letters*; volume two included Harriet's memories, of which the following are extracts:

... I remember the arrival of some French émigrés at Ridgeway in 1799, especially the Comte de Castries, who occupied a cottage on a barren heath about a mile and a half from our house. We went sometimes on foot to pay a visit to this poor nobleman in his desolate sanctuary. I recollect how shabby his clothes were, and yet withal he preserved an air of dignity. His hair was powdered and tied; he wore knee breeches with buckles and white stockings. He offered us some dry bread which he took from a cupboard, and some very weak beer in a teacup, which Miss Davies enjoined us to accept lest we might give M. de Castries pain by refusing. I remember feeling great pity for his fallen condition. He spoke a few words of English to us with a bad accent, and when he subsequently came to dine at our house, he ate ravenously...

In September, 1797, when I was about three years old, I can remember seeing the Volunteer Regiment of Horse, in which my Father and most of the neighbouring gentlemen served as privates, exercising at Townhill, the seat of Mr Nathaniel Middleton (the friend of Warren Hastings): and being taken to Eaglehurst, near Calshot Castle, on a visit to Colonel de Crespigny and Lady Sarah, the daughter of the Earl of Plymouth. The Colonel was a warm admirer of Mrs Lewin: he was of a vivacious character, and of some talent...

In 1799 my mother's sister, Miss Charlotte Hale, came to stay with us for a few months; and as at that time we had no governess, I was placed under her tyrannical rule, as it was thought time that I should learn something. My aunt, Miss Charlotte Hale, was at that time a fine, dashing young woman, full of spirits and fond of pleasure, much admired by the officers of a Dragoon Regiment which was quartered close by at Southampton. A Colonel Affleck and Major Moore were her forward adorers. In August, 1798, my mother was brought to bed of a son who was called Frederick... after his birth we girls had less attention than before. She was very fond of her male child, and spent much time fondling and caressing him, though she did not suckle him herself. The boy had a wetnurse named Hedges, who used to teach me knitting;

The Lewin children c.1807, from left: Frances, Harriet, Frederick Mortimer, William Charles James, and Charlotte.
(FROM A PRIVATE COLLECTION)

and Aunt Charlotte was almost as fond of the infant Frederick as his own mother. I had a perfect dread of my Aunt, who kept me close at lessons and needlework with harsh authority, and more than once whipped me with a rod for not knowing my French dialogues...

1800: About the month of May in this year, prior to our going to Torquay, a camp was formed on Netley Common, a vast open heath, about a mile from Pear Tree Green. It was under the command of Lord Moira, and the troops encamped there were destined to operate a descent on the coast of Holland, England being at that time at war with the French Republic. To this Camp our governess used to conduct us three children of an evening: and I remember distinctly the general aspect of the tents, the music of the military band playing before the Commanding Officer's tent, and the women in pits dug out of the ground, cooking and washing linen, etc. The traces of these holes remained up to 1839. A friend of our family, General Shireff, lived at this time at Old Alresford, about fourteen miles from Ridgeway. He had served with my grand-father, General Hale, and the connection extended to General Hale's children. He had three daughters and one son, who was bred to the sea. At the house of this worthy and gallant veteran we paid a visit in the autumn of 1800, and I was kindly noticed by the ladies, who constantly termed me 'the Empress' from the bombastic title bestowed on me whilst an infant. I recollect feeling a great awe of Miss Eliza Shireff, a fine, tall young woman of great spirit and energy, as well as a certain jealousy of the affection she testified to my elder sister Mary, also a guest at old Alresford. Mary was at this time fifteen years of age, very pretty, beautifully formed, and clever for her age. She never courted my confidence, and I was far too shy and susceptible to tender it to one so much older than myself. We were, moreover, excessively different in almost every particular, and never had any intimate communion up to the hour of her departure for Madras several years later...

1802: One of our servants bathing in the Itchen River ruptured himself and shortly after died. When laid out in his shroud we were taken to see the corpse. This was the first time I ever saw one who was dead. The impression this made upon me was deep and solemn. Poor John Wagstaff was a fine young man of about twenty-seven years of age and comely to look upon. About this period my mother's nephew, Henry W. Yeoman, and his mother, Mrs Yeoman (Anne, who was my mother's twin sister), came to visit us. They arrived somewhat unexpectedly late at night, and young Henry Yeoman was put into my bed with me, where I was lying asleep for the night — he and I being about ten years old respectively. I mention this slight circumstance as shewing how little was thought in those days of what we now call 'indelicacy'. We did not know each other, and I recollect feeling exceedingly annoyed at a great boy being bundled into my press-

bed with such scant ceremony; but we soon fell asleep and never thought more about it till the morning, and the next day another bed was provided for my cousin...

1803: The neighbours instituted a kind of social club which consisted in each house providing an evening's entertainment once a fortnight; there was card-playing, dancing and music, with light refreshments. People seldom went to London — the war kept every English family at home, and the ties of neighbourhood were of a truly kind and friendly character. My father and mother confided their family affairs to more than one neighbour, and took counsel with some as to the destination of their sons and other points with perfect reliance on their good feeling and attachment. During the whole of the spring and summer of 1803 the house at Ridgeway was being transmogrified into a Castle with a high tower, from which floated subsequently an ensign, with the Union Jack in the corner, when the Lewin family was in residence. During these alter-ations we children were lodged at Whitlock's farm hard by with Miss Beetham, whilst our parents stayed

Ridgeway Castle.   (FROM A PRIVATE COLLECTION)

with our Grandfather, Captain Richard Lewin, at the Hollies, near Bexley...

1804: In February of this year Mrs Lewin gave birth to a girl who was in due time christened by the names of Frances Eliza, after Miss Frances Rose, daughter of the Right Honourable George Rose of Cuffnalls, New Forest, and Miss Eliza Shireff. This little creature became the plaything and the idol, I may say, of every-body who approached her. The Godfather was a certain William Chamberlayne, a gentleman residing about two miles from Ridgeway at a delightful house which he had built on the banks of Southampton Water called Weston Grove. He was about forty years of age at this period, unmarried, and wealthy, with a singu-lar charm of conversation and a gift for public oratory. He had read much and travelled a good deal. He avoided general society on principle, but with our family he cultivated close intimacy, and we met constantly, sometimes at our respective houses, some-times sailing in my Father's yacht. A maiden sister resided with Mr Chamberlayne, a woman of ordinary capacity, and with no pretentions to attractiveness. Mr Chamberlayne's father had been Solicitor to the Treasury, and had been called upon to make the will of

A watercolour by Harriet Lewin, dated 1814, showing her mother Madam Lewin, William Stewart Rose and Charlotte her sister. (FROM A PRIVATE COLLECTION)

a gentleman named Dummer, who possessed large estates near Winchester and land at Southampton, including Netley Abbey. Into the entail of this vast property Mr Dummer authorized Mr Chamberlayne, senior, to insert the name of his own son William Chamberlayne, Mr Dummer having at that time not the remotest idea that his own heirs would fail, and the name was inserted only to prevent the slight possibility of the property passing to the Crown. By a singular chance all the heirs died, and Mr William Chamberlayne became possessed of the whole property, on the demise of Lady Holland, who was the widow of Mr Dummer and had married secondly Mr Nathaniel Dance, an artist, whom she managed to get Knighted under the name of Holland, to efface the memory of his own humble patronymic and trade...

I was of a remarkably energetic disposition from early childhood, and took great pleasure in any bodily exercise requiring skill and even personal danger. I could never content myself with the insipid recreations common to girls at that time, but sought amusements which required bodily agility, nerve, and invention. For instance, the River Itchen washed the shores of my father's grounds, the fine oak woods reaching to the river's marge. The fisher-folk were in the habit of mooring their boat to the sedgy shore, and whenever we girls could espy an empty boat we seized each an oar and shoved off into the river; but usually happened that the boat was dirty and half full of water so that on our return our clothes gave ample evidence of our employment, for which we duly suffered. My father's yacht sometimes lay at anchor off the wood, and we would persuade the sailors to fetch us off in the yacht's boat, and my sister Charlotte manfully bore me company in these adventures. We both had robust bodies, uncommon courage and agility, and were fertile in resource and expedient at a pinch. Our brother little Frederick, too, who by this time was six years old, began to take

part in our sports, being a truly gallant and plucky little fellow who, for his age, was hardy and enduring. I used to be an expert climber of trees; would cross over bogs and mud flats in mud pattens; ride horses bare backed when we could catch them, with a bit of string round the nose by way of halter, or we would drag the child's chaise through the woods, racing down the steep descents and often getting upset at the bottom. Sometimes we would climb to the top of the faggot stack and lie in hiding there, making clay figures for hours together, whilst Miss Beetham would fruitlessly pursue us, screaming, through the grounds. In the wintertime we were incessantly on the ice, sliding or snowballing, for skates we could not afford to buy, or making fires in remote parts of the wood to roast potatoes which we appropriated from the garden; anything, in short that could get us out of the neighbourhood or proximity of Miss Beetham...

Long after we were twelve years of age my sister Charlotte and I were flogged by my Father, who laid us across his knees for the purpose, at Miss Beetham's request, for climbing a bricklayer's ladder, without giving ear to anything we had to say in our defence...

On November 2nd my Father and Mother took us all to Southampton to see the King come in from Cuffnells, Mr Rose's place near Lyndhurst, where he had stopped a night or two 'en route' from Weymouth. We were posted at a window in a friend's house nearly fronting Colonel Heywood's residence above Bar, at which King George III was expected. I have a distinct recollection of the King's appearance, and of the whole scene indeed, as it naturally made a vivid impression on my childish imagination. The King came down the road from Moira Place at a hard canter, Mr Rose riding at his horse's flank, and his equerries trotting on each side but a little behind. He was dressed in a single-breasted dark green hunting frock (this was the uniform of the New Forest Verdurers, and he wore it in compliment to his host, Mr Rose), with gilt buttons, light. Kerseymere breeches, flapped waistcoat, and high boots without tops, shewing part of the white stocking at the knee. He had on a small plain three-cornered hat, with a good-sized black ribband cockade; his hair was powdered, and he wore a pig-tail tied pretty closely to his head. There was an immense assemblage of people to welcome the King, but no sort of decoration or flags of any kind. The King lifted his hat and bowed to the people as he reined up opposite Colonel Heywood's door. Mrs Chaloner and one of her daughters was presented to the King as related to Admiral Harvey, and the King kissed her, as we were told, whereat I felt an immediate pang of envy at her good fortune...

I grew tall for my age and naturally stooped a little, as most growing girls do. To counteract this tendency a collar was sent for from London, which I had to wear all day. The throat was enclosed by the iron spring, which was clasped behind by a steel stud; the arms *were pinioned in the shoulder straps. The centre, made of sheet-iron and covered with red morocco leather, pressed against the back, and was secured in its place by a belt round the waist. I was condemned to endure this torture during my waking hours, but whenever I got out of sight of Miss Beetham I prevailed on the gardener or any benevolent domestic to release me for a space, having it buckled on again before going back to the house. The misery which this accursed instrument caused me is one of the bitterest grievances of my youth; indeed, I am persuaded that to the use of this horrid invention is traceable my tendency to have bad headaches in after life...*

Mrs Lewin, accompanied by her eldest son and daughter, set off for Cleveland to visit her father, General Hale, in July, 1805, returning in September. During her absence we remained under the direction of Miss Beetham at Ridgeway, leading the dullest existence possible. About this time my father was led to entertain the idea of bestowing his daughter Mary in marriage on Mr Hippesley Marsh, as a friend of his, Sir Thomas Strange, Judge of the Madras High Court, wrote urging Marsh's claims... On another occasion we attended a single stick match at Botley under the direction of the celebrated Mr Cobbett, who presided on the platform and gave prizes to the successful competitors out of his own pocket...

My Father took in the Courier *newspaper, and never permitted any one to read it before himself. One morning in November, 1805, he ordered me to open and dry the paper for him, he being busy buttering his hot roll for breakfast. I did not then breakfast in the Parlour, but often went there at Papa's breakfast-time to wish him good morning and kiss him, a ceremony he never dispensed with to his last moment of conscious existence. As I held the paper before the fire I was attracted by the sight of many lines printed in large Capital letters, and I read the lines out loud and remember the shock it gave my Father when I uttered the concluding words. The news announced was the great Naval Victory of Trafalgar, and the last sentence was 'Lord Nelson was killed in the action'. The neighbours all ran about to each other's houses discussing the important news and lamenting the death of our great Commander. The fear of Napoleon Bonaparte had indeed for some years past formed a standing terror to all who, like ourselves, lived near the English Coast. Our nursemaids would tell us that 'Boney' would catch us if we broke bounds, and whenever a suspicious vagrant made his appearance he was at once set upon as a French spy. Every gentleman's son was encouraged to learn the manual exercise with a toy musket by his nurse, she assuring him that his duty was 'to fight the French and beat Boney'. The exultation caused by the victory of Trafalgar afforded a temporary encouragement to the Hampshire folks of their being able to resist Bonaparte's power. All sorts of demonstrations took place in celebration of the*

event, and a ball was given at Southampton to which everybody went. I, of course did not go, being too young at thirteen.'

Footnote: The Lewin family sold Ridgeway to James Ede c.1820, and upon his death in 1840 his widow let it to Revd W.S. Fowler. By 1850 it was owned by F.M. Lewin and c.1855 the 'castle' was replaced with a less pretentious house. Various residents followed including Revd A.C. Crick (Curate of Peartree Chapel) and Herbert 'Mornington' Cannon, one of the country's top jockeys at the time. In 1915 the Ford Motor Company considered building a motor works on the land and purchased it for £5,000, but decided on a site at Dagenham instead. The estate was again sold and c.1920 the house demolished; the estate became a golf course before being developed during the late 1930s.

Heathfield House
Updated from *The Lost Houses of Southampton*
Jessica Vale BA

Heathfield House was built some time between 1814 and 1840 on high ground beside the West End Road which was previously part of Bitterne Common. From at least 1840 to 1856 it was the home of the Revd Charles Davy and his family. One of his daughters married the younger son of Sir William

Heathfield House, West End Road, c.1932.

During the 1930s Heathfield became a hotel and produced this booklet.

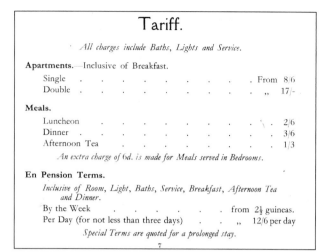

Tariff.

All charges include Baths, Lights and Service.

Apartments.—Inclusive of Breakfast.

Single	From 8/6
Double	„ 17/-

Meals.

Luncheon	2/6
Dinner	3/6
Afternoon Tea	1/3

An extra charge of 6d. is made for Meals served in Bedrooms.

En Pension Terms.

Inclusive of Room, Light, Baths, Service, Breakfast, Afternoon Tea and Dinner.

By the Week	from 2½ guineas.
Per Day (for not less than three days) . .	„ 12/6 per day

Special Terms are quoted for a prolonged stay.

Above: *The hotel's tariff makes interesting reading. Extras included accomodation for visitors' servants at 10s.6d. per day and garaging for cars at 1s.0d. a night (small cars) or 1s.6d. (large).*

Below: *The dining-room of the Heathfield Hotel, 1934.*

Richardson of Chessel House. In 1859 Robert Richardson, who may or may not have been a relation, was living at Heathfield House, but he had moved away by 1863 when George Atherley, a Southampton banker, was in occupation. By 1867 Heathfield House had been bought by Gen. H.P. Raymond, a county magistrate, whose widow continued to live there until 1909 when the property was acquired by William Rivett-Carnac. Within two years, however, he was succeeded by Mrs Wells, who remained at Heathfield until c.1919.

In about 1920 Heathfield House became the home of Mr and Mrs Beazley. After Mr Beazley's death c.1931 his widow opened the house as a private hotel which was taken over in 1936 by Capt. G.J. Quinn. A brochure produced at the time gives an interesting glimpse of the rooms and tariff. By the end of the Second World War Heathfield House was being used as St Jude's Nursing Home and was run by Miss Beale. In 1956 Mr and Mrs Jackson took over the nursing home but restored the house's proper name.

Heathfield House existed without major alterations from its original form until 1981, although much of the grounds were sold for housing, and the original cast-iron verandah on the west side of the house had been demolished. The house itself was demolished at the end of 1981, to be replaced by Homepoint House, a block of sheltered accommodation. The stable block was converted for accommodation some years ago, and is now called Heathfield Cottage.

Tragedy at Hum Hole
Denis Abraham

On Boxing Day, 1905, there was an empty place at the dinner table in the servants' quarters at Heathfield House, in Bitterne. Frances Mary Edwards was missing.

Miss Edwards had worked as a domestic servant for Mrs Raymond at Heathfield House for some six or seven years, but had been unwell with depression for about 18 months. She had, at one time, threatened to drown herself, but when her mother had told the doctor, no action had been taken. Recently she had returned to her work, and for two months had continued with her usual duties.

When she did not appear for her meal, a search was made in the house but she could not be found. Hayward, the groom, and Miss Maud Williams, who was living at Heathfield House at that time, searched the gardens. Halfway towards the nearby wood they met Mr Seymour and Miss Williams stopped to speak to him and sent Hayward on to the wood. After a short while the groom came rushing back with Miss Edwards's cap, which he had found by the side of the pond at Hum Hole, but he had not found Miss Edwards. Miss Williams and the groom returned to the pond where they saw something white. This turned out to be the body of Miss Edwards.

The County Coroner, Mr Bernard Hayfield, held an inquest into the death of Frances Mary Edwards at the Angel Hotel in Bitterne. Mr Cecil Edwards, brother of the deceased, of Osborne Road, Portswood, told the coroner that when he had seen his sister last she had been in good spirits, even though a few days before she had been very depressed. Edward Beckett, a butler, stated that when the deceased had not appeared for dinner he sent a maid to look for her. The deceased had left her cap on the bridge some 30 yards from the pond, which was about a quarter of a mile from the house.

Dr E. Hall stated that he was called to Heathfield House to examine the body of the deceased. Clothing was not torn and there were no signs of violence. Death was due to drowning, in his opinion.

PC Bunce reported that where Miss Edwards had entered the pond she would have had to force her way through growing wood and it would have been practically impossible to have fallen in accidentally. A verdict of suicide during temporary insanity was returned.

Frances Mary Edwards was buried in Southampton Old Cemetery in Hill Lane. The inscription on her gravestone reads:

In memory of FRANCES MARY EDWARDS beloved daughter of JOHN and FRANCES MARY EDWARDS died 26th December 1905.

She was 35 years old. We owe this story to the late Arthur Abraham, of Panwell Road, who mentioned the event to his nephew Denis Abraham in the 1960s. Arthur could remember when this tragedy happened.

The Fire at Heathfield
Gerry Philpott

Three Southampton firemen were badly injured in a fire at Heathfield on Tuesday 10 March 1931 when they were buried under a bell tower which collapsed; they were dug out of the debris semiconscious. The scene of the fire was a 60' x 25' two-storey building in the grounds of Heathfield in West End Road, the residence of Mr and Mrs H.J. Beazley. One end of the building was a gardener's cottage, and here Mr and Mrs F. Mansbridge were living, whilst the rest of the building was used as garages; over the centre was a bell (used to summon servants) and clock tower.

The fire was discovered at about 10p.m. by a maid at Heathfield who saw flames and smoke issuing from near the garage. She at once raised the alarm and the fire brigade were called by telephone. Two fire appliances (Nos 4 and 5) and their crews from Woolston Fire Station were quickly on the scene, under Station Officer A. Westbrooke, and in less than an hour they had the fire well under control. Just before 11.00p.m. Station Officer Westbrooke and Auxiliary Firemen L. Patterson and A. Davis, went up to the room over the central garage to deal with a section that was still burning. A hose was passed up to them, but immediately there was a terrific crash and the roof and tower above fell through to the ground. The three men were buried under about two tons of debris and were extracted with difficulty. The other firemen rushed to their aid and some of the crowd of people who had gathered assisted. It was at once obvious that the three firemen were severely injured and they were carried into Heathfield where first aid was rendered until the arrival of Dr Knowlton and the ambulances to remove them to the Royal South Hants & Southampton Hospital.

The supposed cause of the fire was the ignition of petrol; the motor garage was burnt out and a six-cylinder Wolseley car destroyed.

As a result of the accident Westbrooke and Patton each lost an arm, and Davis suffered severe back injuries and was told he may never walk again. He did eventually, returning to operational duties and completing his service to retire c.1961 as a sub-officer stationed at Woolston.

Peartree House and Major General Shrapnel
Keith Marsh

By the end of the sixteenth century the medieval Bitterne Manor House was falling into a state of disrepair. Rather than repair, the inhabitant, Francis Mylles, sought permission from the owner, the Bishop of Winchester, to remove some of the stone from the building for a new house on Ridgeway Heath. Permission was obviously granted as the new home was built and named Peartree House. Francis Mylles died in 1618. In 1613 daughter Philippa married Captain Richard Smith, a former Governor of Calshot Castle, and they became the occupiers. The house was in the ownership of the Mylles family for two centuries until the last of the family died in 1780; another Francis, the great-great-grandson of the builder, is recorded as living there until 1767. Sometime during the eighteenth century the house was enlarged and had the castellated parapet and stucco front added.

At this time the area was predominantly heathland, with isolated hamlets and dwellings where the inhabitants struggled to make a living by farming and labouring. Along the coast fishing could be added, and at the village of Itchen, ferrying across the river. Itchen itself fell within the parish of St Mary's, Southampton, so attendance at church required an open boat trip across the often turbulent river or a six-mile walk via Mansbridge, which was the nearest bridge. Attendance at church was compulsory with a shilling fine for non-attendance, which for many was a week's wages, so Capt. Smith, a devout Christian, resolved to build a chapel for the locality at his own expense, and applied to the Bishop of Winchester,

Above: *Peartree House, c.1937, built in the late-sixteenth century using stone from Bitterne Manor.*
(*HANTS RECORD OFFICE, 65M89/Z211/443*)

Left: *Major General Henry Shrapnel (1761–1842).*

Dr James Montague, for a licence to build a chapel-of-ease at Peartree. This was granted in February 1617, and more stone was reclaimed from Bitterne Manor for the building of Jesus Chapel. But St Mary's was in a dilapidated state at the time and the rector there was concerned about the potential loss of income, so several safeguards were put in place: for instance, marriage and burial fees still had to be paid to St Mary's, and parishioners living west of the river could not attend Jesus Chapel without the rector's permission. Furthermore, Captain Smith had to guarantee a salary of 20 marks a year (£13.33) for the curate and provide him with a small house.

Perhaps the most famous resident of Peartree House was Major General Henry Shrapnel, the inventor of the exploding artillery shell, who lived there from c.1835 until his death on 13 March 1842. He was born in 1761 at Bradford-on-Avon and entered the army as an artillery officer; he used his own money to develop military inventions. At the retreat from Dunkirk in 1793, two of his ideas were put into use: a method of skidding gun carriages over sand, and the use of decoy fires to fool the enemy.

As a lieutenant he invented an anti-personnel projectile that was fired from cannons and exploded above the enemy, an explosive charge showering them with lead shot or spherical bullets and fragments of the shell case. Case shot had been used at Constantinople in 1453, and in 1573 a German, Zimmerman, had added a time fuse to it, but Shrapnel's invention was the first air-bursting shell that resulted in 'directional velocity' being given to the shot it contained. This was adopted by the British Army in 1803 and used for the first time in 1808 against the French, with the Duke of Wellington and the commander of the artillery, Sir George Wood, testifying to its effectiveness. On 21 June 1815 Sir George wrote to Shrapnel from Waterloo, saying that without his shell it was doubtful whether the British would have retaken La Haye Sainte farmhouse; so

his invention had turned the tide. However, the duke was concerned about public opinion on the weapon, so its use was kept quiet, depriving Shrapnel of fame and honour.

Shrapnel was promoted to colonel in 1813 but financial recognition for his inventions was not forthcoming, though he was granted a pension of £1,200 for life. He retired from active service in 1825 with the rank of major general, but became a colonel commandant of the Royal Artillery in 1827, and a lieutenant general ten years later. It was not until the 1830s, when he was living in semi-retirement, that Shrapnel began receiving recognition for his inventions. Whilst a guest of William IV at Brighton, the King acknowledged his contribution, intimating that a knighthood was to be conferred, and in 1837 Shrapnel received confirmation from Windsor Castle. But the King died before the ceremony took place and nothing more was heard of the honour. So Shrapnel's final years were marred by disappointment, with the recognition which he undoubtedly deserved eluding him. Indeed, his invention was not known as the Shrapnel shell until 1852, and of course now the word shrapnel refers to all bursting fragments and splinters.

Although he was one of the area's distinguished residents, he seemed to avoid the local social round, and his death passed almost unreported, except in the *Hampshire Advertiser*, which mentioned some of his inventions: snuffers, corkscrews, and a regulating pivot pen. He was buried in the family vault at Holy Trinity, Bradford-on-Avon. After his death his widow and daughter moved to Shirley.

Another family that lived at Peartree House was the Cruikshanks, who were very active in promoting education, and who lived there from 1893 to 1917. During the 1930s most of the land surrounding the house was sold for housing, ruining its tranquil setting. Then in 1949 it was bought by Southampton Council and used as a home for elderly people.

Townhill Park House
Ray Marsh

Townhill Park House is certainly the most notable of the remaining large houses which were built in the Bitterne area during 1700–1800. It was built in 1793 for Nathaniel Middleton replacing an earlier farmhouse on land purchased by him around 1787 from John White. The house and surrounding estate was bought by William Hallett in 1820 and by Caleb Gater around 1859; in 1897 it was sold to Sir Samuel Montagu (created Baron Swaythling in 1907) who passed it to his son Louis and his family as a country residence in 1911.

Louis commissioned Leonard Rome Guthrie, a young architect, to rebuild and enlarge the original

A cross-section of Shrapnel's exploding shell.

The garden staff at Townhill Park House c.1925. Back row, left to right: *Arthur Gosling, Ernest Puttock, Bill Fanstone, Gus Line, Tom Phillips, Arthur Razy, Bill Moody;* middle row: *Billy Lee, Bert Cowley, Fred Hayes, Tommy Millon, Fred Rose (head gardener), Bill Razy, Harold Spencer, Fred Miller;* front row: *Leslie Soffe, Reg Williams, Bob Moody, Albert Razy, Jack Kinchington.* (BETTY MOODY)

Above: *The pergola across the bottom of the Townhill Park House garden, summer 1950.*

Inset: *The rear of Townhill Park House, 1998.*

house, its completion being delayed by the First World War until 1920. It is interesting to note that the entrance to the original building is now in the basement, the ground level having been raised during the rebuilding. The wonderful gardens and grounds, for which the house is renowned, were created by the celebrated landscape gardener Gertrude Jekyll, being lovingly maintained for many years by a staff of 25 highly skilled gardeners. Queen Mary, a personal friend of Lady Swaythling, often visited the house where she had a bedroom reserved for her exclusive use, and she would take a daily walk in the gardens. The house was painted white both inside and out, and is still called 'the White House' by many locals.

In 1927, Louis, the second Lord Swaythling, died but the new Lord, and the Swaythling family, continued to live at the house until the outbreak of the Second World War when part of it was handed over to the Red Cross for use as a hospital convalescent home. In 1945, the family decided to sell up as by this time the building was too expensive to maintain. Much of the lovely furniture, the wonderful pictures and the family silver was sold, some of the latter being purchased by the Victoria and Albert Museum in London. The whole of the estate, including the House, Upper and Lower Townhill Farms, the extensive grounds and kitchen gardens together with many large greenhouses, covered an area of 324 acres.

In 1948, the house and 30 acres of gardens and grounds were purchased by Middlesex Education Authority for use as a special residential school for girls whilst most of the remaining estate was acquired by Southampton Borough Council for building the area known today as Townhill Park.

The school closure in 1969 brought the house on the market again, to be purchased by Southampton City Council as a College of Technology hostel for cadets undergoing marine engineering courses; responsibility for this transferred to Hampshire County Council in 1974.

It was probably during this period that local residents became more aware of the importance of the nearby 'White House', where many of them were now employed. The popular warden of the hostel, Ralph Coney, enlisted help in a three-year project to restore the cricket pitch to its former glory. For over two decades until 1992 this was used by the Education Eccentrics CC, a club which evolved from the pre-1974 Southampton Education Office side organised by Alan Leonard. They played a full programme of Friday evening and Sunday afternoon matches, occasional Saturday all-day games and truly eccentric annual encounters with Ralph Coney's team (mostly drawn from the College of Maritime Studies, Warsash) on the morning of 27 December – the latter always seemingly blessed with fine weather!

Ralph also became Chairman of the local Scout Group, allowing use of a room for meetings and the grounds for activities – including a mammoth firework display in November. In the daytime, the cadets being at college, various conferences and courses were held at Townhill Park House and, during the holidays, Southampton Youth Orchestra filled the house with wonderful music.

Unfortunately cadet numbers were declining due to a reduction in the number of British merchant ships, so 1983 saw the last intake into the house before transferring students to the Warsash hostel. A limited number of older students occupied the house until 1993 when Hampshire County Council decided they could no longer justify the cost, so, once again, Townhill Park House was put up for sale. After much discussion and negotiation, the house, set in the remaining 20 acres, was sold to the independent co-educational Gregg School and reopened, after many more interior alterations, in September 1994.

Although the exterior of Townhill Park House has retained much of its original elegance, internally it has necessarily had to change with the requirements of each new set of occupants. That said, many rooms retain some vestiges of former glory by way of fireplaces, some panelling and mouldings. The beautiful gardens and grounds, however, had been at times somewhat neglected. In 1997, a group of people met with the Hampshire Gardens Trust and the Gregg School to form The Friends of Townhill Park Gardens, their aim being to restore that part of the Gertrude Jekyll gardens which still exists; in ten years the few people working on this project have made remarkable progress, despite problems experienced with resident deer and other livestock. The gardens are open to the public on several Sundays each year, with occasional access to the house.

Redcote
Bill Hulbert

Redcote was built by the Revd Henry Usborne, Vicar of Bitterne, and was the vicarage until he sold it and moved. The land was originally owned by James Dott of Bitterne Grove, who owned a lot of land in the area following the Enclosure Act of 1812. In 1825 there was a conveyance between James Dott and a

Redcote, Shales Road, Bitterne's first vicarage. In 1904 it became a convent.

Wage increases affect all services, no matter who runs them! The laundry closed on 29 September 1974.

builder named Richard Laishley, of a parcel of land to the north of Botley Road (now Bitterne Road East). Richard Laishley sold some of this land to John Newman, a brickmaker, in 1827 and it was this parcel of land, amounting to three acres, which was bought (by a conveyance dated 22 October 1858) by the Revd Henry Usborne of Midanbury House for £345.12s.0d. On the conveyance it was designated as:

Oak Lodge, Freemantle Common Road, 2006.

... that parcel of land bounded on the north and east by land owned by the widow of the late Richard Laishley, builder, on the south by Botley Road and on the west by the road leading from Botley Road to Harefield Farm.

All the land to the south of Botley Road was part of Sholing Common.

On the land owned by John Newman there were some cottages, lying back from the road, somewhere near the present York Drive.

Shortly after the first conveyance, on 11 November 1858, the Revd Usborne bought the surrounding land owned by the widow of the late Richard Laishley, the whole parcel purchased being about 21 acres. The Revd Usborne sold Redcote to Joseph Stewart Cockerton, possibly in 1887 when he retired as Vicar of Bitterne.

There was an Indenture of Conveyance dated 5 January 1904 between Joseph Stewart Cockerton and Emily Huet, Bridget McEvoy and Aline Prudhomme relating to the property known as Redcote. The three ladies were the original trustees when the property was bought by a branch of the French Catholic Order of Our Lady of Charity. Although Redcote was known as The Convent of Our Lady of Charity of Refuge it was an independent foundation and not answerable to the French Order. At the same time that Redcote was bought, the Charity also bought a small house called The Chestnuts in Botley Road, later to become a nursing home. Redcote was enlarged by building a laundry, dormitories for the women, a chapel and a presbytery for the resident priest.

In 1946 the Charity purchased Langstaff House in West End Road; this was formerly called Shales and was renamed St Theresa's House. There was a legal wrangle going on in 1949 as to whether the Charity could claim exemption from purchase tax, the outcome of which is not known.

Sadly Redcote, like so many of the old Bitterne houses, is no more. Financial considerations made it necessary to sell most of the Redcote estate for residential development, enabling a new convent to be built, whilst the original building has been demolished.

Oak Lodge
Denis and Deirdre Abraham

The early history of Oak Lodge, facing Freemantle Common, is uncertain: a building by that name is mentioned on the tithe list in 1841, although by 1865 it seems to have been called Oak Cottage. It was home to Mrs Martin from 1871 until at least 1883, and to Mrs Briggs, as Oak Lodge, in 1895. Between 1898 and 1922 John Brook-Brown lived there, followed by S.W. Barnaby, JP, upon whose death in 1926 the five-acre property was divided into two lots and auctioned.

The sale particulars give a detailed description of the property: partial central heating, four reception rooms, fitted kitchen, pantry, scullery, five main bedrooms (one with en-suite), nursery, two bathrooms, maids' rooms, tower, conservatory, heated garage, stables, kennels, granary, aviary, cow pens, pigsties, two tennis-courts, squash or badminton court, well-kept lawns and flower-beds, kitchen and fruit gardens, vinery, ornamental pond, orchard, meadow, paddock, mains water, drainage into main sewer, mains gas (electric mains being laid in an adjacent road!). How much would a property like this cost today? The District Valuer's Office valued it then at £3,850.

Southampton Borough Council had decided to set up a Works Depot in the district in 1918, to meet the needs of the borough's expansion, but the purchase of Oak Lodge was not agreed until June 1930. The Borough Treasurer and the Housing Manager agreed to allow the caretaker to continue living there rent free until later in the year when he was found alternative accommodation.

By 1933 Mr Edward Diment, who was District Foreman for Southampton Corporation, was living in the house with family. His daughter, Peg Wilkinson, recalls life there:

I moved to Oak Lodge, with Mum and Dad and my two brothers, from Whites Road (where I was born) when I was four years old, and spent twenty very

Left: *Len Beale and Gwen Whitlock's wedding at West End Church in 1936. Gwen's bouquet was of magnolia blossom from the Oak Lodge garden. Both were keen cyclists, hence the wheels!*

Below: *Wartime at Oak Lodge. Roy, Peggy, Dora and Ted Diment beside a camouflaged council lorry.*

The beautiful oak staircase in Oak Lodge.

happy years there. My dad was the District Foreman, and he was given a bicycle by the Council to enable him to cycle round the different parts of the area. It was a strong heavy old bike, and when he retired he was able to buy the bike from the Council for 2s.6d. (13p).

We moved into the downstairs part of the house which was originally the servants' quarters, consisting of a scullery, living room, two smaller rooms along the passage, toilet, pantry and coal house. Upstairs there were three big bedrooms, bathroom and separate toilet. There was a large cellar where we used to shelter during the war.

When we first moved to Oak Lodge there was a big meadow at the bottom of the yard where I loved to play when I was a little girl. There was a big oak tree to

which someone had attached a swing and grown-ups and children alike used to end up on it.

We used to have big bonfire parties on 5 November, which was also my mother's birthday, so it was a double celebration. I remember lots of relatives came with fireworks, so it lasted for quite a long time. The meadow was eventually filled in to make room for garages for the lorries, and at the beginning of the war they built a decontamination centre on the site – quite a big one-storey building.

Of course there were horses and carts in those days. Five horses were stabled there: Dolly, Violet, Punch and Judy, and Bob (my favourite – a big black horse).

We moved to the flat upstairs in 1940 where we had three bedrooms plus two very large rooms, kitchen, toilet and bathroom. There was a really lovely wide oak staircase leading up to the flat and a landing, which was so big I was able to play on it if we had a wet day. The cornices around the ceilings were beautiful, all shaped like oak leaves and acorns. Another great feature was the lovely dome which was over the stairs and landing, but unfortunately it was shattered when a blast bomb fell on the Common opposite.

Downstairs were offices and storerooms, leading off a very large flag-stoned hallway. The front door was huge and very heavy and never locked, which was just as well for me, as the key was about eight inches long and also very heavy.

There were some lovely trees in the grounds. There was a superb magnolia tree with big flowers that smelt of lemons. My cousin Gwen Whitlock loved them so much that she had her bouquet made for her wedding from some of those lovely blooms. There were also three camellia trees which were quite rare in those days. Two of my favourite trees were what we called 'Umbrella' trees (we never knew the real name); my friends and I used to like playing under them.

I left Oak Lodge to get married in 1951, but still continued to visit Mum and Dad there until Dad retired in 1954. Very happy times.

Oak Lodge Social Club was formed in 1977 to help psychiatric patients by promoting social skills, offering mutual support and offering skilled help from professionals such as a community nurse. Meetings were held on Mondays and Wednesdays with trained staff, and on Fridays for a social meeting without helpers. Summer outings were arranged, as well as a Christmas concert.

The Council no longer have a use for Oak Lodge, which at the time of writing is about to be demolished.

Shales, the Cootes and the Perkins
Keith Marsh

Shales was typical of the gentry's houses built around Bitterne. It was constructed c.1840 to the

Shales House, the home of Admiral Robert Coote from 1864 to 1885.

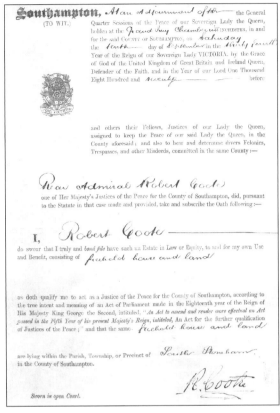

The sitting room in Shales House, c.1883.

Justice's certificate of qualification for Rear Admiral Robert Coote, dated 1870.

(HANTS RECORD OFFICE, Q27/3/624)

Above: Stanley and Maud Coote at Shales, c.1883.

Right: Gardeners Jim Goulden and Bill Heath cutting the lawns at Shales, c.1883.

north of West End Road, and got its name from Shales Flats, the expanse of flat land on the Harefield estate opposite. In 1851 it belonged to Sir Charles Henry Coote, 9th Baronet, MP, for Queen's County (now County Laois, Ireland) who appears in Sir George Hayter's well-known painting of the House of Commons in 1833 (now hung in the National Portrait Gallery). The Coote family have owned extensive land in central Ireland for centuries. In 1628 the then Sir Charles laid the foundations of the town of Moynrath by establishing a linen factory and obtaining the grant for markets and fairs. The present Sir Charles is the premier baronet of Ireland, and he and Lady Coote continue to support the local community.

Sir Charles, 9th Baronet, died on 8 October 1864 and Shales, together with the estates in Ireland, passed to his fourth son, Admiral Robert Coote, CB, FRGS, JP. Robert was born in Geneva, Switzerland, on 1 June 1820, and was educated at Eton. He entered the Royal Navy at age 13 and by the age of 34 had reached the rank of captain. In 1860–63 he was captain of HMS *Victory* and was responsible for reorganising the naval police. He was promoted to rear admiral in 1870, and to vice admiral when appointed Commander-in-Chief Coast of Ireland (1873–76). He served as Commander-in-Chief China (1878–81), being made a full admiral before retiring in 1885. His death in March 1898 was reported in the *Midland Tribune* on 26 March:

> *Deep and widespread regret was caused in Tullamore and district by the announcement of the death of Admiral Robert Coote, CB, which occurred on St Patrick's Day at Arden, Dulwich, London. The deceased gentleman possessed extensive property in Tullamore and district, as well as in Westmeath and Roscommon, and was distinguished by a most benevolent and charitable disposition. His dealings with his tenantry were always marked by humanity and consideration, and even in the liveliest period of the land war no friction ever arose, and most cordial relations were sustained. His was one of those natures of which the milk of human kindness has filled to overflowing, and never became congealed; and many were the practical evidences of compassion and well-directed sympathy which his long and useful life afforded...*

There is a stained-glass window dedicated to his memory in St Catherine's Church, Tullamore, presented by his son, Stanley Coote. A collection of photographs of the Coote family and their servants, taken at Shales between 1884 and 1886, is now in the BLHS archive.

After Admiral Coote's death Shales was tenanted by Dr Harold Browne, Lord Bishop of Winchester, before being sold by auction on 19 May 1897. The sales particulars describe the ten-acre property:

> *... capital dining room... handsome drawing room... nice conservatory... charming octagonal shaped morning room... billiard room... 9 best and secondary bedrooms... 2 WCs... beautifully timbered and most attractive park-like grounds...*

It was briefly owned by Col Bald before being bought by Col and Mrs Perkins. Col Perkins saw military service in the Boer War with the 3rd (Militia) Battalion, The Welsh Regiment, commanding 12 officers and 240 soldiers. At home in Bitterne he played an active part in village life: he was MP for Southampton (1922–29) and honorary colonel of the 5/7 Hampshire Regiment. He was on the organising committee of many local events, and showed great kindness in inviting the child inmates of the workhouse to the estate for their annual treat. In the 1920s Col Perkins officially opened the Bitterne Sports & Social Club's ground in Wynter Road and in his speech he praised the club for rescuing a big field from building operations! He died in 1937.

Sometime between 1910 and 1931 Shales was renamed Langstaff House, and became 'a home for ladies' with a board of trustees. In 1946 it was purchased by the Sisters of Redcote Convent who renamed it St Theresa's and continued to run it as a hostel; the building currently known as St Theresa's was built in the early 1960s as an extension to the old building, with a covered walkway between. In August 1984 the original building, with about half an acre of land, was sold by tender by Fox & Sons, who suggested its suitability for conversion to a nursing home, hotel or guest-house. Instead it was demolished and replaced with St Francis House, a block of warden-controlled retirement flats.

Bitterne Grove
Pete Crawford

Bitterne Grove was built in about 1790 for Richard Leversuch, possibly on the site of an older building. By 1796 it was owned by a retired surgeon, James Dott, who gave sanctuary to a French aristocrat, Toussaint-

An early photograph of Bitterne Grove, one of the finest houses in the area. Certainly it enjoyed splendid views, now enjoyed by the students of St Mary's College.

The view from Bitterne Grove towards Lances Hill c.1920.

Ambroise Talour de la Cartrie de la Villeniere, who was escaping the French Revolution, employing him as a gardener. Dott was considered a little eccentric, thus some incorrectly assume he was the source of the word 'dotty'; Midanbury Lane was at one time dubbed Dott's Lane. He is reputed to have given land on which old West End Church was built, and also an annual endowment to six parish widows, who were given a length of red flannel. This is still administered, though it only amounts to about £3.

James Dott died in 1844 and the house was then owned by Alexander Hoyes until he died in 1857. In 1878 the house, outbuildings and 18 acres of grounds were sold for £6,600 to Major Thomas Bramston Hamilton RA, whose widow remained until about 1900.

In 1910 the property was purchased by a Catholic French teaching order and twelve years later they opened a day- and boarding-school for boys. The house is now the residence of the Brothers of St Mary's College – an independent school for both boys and girls.

Harefield House and Edwin Jones
Keith Marsh

A map of 1806 shows New Farm on the west of West End Road, and in 1815 the 272-acre farm was one of 45 allotments to William Hallet under the enclosure award; the indenture describes it as including Bacon Hill, Shales Flat and Goathouse Bottom. The earliest known evidence of the name Harefield is in the deeds of a property c.1830, which describes Commercial Street as the Road to Harefield Farm.

Harefield House was built c.1840 for Sir Edward

Right: Edwin Jones (1832–96) founder of the well-known drapery store and twice Mayor of Southampton. This drawing appeared in a blotter produced by the company in 1933 to celebrate 75 years of business.

Butler, chairman of the Southampton & Salisbury Railway Company, but he left the estate in around 1856 when Arthur Bailey took up residence. In December that year the estate was extended when the two-acre Sand Pit Meadow was leased from Thomas Chamberlayne for £5 per year for 1,000 years. Arthur Bailey died on 20 October 1858 leaving the estate to Sir Edward Butler, who had died that July, so the property was inherited by his widow, Urania Elizabeth Butler. However, she died on 2 December 1858 so the estate passed to her son, Arthur Paulet Butler. He was a minor so administration was granted to Sir Henry Charles Paulet, who sold the estate in March 1860 to William Stedman Gillett.

William and his family lived in grand style, keeping the grounds immaculately, introducing a flock of peacocks and building an indoor riding school. The undulating estate was well timbered with coverts and plantations, ponds and a stream, whilst the arable land was 'of a sound character and in a high state of cultivation'. The mansion was described as:

... a most substantial erection of the Elizabethan-style of architecture, standing on an eminence approached from the main road by three entrances, by winding carriage drives leading to a bold porte-cochere entrance. On the summit is an observatory with revolving dome fitted with divisional opening, with store room beneath.

In 1886 the farm included cottages, dairy, stables, granaries, poultry houses, barn, slaughterhouse, piggeries and even a manure house! A deep well supplied water and there was a rain-water reservoir and ice house. In the parkland was an ornamental cow house with a starling roost on top, and in Bacon Hill woods was a pheasantry. Rats are always a pest on farms and in his memories Chris Boulton recalled winter evenings spent creeping around with a torch and air-rifle; the victims' tails were nailed to a shed

A picture that epitomises Bitterne life at the beginning of the twentieth century. Mr Thomas the head coachman, and 15-year old Edward Morant at Harefield House c.1910.

door. Foxes were also a problem, and one visited regularly at 12.30p.m. and grabbed a chicken, having learnt when everyone went to lunch!

Each spring the largest pond, with a footbridge to a small island, attracted local children with jam jars to collect frog spawn. The fields all had names: Shell's Field, Longeards Hill, Great Goaters, etc., though local lads seem to have numbered them as well, and great prestige was gained by daring to reach as far as the twelfth field or beyond. And more esteem was earned if you were chased by Ernest Kingman the bailiff!

From Harefield House, a drive ran to the corner of Shales and Balaclava Roads, providing a tradesmen's entrance to the estate from Bitterne village. This led to Shales Road being known as Back Lane until it was named; in dry weather the course of this drive can be seen across the school playing-field.

Perhaps the person most synonymous with Harefield House is Southampton merchant Edwin Jones, who lived there from 1889 until his death in 1896. Born in Romsey in 1832, Edwin was educated at a private school, and apprenticed to a local draper. After periods in Winchester and London, he moved to Southampton in 1860, and rented a small haberdashery shop in East Street with his sister. This was most successful, partly through Edwin's astute deals in cotton, so by 1865 they had moved to larger premises and in 1888 the business became a limited company with an agreed capital of £120,000.

In the late 1860s Edwin married Annette Sharp and moved to Bassett, but she died soon after their daughter Annette was born. In 1870 Edwin entered politics, being elected to the Southampton Town Council. The following year he was elected Senior Bailiff, and he became Sheriff and a magistrate in 1872. Mayor in 1873 and 1875, he led the reception when the body of Africa explorer Dr Livingstone was returned to this country for burial. Besides his political and commercial activities, Edwin was responsible for many elaborate social events, including a Grand Ball attended by 1,600 at the Hartley Institute in 1874 to celebrate the marriage of the then Duke of Edinburgh; this was said by many to be the grandest ball the town had ever seen!

Edwin's marriage to Fanny Louisa White on 13 February 1874 was reported in the *Pictorial World*; headlined 'Presentation to an ex-Mayor', an illustration showed the five-piece fruit service presented to them and the centrepiece is now displayed in the Civic Centre, and is used at civic functions. In 1890 Edwin retired from the Council to spend more time on the estate, and in his obituary the *Southampton Times* reported that 'recently over 2,000 rhododendrons have been planted in a portion of the grounds.'

The Harefield estate was freehold except for Sand Pit Meadow, and in 1896 Edwin corresponded with Tankerville Chamberlayne and an agent, J.M.

This was the centrepiece of a five-piece silver gilt and cut-glass fruit service, presented to Edwin Jones by the Southampton townspeople in recognition of his time as Mayor and in honour of his wedding to Fanny White. This 32-inch high piece is now displayed in the Mayor's Parlour, and is occasionally used at civic functions, but where did the other pieces go?

Pritchard Esq., who were disputing the lease. In one letter Edwin wrote:

If a man takes a plot for 1,000 years solely for the purpose of taking and using the sand on it, when all that sand is gone is not the lease void in as much as the privilege confirmed by the lease is non-existent?

On 10 June 1896 Edwin wrote to Prichard enclosing the indenture for the land; on 30 July Fanny, on notepaper poignantly edged in black, wrote to ask for its return, Edwin having died the day before.

Edwin's first sign of illness was on 27 June, and within a few days he was confined to bed with pleurisy; despite an operation by Dr Trend, Edwin died on 29 July. He was Deputy Lord Lieutenant of Hampshire when he died so would have become Lord Lieutenant the following year. His funeral journey from Harefield House to West End Church, was a solemn affair, the coffin borne on an open hearse bedecked with flowers, the route lined with mourners. On Whit Sunday 1897, a pulpit (donated by his wife and daughter) and a stained-glass window (paid for by public subscription) were dedicated to Edwin's memory in West End Church.

On 27 March 1901 Fanny Jones, Edwin's widow, married Dr Thomas, a widower, who a year later became a director of the Edwin Jones Company. He died on 10 June 1913 reportedly of septicaemia caused by a cut inflicted whilst pruning roses, but the recollection of his seven-year old grandson, Rupert Martin, was slightly different:

It was the custom each Sunday to hold a huge family lunch party. Afterwards my grandfather would take my sister and me, and usually a Bond aunt, for a long walk round the garden and woods, while the others were sleeping off the roast beef. He always used this expedition to gather flowers to take with him to his hospital wards on Monday morning. He was standing on the edge of a stream cutting foxgloves when the bank collapsed and he fell right on top of the open knife which he was using. My sister and I stayed with him while Sybil Bond rushed for help. Too late. The long knife went straight through him. There is a bed endowed in his memory in the South Hants Hospital which he served so devotedly, as well as being Chairman of the Hampshire doctors for a long spell.'

On 17 March 1917 Mrs Thomas signed a tenancy agreement for the farm with W. Harris but on Sunday 6 May 1917 the house was destroyed by fire. It started at about 8.20a.m. when, it is believed, sparks from the kitchen chimney ignited leaves caught on the roof; local boys were often sent up on to the roof to clear leaves, so the fire hazard was well recognised. The following day, under the headline 'Great Fire at Westend - Beautiful Residence in Ruins', the *Southern Evening Echo* reported:

One of the finest homes in Southern Hampshire was completely gutted. The flames swept the whole of the interior, denuding it of everything, and converting all combustible substances into piles of charred rubble. Nothing now remains save the exterior walls, but inside the scene is one of indescribable desolation and destruction.

Whilst a stiff breeze fanned the fire, the fire brigade, villagers and the local police salvaged some of the contents of the house, despite the danger of collapsing upper floors, and a stream of deadly molten lead from the roof. Some say that the building burnt well due to a large amount of butter stored in the roof! Most of the irreplaceable antiques, valuable furniture and priceless oil paintings on the ground floor were saved, but most upstairs were lost; local children recounted seeing beautifully carved settees and trophies from abroad being stacked upon the lawns. Subsequent rumours suggested that the Southampton Fire Brigade were selective when they arrived on the scene, and headed for the cellars to save the vintage wine! However, at least one did more: Winifred Jones's uncle was a fireman, and told her that one of the residents begged him to save the contents of her bureau; her bedroom was already well alight and the bureau locked, so he chopped off the legs and threw it out of the window. The lady, extremely grateful as it contained her jewellery and several thousand pounds, vowed never to lock a drawer again!

The entry in the Fire Brigade Report Book details the fire and the five appliances that attended, and gives the estimated total amount at risk as £21,973. It reported:

... only one jet obtainable from hydrant system after the supply of water to village of Bitterne had been shut off; steamer worked from small ornamental pond.

The *Southampton Times* report on the fire concluded:

... the sympathy of all that place has gone out to Mrs Thomas in her loss. Ever a kind and generous friend and supporter of the many and varied benevolent institutions in the parish and neighbourhood, she has been ever ready and willing to place the grounds of Harefield and the riding school at the disposal of those endeavouring to assist the funds of parochial organisations, while the extent of her private charity is known only to the many who have reason to be grateful to her for her practical sympathy and kindness of heart.

After the fire Fanny moved to Midanbury Cottage; she died on 12 March 1918.

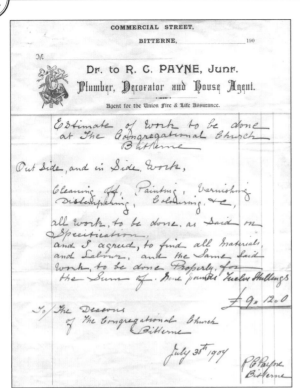

Left: *A dapper George Payne on his 21st birthday.*

Left: *An estimate for decorating work to be carried out at the Congregational Church, 1907.*

Below left, : *R.C. Payne & Son's first premises, Western Place (now the Percy Arms car park) advertising the versatility of the firm in the early 1930s.*

R.C. Payne & Son moved to their current location in 1932. Next door is the first Co-Op shop in Bitterne.

The dedication of a clock at R.C. Payne's premises. A plaque below is inscribed 'This clock has been placed here in memory of Bob Payne who died on 12 January 1999. He was one of Bitterne's gentle men who helped many people in a quiet way.' Those attending included June, John, Carol and Jane Stockley, Len Cooper, George, Peggy and Debbie Payne, Iain Steel, Sarah, Ian, Peter and Ruth May Abrahams, Margaret Coleman, and David and Christine Murphy.

(SOUTHERN DAILY ECHO)

Chapter Three

R.C. Payne & Son
George Payne

R.C. Payne & Son was established in 1887 in the village of Bitterne. Although generally painters and decorators they tackled practically anything. A letter heading dated 1913 depicts a plumber in one corner and a horse-drawn hearse in the other, whilst exhorting the public to use the company as gasfitters, house agents, glaziers, paperhangers and undertakers.

There were three R.C. (Robert Chapman) Paynes. The first (Bob) lived and worked from a house in Commercial Street (now the Percy Arms car park). He died in 1942. In the 1930s the company moved to the existing premises in Bitterne Road, the home of the second 'RCP' (Young Bob) who died in 1982 and was succeeded by his son, the third 'RCP' (Bobby) who died in 1999. The impressive clock on the front corner of the Bitterne Road premises was donated in memory of Bobby Payne by his family and friends in the year 2000 and the plaque simply reads 'He was one of Bitterne's gentlemen, who helped many people in a quiet way.'

Family involvement was much in evidence – the original R.C. Payne's brother George worked for the firm and in turn I, his son also George, joined the company in 1946 following war service with the Royal Marines, and still retain an active interest in the business today.

In the early years the number of funerals carried out was comparatively few. A hearse was rarely provided, the coffin being carried by pallbearers through the village to the appropriate church or churchyard. For the more affluent, horse-drawn hearses and coaches were commonly used until the late 1920s and it is still possible for the company to provide this service today.

Until the rationing of food in the Second World War, the firm was also well known as 'Refreshment Caterers', and although everyone was involved, this was really the province of Lucy, wife of the first 'RCP'. Unlike her husband, who was known to have a short fuse, Lucy was lovely lady and was referred to by many who knew her as the 'Angel of Bitterne'. Over the years many Bitterne people were served at numerous functions where the firm were employed as caterers, such as at garden fêtes, sports meetings, Sunday School outings and, of course, wedding receptions.

The bulk of the work up to the 1960s was mainly painting, decorating, repairing and the maintenance of homes and buildings in Bitterne and the surrounding districts.

After the end of the war the huge new housing estates at Harefield, Thornhill and Surrey House, Sholing were built and by the 1970s the number of funerals carried out increased dramatically and it was at this time that all other work ceased and the firm became solely undertakers or, as they are generally known nowadays, funeral directors.

Bobby, the last 'RCP', sold the company in 1989, but it still continues today under new ownership. The premises were completely restored and renovated in 1991/2 and again in 1999, and now provide full professional facilities with tastefully appointed chapels of rest, a service chapel, selection room, meeting room and reception rooms.

In 1997 branch offices were opened at Shirley Road, Shirley and at Woodmill Lane, Bitterne Park. These enable the company to provide a comprehensive service to a wider community within Southampton.

Over 100 years after its formation, R.C. Payne & Son still offer and provide an efficient, dignified and sympathetic personal service with a highly trained and experienced staff who continue to place great emphasis in being caring family funeral directors.

I was employed as a painter and decorator, though over the years I became a 'Jack-of-all-trades' and carried out work in most of the building industries. Not many funerals were carried out at that time. One of the conditions of employment was that you had to be prepared to be a pallbearer when necessary – this was my introduction to the funeral business.

Over the past sixty years there have been many changes in the funeral business as there have been elsewhere. The original crematorium in Southampton at South Stoneham cemetery was first used c.1929, but in the immediate postwar years most people still preferred burial – about 80 per cent. Nowadays the numbers are almost the complete reverse of that. The majority of people died at home, but even if they passed away in hospital or elsewhere, they laid at home in their coffins until the day of the funeral. Chapels of rest were only just beginning to be provided by funeral directors. Coffins were of solid elm or oak, and were made for each individual. Today coffins are practically all factory made and there is a huge range to select from – veneered oak and mahogany, solid oak, mahogany, pine and elaborate caskets. With the advent of environmentally friendly woodland burial sites, bamboo or wicker coffins are now supplied and for those who often remark, 'a cardboard coffin is all I want', these are also available.

In conclusion, I can say quite honestly that I have enjoyed my working life with R.C. Payne & Son. My greatest memories will be of all the people I have met, from the early days when working in their homes as a decorator, etc., up to the present when in latter years I have been involved with them during their times of bereavement. Inevitably I have arranged the funerals of many of the friends and acquaintances I have made through my work over the years. I hope and trust that my friendship has helped these families through this sad period of their lives.

The Sandpit
Eddie Croxson

The Sandpit was secured for the village of Bitterne under the Enclosures Act of 1812 implemented in 1814.

The subsoil in the area is very stony as can still be seen in Panwell Road (one of the very few unmade roads in the City of Southampton). Not only is the surface stony but the subsoil at a depth of no more than two meters is solid sand. Both of these materials are useful for building.

In Victorian times the whole area east of the River Itchen was being built upon and there were several brickworks and gravel and sand excavations being undertaken. This meant that Bitterne Sandpit was no longer used and it was levelled off and used as a play area. In about 1920 the Borough Council decided to enclose the area and make it into a recreation-ground for general use. Following complaints by the local residents in 1935 about the noise at night from young people, the ground, which already had a fence for much of its length and width, was finally enclosed and fitted with gates, which were closed at dusk and opened at 9a.m. daily. It was a common practice to enclose such grounds and to lock them to stop any naughty goings-on at night. Unfortunately the Council in their zest for a well-behaved ground failed to realise that people had been using this common land to go from Pound Street to West End Road for as long as anyone could remember and they had closed all access. After consultation a compromise was reached whereby a pathway was provided which allowed people to walk between the two roads but it was at considerable expense since they had provided a fence alongside the last property on the south end and now they had to put in a new fence and a gate a few yards further north. The locals benefited from the mistake because they were provided with a tarmac pathway and even a street lamp that enabled them to see their way through. Toilets were built beside the new pathway and a new shed in which the park keeper could keep his tools was also provided.

There were two roundabouts and two seesaws for children to play on and a circular pit was dug and filled with sand for the younger children. On Boxing Day each year the local public houses held an informal football match. It was just a 'kick-about' game as the surface and slope of the ground did not lend itself to organised games.

The best part of the ground for informal cricket and football games by the older children was along the West End Road side but complaints were made by the tenants of the local houses that children were damaging their fences by climbing to retrieve their balls. Eventually a high fence was put up and everyone was happy. But this happiness did not last long.

With the threat of war in 1939 local authorities throughout the country began to dig trenches and build air-raid shelters for the general public to use. Mechanical diggers were cumbersome things then and most of the shelters, including the one in Bitterne, were dug by hand. They were about 5ft deep and zigzagged over some 30ft in length, the idea of the zigzag being that a direct hit by a bomb on the shelter would not affect all the occupants.

Later on during the war it was considered necessary to provide water tanks for the fire service to use in the event that the mains water pipes were damaged. A tank was built on The Sandpit recreation-ground alongside Pound Street. When the war ended both the water tank and the air-raid shelter pit were filled in and the park benches were traditionally used in

The view across The Sandpit from outside Alf Prowse's barbers, 45 Pound Street, October 1971. A wooden fence masks any view today.

The last remnant of The Sandpit recreation-ground, 2006.

the day time by the retired men who had to escape from their homes to enable their wives to do all the housework and in the evening they were occupied by courting couples. No longer did the Council lock the grounds at night, neither did they employ a regular park keeper. The roundabouts and seesaws were damaged to an extent that only one of each could be repaired and used by the children. The iron fences were never replaced. Because local people began to use the park as a car park, the authorities installed a low wooden fence to prevent vehicular access along Panwell Road.

In 1963 the *Southern Daily Echo* carried an article informing residents that the planners had decided to install a road to carry the traffic away from the shopping centre and that this would signal the end of The Sandpit. It was 20 years before the bypass was completed, with the result that the only piece of recreation-ground in Bitterne was lost.

South Stoneham Workhouse
Keith Marsh

The Poor Law Amendment Act of 1834 is often considered one of the most significant pieces of social legislation in British history as it swept away an accumulation of poor laws going back 500 years. These included prohibiting the giving of relief to able-bodied beggars, requiring those receiving relief to wear badges, and threatening vagabonds with three days in the stocks. The cost of looking after the poor had been increasing, and this was met by the upper and middle classes through local taxes, but there was a suspicion that the poor were being paid to be lazy and avoid work. The new law introduced a national system for dealing with poverty and its relief, based around the union workhouse; the union became a slang term for the workhouse.

In 1833 a Poor Law Commission was set up to examine the situation, and their recommendations to Parliament resulted in the Poor Law Amendment Act. This stated that:

* no able-bodied person was to receive money or other help from the Poor Law authorities except in a workhouse;
* conditions in workhouses were to be made very harsh, to discourage people from wanting to receive help;
* workhouses were to be built in every parish or, if parishes were too small, in unions of parishes;
* ratepayers in each parish or union had to elect a Board of Guardians to supervise the workhouse, to

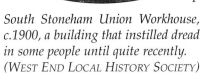

South Stoneham Union Workhouse, c.1900, a building that instilled dread in some people until quite recently. (WEST END LOCAL HISTORY SOCIETY)

collect the Poor Rate and to send reports to the Central Poor Law Commission.

The South Stoneham Union was formed on 25 March 1835 and comprised nine adjacent parishes: Botley, Bursledon, Chilworth, Hamble, Hound, Millbrook, North Stoneham, St Mary's Extra and South Stoneham, which then included Bitterne. (In 1894 parishes were reorganised and these nine were divided to form another eight parishes, including Bitterne.) Guardians were elected by each parish to serve on a Board of Guardians: the workhouse management committee. In 1837, J.R. Best Esq., Chairman to the South Stoneham Union, commented on the new law in a pamphlet he wrote, *The New Poor Law in Practice*, which included amusing examples of the issues faced by the Guardians. Shortly after the law was introduced a number of scandals hit the headlines (the most notorious being at Andover, where it was reported that half-starved inmates were eating rotting flesh) and in response the government introduced stricter rules and set up a system of regular workhouse inspections. However, inmates were still at the mercy of unscrupulous masters and matrons who treated the poor with contempt and abused the rules.

A workhouse existed in West End before the South Stoneham Union was formed, and initially this building was used, but by 1848 it was considered inadequate so a new building, consisting of a central corridor with four pairs of parallel wings off it, was constructed at a cost of £7,000.

Conditions inside the workhouse were deliberately harsh, so that only those who desperately needed help would ask for it. Families were split up and housed in different parts of the workhouse. The poor were made to wear a uniform and the diet was monotonous. There were also strict rules and regulations to follow. Inmates, male and female, young and old, were made to work hard, often doing unpleasant jobs such as breaking stones. Children could also find themselves hired out to work in factories or mines. The 1881 census shows that occupations of the 222 inmates of the South Stoneham Union Workhouse included washerwomen, labourers, domestic servants, bricklayers, seamen and a whitesmith. Political correctness was not as it is now: eight were described as lunatics whilst another three were idiots. Although most inmates were from the union's area (four were born in Bitterne: Amelia Blandford, Thomas Hooper, George Jewell and Frank Powell) some were from afar: Durham, Blackburn, Scotland, Ireland, Egypt and the East Indies. And some were born in the

The lads from the South Stoneham Union Workhouse c.1885, during an outing to Shales.

Left: *The workhouse wash-house c.1905.* (WEST END LOCAL HISTORY SOCIETY)

Below: *An invitation to Mr F. Wylde.*

Councillor J. and Mrs. Brown
request the pleasure of

Mr F. Wylde

company to a Three Hours' Char-a-banc Drive,
Tea and Garden Party,
on the occasion of Councillor Brown's Birthday,
Saturday, September 25th, 1926,
at 29 Dean Road, Bitterne.

Char-a-bancs leave Houndwell Park, Southampton
at 1.30 ; returning at 8 p.m.

Below: *Men from the Southampton Workhouse (now part of City College) were invited to tea in Cllr John Brown's garden in Dean Road, following a charabanc ride.*

workhouse. Also living in were the master and his family, and five officers (two teachers, a nurse, cook and porter).

Although conditions were austere, the occasional outing was arranged for inmates, usually to the grounds of a local benefactor's home. An article in the *Southampton Times* newspaper in July 1883 records:

The Chairman of the Board held at the workhouse, West End, mentioned that on Saturday last Mrs Coote of Shales, Bitterne, had with her usual kindness given her annual treat to the children of the house, who had been bountifully entertained and he begged to convey the grateful thanks of the members to Admiral, Mrs and Miss Coote for this and their great interest and kindness in the welfare of the inmates.'

The building was renamed the Eastleigh Workhouse in 1920, then in 1929 it became the West End Public Assistance Institution, finally becoming Moorgreen Hospital upon the creation of the National Health Service in 1948. Many of the workhouse's buildings survive, acting as a reminder of its original purpose and a catalyst for the fear and dread that many older local residents have of going there!

Share Drug Stores
Irene Pilson

Alan Prince is a Bitterne lad who attended Bitterne and Taunton's Schools before going on to university. Mr Mew and Mr Wetton were two teachers he especially remembers, though by his days the boys called him 'Tosher' Mew whereas earlier he had always been 'Pussy' Mew. Sylvia Tizzard, the daughter of the Deacon Road builders, and Alan Prince from the Brownlow estate had known each other from their schooldays, and eventually they married and started their prosperous business with a shop in the district where they had grown up. Since they founded the Share Drug Stores in 1971 when Alan was in his late twenties, the husband and wife team have gone from strength to strength. By 1984 they already had a chain of 50 shops, mostly in the South, but extending

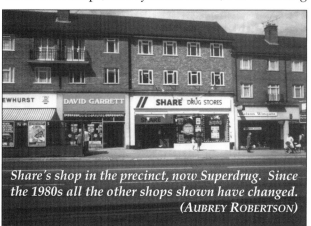

Share's shop in the precinct, now Superdrug. Since the 1980s all the other shops shown have changed.
(AUBREY ROBERTSON)

to London, Hereford and Plymouth. Having outgrown their headquarters on the Nursling industrial estate, they then moved to a 72,500sq.ft office and warehousing complex built by Taylor Woodrow at a cost of £1.85 million on the same estate.

By the mid-1980s, the spacious and very popular Share Drug Stores, that have gone such a long way from the original small shop, had attracted the attention of another very successful firm, Kingfisher plc, owners of Woolworths. On 16 February 1988 a headline in the *Daily Telegraph* announced 'Woolworth £32 million cash offer for Share Drug'. Only Boots had a larger share of the market, and Alan said that the company could have remained independent for several years, although it would probably have become 'pretty uncomfortable' sandwiched between these two big companies. So, at the age of 44, he and Sylvia decided to accept the Kingfisher offer and retire. From that first shop in Bitterne to 145 specialist stores is a record of which they can both be proud.

Like Share Drug Stores, Superdrug Stores plc was originally founded by a family, the Goldsteins, with one store. From 1964 they developed the business, eventually selling it to Kingfisher in 1987. Superdrug has subsequently had several owners, currently the Hong Kong based company Hutchison Whampoa – a far cry from its family origins. Superdrug now employs over 12,500 people in 700 stores in the UK, including one in Bitterne. Coincidentally Share took over the shop that Superdrug now occupies when one company, whose general policy is not to have shops in precincts, pulled out of Bitterne when the precinct was built. That company was F.W. Woolworths!

Bitterne Fire Brigade
Alan House

In October 1896 it was decided that Bitterne should have its own fire brigade so volunteers were called for and 16 'strong, able-bodied' men applied. Ten

Bitterne Volunteer Fire Brigade, thought to be outside of their 'shed' in Almatade Road, c.1913.

Above: *A picture taken in August 1944 showing a group of CD (Civil Defence) and ARP (Air Raid Precautions) Wardens from Bitterne & Peartree Ward Post 6, gathered around a trailer pump. It is curious because the CD and ARP Wardens did not normally fire-fight, so perhaps the pump was just a prop, although the man on the left may have been a Warden Fire Guard.*

Bert Instone's fire brigade pass, dated 1940.

Above: *The fire at Gusters ironmongers on 30 July 1969 resulted in a salvage sale with many fire-damaged bargains to be had.*

Below: *Fireman Peter Jupe from Woolston Fire Station (left) tackling a night-time thatch fire in Pound Street in the 1960s.*

attended a meeting in December and were enrolled as members of the Bitterne Volunteer Fire Brigade. Sergeant Major Moody, of the 1st Hants Artillery, was appointed captain of the new brigade. The South Stoneham Rural District Council, which included Bitterne, offered the Parish Council hydrants and an appliance and arranged for the supply of a hose-cart plus hose, axes and associated equipment at the cost of £64. A plot of land to house the equipment was sought and on 20 December 1897 a tenancy agreement was signed by Cllrs Charles Witt and Isaac Barrett, and William Adcock, for the erection of a 'fire shed' on the latter's land in Chapel Street, at a rent of £5 per year.

The minutes of the annual meeting of the Parish Council on 14 March 1898 recorded that a Fire Brigade Committee had been formed, the fire station had been completed, and hose-cart and appliances were on site and fully operative. A partial issue of uniform had also been purchased at the following costs:

Shand Mason & Co. (fire brigade supplier
   of the period)   £66.2s.6d.
Messrs Witt Bros   £4.1s.3d.
Mr Vine (purchase of belts)   £2.5s.6d.
Edwin Jones & Co (purchase of boots)   £6.10s.6d.
   £78.19s.9d.

Captain Moody became caretaker of the new station (being paid £2 per year) and 21 hydrants were installed, resulting in an annual tax of £10.10s.0d. on the parish.

By the meeting of the Council on 6 March 1899, many practices of the brigade had taken place, new tunics had been purchased from Mr Thorn at a cost of £9.8s.0d. and identification plates had been fixed to the houses of firemen so that fires could be reported more easily. A fire on Bitterne Common had been attended by five men with the hose-cart.

At the meeting in March the following year it was reported that the hose-cart and appliances were in good repair and that several more practices had been held. The question had arisen regarding the brigade's attendance at fires outside the parish and it was agreed that the person who called for assistance should be asked to pay 15s., to be divided equally between the firemen who attended.

Steps to improve the drying of the canvas hose to stop it rotting were taken in 1901, and at the meeting in March 1902 it was reported that the brigade had 'turned out smartly' to a fire at Lankester & Crook's store in the High Street. They were congratulated for 'preventing what might have been a disastrous conflagration'. Applications had been made by the Council to various insurance companies for reimbursement of expenses incurred, and a payment of £7.17s.0d. was received.

The March 1905 meeting heard that a fire at Adcock Grocers had been the biggest incident yet attended by the brigade, and the insurance company had paid out 5 guineas (£5.5s.0d.) for their services, enabling the purchase of two life lines, nine pocket lines and six new canvas buckets for the hose-cart. The following year a fire at Moorlands Farm resulted in insurance payments of £2.18s.6d.

By 22 March 1909 all members of the brigade were insured under the Workmen's Compensation Act. Captain Moody was still the officer-in-charge but the caretaker's duties were by this time shared between four men, each with a small salary. Several properties in the parish could not be reached with the existing hoses so £14 was spent on purchasing an additional 300ft, and hydrant marker plates to be installed for the first time.

The Martin Hall in Brook Road had become the headquarters for the Parish Council by March 1913, and it was agreed to build a new shed on the side of the hall to house the fire brigade's equipment. Tenders were received for erecting the new fire station and the contract was awarded to Mr A. Fly of Bullar Road at a cost of £30.4s.0d., provided he paid trade union wages as paid in the District. It was decided that a lamp with its glass marked 'Fire Station' should be fixed to the front of the main building.

The brigade members on 17 April 1913 were: T. Moody (Captain), E. Millar, A. Burgess, H. Rockett, C. Thornton (the Call Boy), W. Whitlock, H. Burgess, W. Burgess, A. Thornton; W. Birch was to replace H. Plumicott. As there were few telephones, the means of calling out the firemen was by the Call Boy.

On 24 July 1913 it was suggested that the brigade test the new hose and equipment at Bitterne Manor, situated in a box on the wall of the sewerage works. In October a uniform was provided for the Call Boy by Edwin Jones at a cost of 10s., but an inspection in the first week of December 1913 showed that other uniforms and boots were in poor condition. A contract was awarded to Edwin Jones for the supply of tunics and trousers at a cost of 45s. per man; trousers had a red side stripe and the tunics had brass buttons for the firemen whilst the Captain had white metal buttons; the tailor attended the station to measure each man. Two new pairs of leather boots were ordered from Mr Martin in the High Street whilst the other boots were repaired. The new uniforms were issued on 12 November.

A. Thornton had joined the army in 1913 and, having first asked H. Plumicott to rejoin to replace him, Mr Fisher had done so by May 1915, whilst W. Whitlock was appointed as Vice Captain in support of Captain Moody.

A report was submitted in July 1914 regarding a fire at Heather Cottage; another in March 1916 made reference to a fire at the Fox and Hounds public house. Later that year it was agreed to fit candle lamps to the rear of the hose-cart, and to provide certificates proving brigade membership for firemen called up for military service; two members had joined the army and a replacement Call Boy was being sought. Mention was made of new boots for Mr Plumicott, as he had been persuaded to rejoin.

A serious fire destroyed Harefield House on 6 May 1917. The blaze was fought by members of Bitterne Brigade together with the Southampton and West End Brigades, but fire-fighting was seriously hampered by poor water pressure in the main feeding the hydrants. A few days later it was reported that Mr Whitlock had resigned from the brigade and that Mr Hammett had joined. He lived next door to the fire station and was one of the key-holders, a list of the others being displayed on a notice-board. At this time four brigade members were serving in the army and they had still not recruited a Call Boy. Cllr Seymour drew the Fire Brigade Committee's attention to the smoldering hay at Howard's Yard and it was resolved to write to the yard pointing out the possible danger!

In July 1919 the Council considered the state of the brigade to be unsatisfactory, and resolved that Cllrs Brown and Bailey would call on the brigade members, then listed as being Moody, Rockett, Hammett, Burgess, Burgess, Burgess and Plumicott. On 29 July the Bitterne Celebration of Peace was held at Harefield and the brigade was given permission to attend; indeed Messrs Moody and Burgess were on the sports committee.

A year later the Council sent a letter to Captain Moody asking him to attend the fire station more frequently; Cllr Shapland had visited and noted the poor state of the equipment, and it was agreed to write to Captain Moody stating that if the appliances were not maintained in better order the 10s. per quarter he was paid would be discontinued. In September the payment was suspended but the next month the Chairman reported that the appliances were now in a satisfactory condition and the payment was reinstated.

In November 1920 Bitterne parish was absorbed into the County Borough of Southampton, and the following April Bitterne Fire Brigade, consisting of nine firemen with a hose-cart and ancillary equipment, was disbanded. In January 1921 a motor fire-engine had been placed in service at the Woolston Fire Station and it was felt that this, together with those at the fire station in St Mary's, could adequately protect Bitterne residents.

The only other fire station that has existed in Bitterne was during the Second World War when an Auxiliary Fire Service (AFS) station was established. Station 'J' was activated on 1 September 1939, just two days prior to the outbreak of war, at Halletts Garage, Cobbett Road, but the need for more room resulted in a move to the Bitterne Drill Hall in May 1940. A garage adjacent to the Red Lion gave addi-

tional room for towing vehicles and trailer pumps, and from January 1941 personnel were accommodated in the Congregational church hall, Dean Road. When an air-raid warning sounded, one crew from Bitterne would deploy to their 'action station' on Peartree Green, thus spreading resources and reducing risk. With the formation of the National Fire Service (NFS) on 18 August 1941, the Bitterne station became part of No. 16 Fire Force with the designation 16A 3Y, continuing in existence until the stand-down of the NFS in 1945.

Eric Thompson, Registered Plumber
Keith Marsh

Although not a Bitterne lad (he was born in Fareham in 1931) Eric Thompson became greatly involved with the district when he moved into 66 Pound Street in 1971.

Eric's team and their vans, c.1985. From left: Derek Perdue, Nigel Green, Ken Rousso, Paul Harvey, Nigel Lewis, Eric.

Below, inset: *Eric with a part of his collection of toilet chains.*

Bitterne Hardware at the bottom of Lances Hill was Eric Thompson's venture in retailing. The fanlight windows are of historical interest, bearing the words 'The Garden Suburb Centre' the name by which the Chessel estate was developed in the 1920s.

He always enjoyed the outdoors and spent much of his youth boating and sailing around Fareham Creek, and cycling, later motorcycling, further afield. He excelled in amateur dramatics, and as a Boy Scout he even had breakfast with The Chief, Baden-Powell. He undertook a plumbing apprenticeship at school and after National Service in Egypt and a spell as a travelling salesman he moved to the area. Here he returned to plumbing, culminating in setting up his own business, well known locally as The Complete Plumbing Service.

It was this trade that led to his appearance on the popular Sunday evening BBC TV show *That's Life* hosted by Esther Rantzen. The programmes were a blend of curious abilities, consumer problems and humorous anecdotes, and the 1976 series included a weekly unusual collection feature. These were proving hard to find, however, so when one of the show's production team was using Eric's plumbing services they persuaded him to assemble a collection of loo chains! Eric quickly gathered together several dozen, including some just borrowed, and displayed them to the nation.

That's Life was not Eric's first broadcasting experience for in the late 1960s / early 1970s he spent much time in hospital broadcasting and had his own Sunday programme: *My Favourite Things*. He was also an early master of home videoing, and indeed recorded many local events including the revived Bitterne carnivals.

Having moved into a building that was once one of the most popular shops in Bitterne (Tickle Fancy's sweet shop) it was inevitable that Eric would develop an interest in local history, and he wrote the BLHS Local Papers, *A Diary of Bitterne*. But Eric was always proud of his trade, so his booklets show the author as 'Eric J.A. Thompson, RP' (for Registered Plumber). His trade also gave him access to normally inaccessible places (roofs, high office blocks, etc.) and Eric always had his camera with him to make the most of such opportunities.

Eric passed away in 1999, but the BLHS is extremely grateful for his bequest of the remains of his loo chain collection, and of many photographs which now have historical significance.

Eric is not Bitterne's only TV star. In the late 1960s the Smith family of Glenfield Avenue appeared in the popular quiz show *Ask the Family*. On the big screen, Mike Ballan, then living in Cheriton Avenue, being Britain's shortest man at just 2ft 11ins tall, secured roles in the films *Labyrinth* (as a Goblin, 1986) and *Return of the Jedi* (as an Ewok, 1983).

The Two Bitterne Libraries
Barbara McCaffery

Bitterne must be one of the few villages that can boast of having a library at each end, the first being built in 1939 to meet the needs of extensive residential development in the area. The library was located on the junction of Cobbett Road and Bitterne Road on land donated by Revd F.C. and Miss G. Vaughan-Jenkins, where once tennis-courts stood. The single-storey building is of best quality red bricks with stone facings, and cost £9,520, which included £1,320 for furniture. The main entrance hall and reception area has direct access to the lending library on the right, with the junior library and reading-room to the left. Brick flower-beds flank the front doors. Opened on 16 May 1939 with a stock of around 9,000 books, Bitterne Library (as it was named at the time) was said to have had the air of an Odeon cinema or transatlantic liner with its art deco interior of wood panelling and rounded furniture of Austrian oak lime; some windows were even shaped like portholes. With Miss Higgins as Librarian, it soon became the busiest branch library in Southampton, and during the Second World War its flat roof was put to use for fire-watching duties.

In 1960, to meet the increasing needs and further development of the district, the local authority approved the proposal for a new library in the Bitterne area, the first permanent library to be built in Southampton since the war. The old cottages that occupied the plot of land on the corner of Commercial Street and Bitterne Road were to be pulled down and borough architect L. Berger was commissioned to design the building and furniture for the new Eastern Library. His design was a very modern building with huge windows dominating the front and back, and to break up the great expanse of glass at the front, a mural was displayed between the separate entrance and exit doors. These doors were heavy and especially difficult to open for those visitors who had a pram with them, whilst the area between them was referred to as 'the greenhouse' by staff who joked that tomatoes could be grown there! The interior was split into three distinct sections: an adult reading area, a children's reading area and a junior study room, along with plenty of open space and seating for readers to browse over their selection. It was the first library in Southampton to have its own walled garden, with a fishpond and trellised seating area; under the tender care of the various janitors it won three certificates in the Southampton in Bloom competitions in the early 1990s.

The library opened to the public on 10 September 1963, with a small ceremony in the presence of the Mayor of Southampton, Alderman R.F. Pugh and the first book was issued to Mr A.G. Steavenson by Cllr L.N.C. Squibb, Chairman of the Public Libraries Committee. The staff consisted of Miss Molly Boyd (who was to be Librarian there until she retired in 1982) and three library assistants. Within three weeks of opening an estimated 6,000 books a week were being borrowed, a third of them on Saturday.

During the early 1980s Eastern Library had two writers in residence, David Benedictus and Maria Fitzgerald, who held workshops and provided encouragement to budding writers. Late-night novel readings were also held, with various novelists reading their latest epics in their entirety; one such event with the author Barbara Trapido did not finish until 5 o'clock in the morning!

I came to work at Eastern Library as a young library assistant in 1987. I had worked for two years at the Woolston branch, and was often sent to cover at Eastern when they were short of staff and found that I enjoyed the busy atmosphere of this bigger library and so transferred when a vacancy arose. That was before computerisation when everything was done by hand: when someone joined the library four, sometimes eight, tickets had to be written out with their details, a job done during quiet periods of the day. But on a Saturday there was never a quiet moment and I remember it was always a frantic rush to get all the tickets written out and filed away before we closed. It was, however, a prime job as it meant you could sit down, whilst the more junior staff were left running from counter to counter serving visitors and trying to shelve the returned books. In the late 1980s the BLHS found a temporary home in the study room of the library were artifacts and memorabilia were displayed, along with books on Bitterne and the surrounding area. A steward from the society was often on hand to assist with any public queries.

In 1989 an Urban Regeneration grant enabled restoration work to be carried out at Bitterne Library. The original furniture was repaired and recovered in green leather and new bookcases were installed in keeping with the original art deco design. It was a moment of pride for Doreen LeHuquet, the Librarian, when a carpenter removing and altering some of the wood panelling spoke admiringly of both the wood and the original workmanship as her father was a carpenter/joiner who had worked on the building.

With increasing confusion over which of the two libraries was Bitterne Library, it was decided to change the name of the Bitterne Library to Cobbett Road Library, thus reflecting its location. Another distinguishing feature of this library is the statue, erected in October 1991, of local reader Dot Winteridge reaching out for a book. Commissioned by Southampton City and Hampshire County Councils the statue, designed by Kevin Atherton, provoked a lively debate in the local press about the merits of spending public money on art.

The 1990s saw modern technology reach both libraries. At Eastern Library, along with computerisation, came a refurbished entrance and counter, with automatic double doors replacing the separate entrance and exit doors. The mural was taken down and carted away to where? Nobody knows!

The Eastern Library, 1963. (Bitterne Library, SCC).

Right: Art Within Reach: Dot Winteridge and her statue before it is erected against Cobbett Road Library, October 1991. She had been borrowing books there for over five decades.

Designed by William Mitchell and made of glass-fibre, Eastern Library's colourful mural was once described as 'a jellyfish having an affair with a poached egg.' Alas it has now gone. (BITTERNE LIBRARY, SCC)

Inside the new Eastern Library. (BITTERNE LIBRARY, SCC)

The installation of computers meant the end of what was, to me, the ultimate job of a librarian: flicking through trays of tickets and books cards searching for the correct card to put back into the book, then handing the tickets back to the reader saying 'Four tickets for Mrs Smith'. It had been much easier to get to know our readers then. Today we have nothing to hand back and readers have often moved away to the shelves before we have finished scanning the returned books. A few years later computers were introduced for public use, changing the whole ambience of the library: in place of the rustle of book leaves and the occasional hushed word, we hear the tap-tap-tapping of keyboards and the chatter of the children as they play weird and wonderful games, not to mention the occasional mobile phone and conversation!

In May 1999 Cobbett Road Library celebrated its diamond jubilee, holding a birthday tea party for readers and former staff, and as part of the celebrations, Martin Pavey, the Librarian, initiated a twinning link with Freshwater Library on the Isle of Wight, also celebrating its 60th birthday. Eastern Library celebrated its 40th birthday in September 2003 with a 'This is your life' party for past and present staff and friends who got together and shared fond and funny memories of their time at the library. It was at this gathering that the announcement was made that Eastern Library was to change its name; Eastern Library was to become Bitterne Library. Bitterne Library was finally in its rightful place!

Over the past decade, the need for two libraries in close proximity, has often been questioned, but each has its own character and unique way of serving the community so, for now, Bitterne is happy to have a library at each end!

Henri the 'Onion Johnny'
Magali Delporte

Until 5 January 2004, Henri Argouarch was a familiar personality around Bitterne and indeed the area around as far as Hythe and Romsey. He smelt of onions, not the acrid odour of raw onions, but a pleasant, sweet aroma, the natural smell of a true Onion Johnny, a man who lives with onions.

To qualify as an Onion Johnny, you must be a Breton from the vicinity of the harbour town of Roscoff (Henri is from Tregor Plougoulm, only a few miles from the town) and spend four to six months of the year across the Channel in Britain selling your very special oignons rosés de Roscoff. Pink in colour and sweet to taste, Roscoff onions will keep for months, then melt as they are cooked. The trademark name Johnny, or Petit-Jean, originated in the 19th century when English customers found that most sellers who turned up on their doorstep were called Jean and many of them were as young as ten. But the Franco-British onion trade itself began in 1828, when a young Frenchman loaded his entire crop on a boat sailing to England and returned with his pockets bulging with silver. Others followed and in the 1920s every major city was inundated with these aromatic Bretons walking the streets in search of customers. Some of the 1,500 men who left Brittany even made it

'Onion Johnny' Henri's membership card to the Association des Marchands d'Oignons.
(MAGALI DELPORTE)

With his bike laden, Henri tours the area. Cutbush Lane is the last quiet lane like this in Bitterne.
(MAGALI DELPORTE)

Above right: *Unloading the bags of onions in September, ready for the start of his tour.*
(MAGALI DELPORTE)

Left: *Henri plaiting his onions.*

(MAGALI DELPORTE)

as far as the Shetland Islands.

Henri was born on 5 November 1935 and his career in onions began in Wales when he was age 14, continuing uninterrupted, except once for the French–Algerian War in 1958 (during which he joined the French Army and went off to fight in the desert). But what made him so special was his mode of transport. While the remaining dozen or so Onion Johnnies have adopted the 'white van' approach, Henri still cycled to his customers. The practical reason was that he didn't have a driving licence, but the truth is that he never contemplated dumping his bike because it was part of his way of life, as it was his father's before him.

Every year, at the end of August, Henri ordered four tons of onions from his producer and packed his suitcase. In early September, he headed for Southampton on the passenger seat of a lorry, with 160 25kg bags of onions in the back, along with 18 bottles of Prince Hernia table wine (which is too expensive to buy here). He rented a room and a garage for £50 a week and stayed until every single onion was sold. He never took time to see the sights as he was here only to sell onions. Every Wednesday and Sunday morning, he prepared the onion strings in his garage, weaving the stalks into the traditional plaits to make up bundles weighing 3.5kgs. On Sunday afternoon he cooked a big stew that would last him for the week (an Onion Johnny doesn't eat out apart from fish and chips on Saturday night). The rest of the week he got up at 6.30a.m., loaded 20 strings of onions on his second-hand butcher's bike and began his rounds. He had a sandwich for lunch and a couple of pints of IPA bitter at the Richmond Inn, Portswood Road, in the evening. And once you became a customer, only death would erase your name from Henri's mental address book.

Of course it was not only the dusty cliché of a Frenchman on a bike that allowed the 69-year-old to earn a living selling onions. Roscoff onions have a distinctive aroma and mature organically by the sea. They are not watery like white Spanish onions so they caramelise nicely without burning. And you can eat them raw, unlike the British ones that burn the mouth.

Now that Henri has retired the nostalgic sight of an onion man on a bike has been confined to history; Onion Johnnies may yet survive, but in the guise of a 'white van man' with Onion Man emblazoned on the sides.

Policing in Bitterne
Jim Brown

I joined Southampton County Borough Police in 1952 and although I never served in the Bitterne Division, I dealt with a number of incidents east of the Itchen, both through living in Sholing from 1954 onwards and as a detective dealing with crimes that included enquiries in the area.

One incident occurred on a July afternoon in 1959, whilst I was a detective. I was off duty at home when there was a disturbance opposite my house. Several drunken youths had assaulted a bus conductor on the No. 3 bus, throwing him down the stairs, and the driver, who knew me, drove his bus to my house for assistance! I knew two of the youths who lived nearby and they knew me. However, they were under the mistaken impression that as I was off duty I had no powers, and I was told where to go! Attempting to arrest the most obnoxious of them resulted in a violent fight, with me and the three youths crashing through a garden fence and me ending up on the ground being kicked and punched. I received several bruises and lacerations, including four broken ribs, but Bitterne officers were quickly on the scene and the youths were arrested and charged with assault and public disorder offences. I spoke on their behalf at Court as they were local lads known to me, and instead of almost certainly receiving prison sentences, they were heavily fined.

The most important case that I was involved in was the tragic murder of nine-year-old Margaret Dawkins whose body had been found with 37 stab wounds, near the stream in Mayfield Park in February 1960. As a member of the murder squad I was called out from home and reported to Bitterne Police Station at 6.00a.m. The next nine days consisted of 12 to 14 hours a day of

Bitterne Police Station, Christmas 1920. Second from the left is PC Tyrrell. The sergeant at this time was Ernest Baugh. (MARY TYRRELL)

PC Jim Brown on point duty (directing traffic) on The Avenue.

Bill Ainslie receiving his Long Service & Good Conduct medal from the Chief Constable, Sir Douglas Osmond, in 1976.

PC James of Whites Road on police horse Warrior. Warrior was bought from the army after the First World War and presented to Southampton Corporation by Miss Hilda Moore; he attended many civic events including the freeing of the Lances Hill toll.

Right: *PC Ray Dyer, known affectionately as Tiny.*

In March 1963 the police vacated the Victorian Police Station, built in 1858, prior to its demolition and rebuilding.

(SOUTHERN DAILY ECHO)

continuous door-to-door enquiries, interviewing and eliminating suspects. At one stage a young man with a history of violence was arrested, his mother having burnt his trousers because they were stained with blood, but he was found to be not responsible. Many years later a man was arrested whilst hiding in bushes and admitted the murder; he took the police to where he had hidden the knife, thus confirming his guilt.

My final Bitterne incident took place in August 1962 when I was a detective working the 'late turn' at the Civic Centre. This meant doing 'split shifts' (being on duty from 9a.m. to 1p.m., then again from 8p.m. to midnight) and because of a backlog of paperwork, I had worked through my off-duty period. At 11.30p.m. I was tired and ready to go home, but a call was received that a girl had been stabbed and taken to the RSH Hospital's Casualty Department. I attended with the late Det. Sgt Bill Pritchard, but had to wait until 12.10a.m. before we could interview the victim. Her story was that her boyfriend had just been released from prison and on discovering that she was pregnant had quickly worked out that he couldn't have been responsible. A violent row developed resulting in him stabbing her in the chest before running away. She had two sets of two small puncture wounds, half-an-inch apart, in her left breast and had narrowly escaped suffering a fatal blow. Her boyfriend (I'll call him 'Tony') was known to me as I had dealt with him in the past, and his description was circulated as 'wanted' before we eventually went off duty at 3.10a.m. As I drove up Lances Hill on my way home I saw 'Tony' walking down the road towards me. I stopped, got out of my car and walked towards him: he recognised me and ran off, throwing something into a front garden as he did so. I caught and searched him, finding a bank bag full of change together with a large number of pills. Bitterne officers searched the area and a pair of bloodstained scissors was found in a garden.

'Tony' readily admitted the stabbing and also breaking into Garretts Chemists in Bitterne Parade, from where he stole the cash and pills; he was an addict. He was charged, and appeared before the magistrates for a remand in custody. I called in at Garretts on my way home to have the bank bag identified and take statements, then went home to bed, after having been on duty for over 28 hours. But I still had to report for duty at 8p.m. that evening!

Bill Ainslie

I joined the Southampton Borough Police as a cadet in 1950 before doing my National Service in the RAF as a 'Snowdrop' (the colloquial term for an RAF Policeman). On completing my National Service in 1954 it was only natural that I become a policeman and rejoin the Southampton force.

My first spell of duty at Bitterne started c.1959 at the old station, a Victorian building originally built for the Hampshire Constabulary, before Bitterne was brought within the boundaries of Southampton. I can recall many happy times with colleagues like Len Thorne, Dave Stanford, Joe Churcher, Joe Casson and many others. There was a kitchen on the upper floor, where the 'reserve man', Pete Sibley, cooked delicious breakfasts, which we consumed sitting round a large table in the Mess Room.

I remember there were 11 beats in the Bitterne Division with the boundaries usually along the main or busiest roads. In addition, there were two main road patrols, one at Bitterne and another at Woolston. Although these two patrol areas were smaller they were very busy with traffic, schools and shops.

It must be noted that at this time we did not use radios, except in motor vehicles, and our main means of communication was by telephone pillars and Police Boxes. We were required to report in at a certain time and if you were more than two minutes late you were likely to be in trouble with your sergeant! There was, however, a good relationship with the general public, which we found we could use with great confidence.

An example: I was just about to report in from the pillar at the junction of Victoria and Portsmouth Roads, when the light on the top started flashing, indicating a call. I was directed to Lankester & Crook's shop in Obelisk Road, where an intruder alarm had been tripped. I was on foot patrol, but as I left the pillar, a car came across the junction heading my way so I stopped it, explained the position to the driver, and he drove to the shop. Not only that, he told me that if I went over the gate to the rear yard, he would stay and watch the front. As I entered the yard I saw a man clutching a large carton running away. He jumped a small wall and it was fortunate I did not follow without checking as the drop on the other side was about 8ft! I was by myself with no means of communication, but I did have my whistle! I attracted the attention of people living nearby who were able to pass on the description to the car carrying my colleagues to the scene. They found the suspect in a pub having a quiet drink and later recovered all the stolen goods. This was not an isolated incident and demonstrates the helpful attitude of the public at that time.

Police officers always seem to have had a severe look but at times you could have a little fun at the expense of the public. Whilst manning the very busy pedestrian crossing at the top of Lances Hill I was approached by one of my neighbours, a matronly lady. In front of the large crowd she said in a very coy, but coquettish manner 'Oh, officer, can you see me across the road?' 'Certainly, Madam' I replied, and promptly, to the amusement of the waiting crowd, I took her hand and walked her across by herself! Halfway across and out of earshot she whispered 'You rotten b*****!'

One advantage of living in the area was when my wife and I were expecting our first child in 1960. I was on 'nights' and as the baby was already overdue, I was allowed my home beat. I arranged that when passing my house I would ring my cycle bell and if I *was needed, my wife would let me know. All went well, and I received signals that everything was alright until I got home just after 6.00a.m. Then my wife told me she had commenced labour at about 3.00a.m.; our daughter, Carolyn, was born at 9.30p.m. that evening. Nurse Hibbert, the midwife, allowed me to be present at the birth, something that was unusual at that time, but I explained that the experience would be good for me, if I ever had to deliver a baby.*

In 1967 the Southampton force was amalgamated with the Hampshire Constabulary. There were good things about the amalgamation, but the new hierarchy decided to split Southampton into three separate areas controlled from Winchester. The following year team policing was introduced at Bitterne, and as I was attracted to this new concept, I applied for a transfer back there from the Civic Centre. The new Bitterne Police Station had been built, patrol officers would use Panda cars and there would be Community Beat Officers responsible for their own areas. As I remember, Les Smith had the Sholing beat and Geoff Mitchell was responsible for Thornhill.

One night we attended an alarm call to Warsash, out of our division, but we were the nearest available response team. The premises were surrounded and we awaited the arrival of the key-holder. Upon entering the bar with him a man behind the counter said 'Right gents, what would you like to drink?' We looked at the key-holder and he looked at us, and we asked each other if we knew the man. The reply was negative, the 'barman', of course, was the burglar, who was arrested and kept in custody to be dealt with by the local bobby the next morning. The relationship between police and offenders is not always severe and formal, and even crooks have a sense of humour!

Many people will remember PC 'Tiny' Dyer who had a special duty to control traffic at Bullar/Bitterne Roads junction during 'rush hours'. He had his own somewhat unorthodox method of control, but everyone loved him for his cheerful approach. One morning a sleepy motorist was not quite on Tiny's wavelength: Tiny resolved the situation by banging his fist on the roof of the car and shouting 'You're here to drive your car, not to sit there picking your nose!' causing merriment all round, including to the lady passenger.

I enjoyed both my periods at Bitterne. There were officers who had served in the borough force so had a great deal of local knowledge as well as a good relationship with the public. In 1970 I was promoted from Bitterne, then retired after 25 years' service in 1979.

Herbert 'Tiny' Dyer

PC Herbert 'Tiny' Dyer, an unmissable figure at 6ft 4ins, with an unorthodox approach to traffic control, is fondly remembered as Bitterne's very own Dixon of Dock Green. He became a legend in his own lifetime, and years after his death he is still remembered with affection. Inevitably, with his height, he was always

known as 'Tiny' by colleagues and the public alike, but he is probably best known for the unique style of point duty by which he kept the traffic moving at the former five-road junction at the foot of Lances Hill.

During the 1960s, before the building of the gyratory system that preceded the traffic lights, the junction of Bitterne Road, Bullar Road, MacNaghten Road and Athelstan Road was a traffic bottleneck. This was Tiny's domain; with the large and jovial PC Dyer on point duty the traffic was kept flowing. 'His methods are unorthodox as he shouts, cajoles, instructs and waves his arms about,' said a *Daily Echo* report from the 1960s on PC Dyer. 'Motorists tell how he waves his arms like a windmill, cavorts like a blue-uniformed Nureyev, shouts like a Town Crier and sometimes even charges like a bull.' Many a time Tiny could be seen taking a shortcut through the clump of bushes that stood in the centre of the roundabout or jumping on the back platform of a bus to get to another part of the junction.

So respected was he by motorists that when he became unwell with appendicitis the *Daily Echo* carried regular bulletins on his recovery and the date he would be back on duty. At Christmas, gifts (including turkeys) were said to bounce into Bullar Road, tossed from car windows by the grateful public. Tiny's popularity was phenomenal, with many letters of praise being sent to his chiefs. His celebrity image was firmly established in the summer of 1969 by the 12th Itchen North Scout Group; they didn't want the Mayor or some dignitary to open their fête, they wanted Tiny and they got him!

Tiny, who lived in Woolston, joined the Southampton County Borough Police in September 1946 after serving in the Royal Air Force during the Second World War. He served a total of 30 years, through an era when people's perception of a policeman was Jack Warner's television portrayal policing in *Dixon of Dock Green* rather than the cast of *The Bill*. On his retirement, Tiny said:

I was, I suppose, somewhat unorthodox, but no one was in doubt about when to stop and when to go. I was enthusiastic. I enjoyed myself. I got to know a lot of regulars and they got to know me.

Following retirement in 1976 he became a leading figure in the Mormon Church in Southampton, and died in November 1989.

Adapted from the *Daily Echo* feature (24 February 2006)

Ovens for the Royal Yacht *Britannia*
Colin Packham

Kempsafe Ltd, an engineering company based in Quayside Road specialising in the manufacture and supply of marine catering and laundry equipment, was contracted in 1979 by the Ministry of Defence to supply various items of cooking equipment for the Royal Yacht *Britannia*. The company also supplies equipment to the Royal Navy, Merchant Navy, tugs, large yachts and the cruising industry.

The items required in 1979 were hot cupboards, a grill unit, a fryer and two heavy-duty double ovens (the vertical type, one oven over the other), all to be to 'ministry standard'. A good contract for a small company of about 20 strong.

There were problems manufacturing for the *Britannia*, mainly with the electrical supply. Being a relatively old ship, having been built in 1954, this was 220V direct current, requiring heavy-duty switches and contacts which, by 1979, were getting hard to find. The other problem was that the manager/designer at Kempsafe, in a fit of enthusiasm, asked the royal chef 'Sandy' if there was anything special he would like on the oven for the royal galley (the other was to go in the crew's galley): easy, robust, solid, sailor-proof, or...? However, Sandy's request for the royal one was a bit unusual: same robust standard, but could he cook a soufflé with the oven door open so he could watch it rise? The cooking temperature would be 700°F.

Yes, and Kempsafe offered asbestos underpants but they were declined!

Sainsbury's in Bitterne
Keith Marsh

John Sainsbury, dairyman, opened his first shop in 1869 in Drury Lane, Holborn, but it was not until 1954 that his company opened a shop in Southampton, on a bombed site in Above Bar. Some 11 years later they opened the Bitterne shop, built by Braziers on the site of the Carpenter's Arms. It was opened on 23 March 1965 by Lord Sainsbury, grandson of the founder, who cut a ribbon and welcomed the first customer, Mrs Isobel Voges of Tatwin Crescent, Thornhill.

Sainsbury's was not, however, the first supermarket in the district. Fine Fare (a subsidiary of Associated British Foods) had opened at 407/411 Bitterne Road c.1957, bringing to shoppers the concept of self-service with a basket and paying at a row of tills on the way out. But Sainsbury's was a

J. Sainsbury's original premises on the site of the Carpenter's Arms which stood on the corner of Maytree Road. What a wonderful array of prams parked under the canopy!

larger shop with more choice: according to the *Southern Evening Echo* 'the housewife will be able to buy practically every household commodity'. There were wide aisles for shopping trolleys, conveyors at the tills, automatic doors, and a staff of 80 under the Manager, Mr R. Cunningham.

By 1972 the Bitterne branch was so busy that expansion was necessary so the company acquired the adjacent Angel Inn, and after several months of building and refurbishment, the shop reopened with three times the floor area. Other significant changes were made such as adding a rear entrance and moving the loading bay from Maytree Road to the rear. As Sainsbury's trade grew, Fine Fare's diminished and in April 1982 it became a Shoppers Paradise, finally closing in October 1984.

The construction of the bypass introduced stiff competition for Sainsbury's as the plans included a new supermarket facing West End Road, Safeways, yet both seemed to flourish. The creation of the precinct did spark rumours that Sainsbury's would close as they disliked having shops in precincts (the shop in Above Bar having closed when that road was pedestrianised), yet it remained open. In March 2004 Safeways plc was bought by Morrisons and shoppers expected the competition to continue. However, the financial burden led Morrisons to dispose of many of the new acquisitions. The shops were disposed of in groups and Bitterne was put with eight other shops, including Andover, Eastleigh and Slough (taking 'multi-buy' to a new level!).

It is rumoured that Sainsbury's wanted some of the other shops in order to move into new areas, so were forced to buy the Bitterne store as well. Sainsbury's closed and refurbished their original shop in the precinct, then the shop in West End Road, the latter becoming an outlet for clothing, furnishings, electrical appliances, etc. The former remains a grocery supermarket, but now has a monopolistic position in Bitterne, and seems to be reducing its lines whilst striving to serve a still-increasing population.

Fine Fare in the 1960s, where Peacocks is now.
(*AUBREY ROBERTSON*)

	Best butter (½ lb)	Large English eggs (½ doz)	Mature English Cheddar cheese (½ lb)	Wiltshire smoked back bacon (1 lb)	Red Label tea (¼ lb)
1903	8d	7½d	5d	11d	3¾d
1911	8½d	9d	5d	11d	4½d
1927	10½d	9d	8d	1/6	6½d
1937	7½d	1/3	7d	1/6	5d
1947	8d	10½d	11½d	2/-	Not available
1957	1/1½	1/6	1/6	3/-	1/4
1967	1/9	2/3	2/-	5/4	1/5
1977 (i)	27½p (5/6)	57p (11/5)	35p (7/-)	£1.08 (£1/1/7)	16p (3/2)
1987	52p	£1.13	66p	£1.75	37p
1997 (ii)	79p (iii)	99p	£1.34	£2.19	62p
2006 (ii)	76p	£1.35	£1.32	£2.99	46p

(i) Decimal currency was introduced on 15 February 1971, so the 1977 figures in brackets are converted to allow comparison and politians vowed that it wouldn't increase prices!)

(ii) Package weights are now decimalised so ¼ lb has become 100g, ½ lb has become 250g and 1 lb has become 500g

(iii) Now described as 'blended' instead of 'best'

Chapter Four

The Old Chapel
Richard Sheaf

The Old Chapel in Dean Road (formerly Chapel Street until the 'annexation' of Bitterne by Southampton in 1920 and the subsequent change of road names in 1924) is the one remaining chapel of the three that have stood in that road. Even more interestingly, it was only used as a chapel for around nine years. It was built as a Baptist chapel, entirely at the expense of William Francis Mayoss, a deacon of East Street Baptist Church, Southampton, and it appears that he was Christian enough to forgive the fact that he never received any rent despite an agreement to pay some by the fledgling branch. William Mayoss was a grocer from Lower East Street, one of many Nonconformist tradesmen in Southampton.

A licence for the chapel to conduct 'Public worship of God according to the form of worship of the Baptist Protestant dissenters' was applied for on the 14 August 1844 and signed by Charles Nash, a chemist (and later schoolmaster) of Bitterne, and John Rimer, another grocer of Lower East Street. The Revd Green was its first (and only) pastor. He was the son-in-law of Mr T. Morris, minister of East Street Baptist Church. To quote from 'A Brief History' of that church (W. A. Gamblen, 1889):

It was a weakly child from its birth... until about the year 1849 when it appears to have so far declined, that it was not practical to continue the services any longer. The chapel was afterwards sold, and has since been used as a reading room.

The chapel was in fact leased for seven years commencing 1 December 1849 and subsequently sold to the local Church of England (St James, West End) who used it as a chapel to cater for the expanding population of Bitterne while the Church of the Holy Saviour (Bitterne Church) was being built. According to the Religious Census of Hampshire in 1851 (part of the national census) the chapel had 76 free seats and 73 others and the attendance at services reached a maximum of 188 persons.

Once the new church was up and running the building was used as the parish hall, often referred to as the reading-rooms. There is a copy of a poster in the BLHS archives advertising a concert there in 1882. There is also a copy of William 'Castle' Carey's diary in which he recounts arriving from Australia in 1861 and proceeding to build a house and business as coal merchant and fly proprietor in Chapel Street, opposite the chapel, and records joining the reading-rooms on 1 February 1862. A fly was a 2-wheeled, light-weight, horse-drawn cab.

Besides being used for concerts and as a library, soup kitchens were organised there at various times by members of the local gentry, such as Miss Emma Smith of Glenville and Mrs Bucknill of Brownlow. Soup was a penny a bowl if you could afford it and free if you could not. The curate, Revd A. LeFeuvre, in 1909 ran a gymnasium and supplied equipment for the lads of Bitterne. The Parish Council used it for meetings and rates were collected there.

Eventually the time came when the building was deemed surplus to requirements as the church had another hall, Martin Hall as it was then, in Brook Road and they wanted money to finance the building of a Church Institute near the church.

In February 1923 permission was given by the Charity Commissioners to sell the Old Chapel for a sum not less than £200 with the proceeds going to the Church Institute. A notice to this effect was attached to the outer door of the chapel. The Church Institute was eventually opened in September 1932 but did not last long, being destroyed by fire in a bombing raid on 14 March 1941.

The Old Chapel building was sold in June 1923 to George Anthony Olley, a Swaythling estate agent, for £200. He was obviously a shrewd businessman because he sold it four months later to Alfred William Holloway of Wilton Avenue for £300. Mr Holloway turned the Old Chapel into Bitterne's first cinema. On top of the porch he had a projection room built which was only accessible by an iron ladder outside the building. Films were then projected through the central window opening. Francis Brett, an old Bitterne inhabitant whose memories were collected by Irene Pilson, remembered the hard wooden seats and the noise of the films being hand cranked. Southampton Council first gave the building a cinematograph licence in January 1924, subject to the use of a Howarth portable projector. They started having second thoughts in January 1926 when it was reported that the premises were undrained and pail closets (i.e. buckets) were in use and should be replaced by water closets, although the licence was renewed. The work was never done and the records are not clear but some time in 1927 or 1928 it ceased to be a cinema.

Chapel Street c.1913, with the Old Chapel on the right and post office on the left.

The Old Chapel in use as a builder's store by H.W. Small.

Above: *The Old Chapel in 1994, now without its porch and converted into a unique family home.*

Right: *An example of Bob Payne's artistic ability, his drawing of the parish church and school, c.1884.*

Bitterne Church and School, circa 1884

Left: *The interior of the Church of the Holy Saviour. The scene is pre-1925 as the gas lighting was replaced with electric in that year. A later change was the raising of the chancel floor in 1937–39.*

This 1996 painting is by Revd Cyril Harris, father of the then vicar, Revd Paul Harris.

Bitterne Church Mothers' Union pictured on the vicarage lawn, c.1951. The adults are, left to right: *?, Mrs Bovey, Mrs Hunt, ?, ?, Mrs Smith, Revd Harries, Mrs Harries (in front), Mrs Irons, Mrs Stott, Mrs Chapman, Mrs Bowyer, Mrs Shapley.*

Alfred Holloway, by now described as an engineer of Westridge Road, eventually sold the old cinema hall in 1936 to Harry Wakeford Small of 44 Dean Road for £92.10s. Harry Small was a local builder and he and his heirs used the building as a workshop and store for 40 years. (It was finally connected to the drains via those of 71 Dean Road in 1948). By 1987 it was being used as a double-glazing workshop by Bitterne Glass and Mirror Centre of 88b Dean Road but this was deemed unneighbourly by Southampton Council who purchased it for £47,500 in 1987 and re-sold it 22 months later for £28,000 with the condition that it be developed into a private dwelling or dwellings within 18 months. It was eventually converted in 1991 by Robin Dear of 2 Dean Road and at the time of writing remains a spacious private dwelling on four floors with many of the original beams exposed. One of Bitterne's original buildings which has seen a variety of uses over 160 years will hopefully, while all around seems to change, stand for many more years.

Memories of Bitterne Parish Church
Raymond Luker

'I can see the spire, but how do I get to it?' is a common question for today's visitors seeking out the Church of the Holy Saviour, but was surely less of a problem when the building was consecrated just over 150 years ago, as the road through the village then passed the church gate and the trees formed a much smaller obstruction of the view, even to the casual observer who was probably unaware that the structure was only two-thirds complete. Some 36 years elapsed before the matching south aisle was added, providing my first family connection: my grandfather, George Watson, an apprentice carpenter with Chapman, the builders, of Woolston, worked on the construction of the new roof timbers. I cannot help surmising on the nature of the temporary wall and windows needed until the extension was finished.

The main schools next to the church were built in 1856, followed by the infants' building in 1897, where I was enrolled immediately after my fifth birthday in February 1935. Only gradually was I aware of the links between the school and the church on the other side of a high, dense hedge. In the summer we joined in displays on the vicarage lawn – possibly maypole dancing – but finding the route to the garden without trespassing into the house was quite daunting. In December pupils usually performed on the stage of the Institute. On one occasion I was selected to be Joseph in a tableau depicting the Nativity – presumably because of my height – whilst three senior girls recited the narrative from memory. Costumes were made by some of the mums, who used one pattern as the basic robe for Joseph, the shepherds and the wise men; there was a panic when the pattern was mislaid! One of my

friends had her birthday party at the same venue.

Attending Matins at 11a.m. with my mother, we normally sat just in front of the west door, where, after 15 minutes or so, I could watch the procession of my contemporaries, some of whom I knew, departing for their Sunday School classes. Nearly everyone in the congregation walked to church, as the Corporation omnibuses only began their Sunday timetable at midday. I also walked to school, like most of the staff; headmaster Charlie Watson had acquired a car when he moved to Chessel Avenue.

Returning to Bitterne after wartime evacuation and National Service, I found a new vicar in post (Revd Raymond Harries), my sister in Gene John's Bible Class and my mother one of three or four ladies in their best hats permitted to sit in the back row of the choir to augment the boy trebles. Soon mother was promoted from a distributor of magazines to Magazine Secretary, and so every month two bundles arrived from the printers, requiring the instant counting of 67 copies for Mrs Dickinson, who was renowned for the size of her delivery round. The rest, including postal copies, could be sorted at a more leisurely pace.

Next, preparations were in hand for the church centenary. Curate Revd David Tanqueray and my father, Edwin Luker, were asked to act as joint editors for the commemorative booklet A Vista, recently reprinted by the BLHS, for which I designed the cover. The celebrations spanned eight days in September 1953 and my special involvement was playing the violin in a performance of Mendelssohn's 'Hymn of Praise', with the orchestra and augmented choir, conducted by Mr F. Gange, church organist (and well-known shoeshop proprietor). The singers were arranged in two rows across the sanctuary by the communion rail to achieve maximum projection for their voices, and the instrumentalists were led by Stanley Roper, a policeman (now buried near the west door), with the Ortons, father and son, contributing cello and oboe. An extended orchestral introduction had the singers bursting to open up fortissimo in the first dramatic chorus 'All things, all men'. This was a period when our church choir still had the resources to undertake standard cantatas such as Stainer's 'The Crucifixion' and 'Olivet to Calvary'.

A recent survey has revealed a total of 40 memorials, mostly of brass or marble, scattered around the inside of the church, including one hidden behind the communion table in the south aisle, recording prominent as well as lesser-known former inhabitants of the parish. Two of the latter are for my parents, but I wonder how many people now recall the exploits of Captain Dan Parker of the oceangoing tug Turmoil in rescuing the Flying Enterprise?

Some 62 names are listed on the plaque for the First World War and another 43 for the Second World War, and the 11 stained-glass windows – some in vibrant colours like the east window to the side aisle, with its

Vicars of Bitterne
Tune: 'The Vicar of Bray'

The tune was well known and the words were composed by the Revd P.J. Winstone while Curate (1955–58). Hodkinsons have been Parish Clerks since 1863 and continue in the post to the present day.

In Queen Victoria's golden days
Before Prince Albert died sir,
They built the Church on Bitterne Hill:
Afar it could be spied sir.
The Vicar then was named Usborne,
A wealthy man was he sir,
And the Parish Clerk was a Hodkinson,
And evermore shall be sir.
        Chorus:
And this is the law I will maintain
Unto my dying day sir,
That whatsoever Vicar shall reign,
The Hodkinsons will stay sir.

When Naughty Nineties roared their course
In London far away sir,
Our Vicar then was Edward Hill,
He moved from Southernhaye sir.
He wrote his Pax Intrantibus
Above the Vicarage door sir,
And the Parish Clerk was a Hodkinson,
And shall be evermore sir.
        Chorus

When George succeeded lively Ted
And the Kaiser turned and ran sir,
A. Crockett was our Vicar's name,
A stern and low churchman sir.
Some thought his sermons over long,
But not a fig cared he sir,
And his Parish Clerk was a Hodkinson,
And evermore shall be sir.
        Chorus

When Charlestons were all the rage,
And shares just fell and fell sir,
The Vicar visited the sick
And his name was Aldwell sir.
He rode his bike about the place,
And a keen gardener was he sir,
And his Parish Clerk was a Hodkinson,
And evermore shall be, sir.
        Chorus

As George the Fifth declined in health,
Love was our Vicar's name sir,
Southampton spread itself about,
And up the hill it came sir.
The Vicar's ill, but never mind,
Why should you anxious be sir?
For our Parish Clerk is a Hodkinson,
And evermore shall be sir.
        Chorus

James Hodkinson was Parish Clerk from 1863 until 1927 when he was succeeded by grandson Tom.

When George the Sixth became our King,
And Hitler went to war, sir,
B. Allen was our Vicar then,
He raised the chancel floor, sir.
They fired the church, burned down the hall,
Blew off the Vicarage roof, sir,
But the Parish Clerk was a Hodkinson,
And him they failed to move, sir.
        Chorus

When queues and rationing held their sway,
The Army turned up trumps, sir,
And sent us Vicar Pa McKew,
Who raised us from the dumps, sir.
The young and old both loved him well,
But he had little rest, sir.
And his Parish Clerk was a Hodkinson,
As you've already guessed, sir.
        Chorus

Then Ireland gave way to Wales,
[to the pianist]: 'Cwm Rhondda' is the tune, sir
And sent us Raymond and his wife,
Who left us very soon sir,
And many stories still are told,
Of Harries' goings on, sir
You've guessed the name of the Parish Clerk?
Yes, it was Hodkinson, sir!
        Chorus

John Boaden may he with us reign,
For many a happy year, sir
And many a steaming bowl of punch,
Be brewed by Mary here, sir.
But when the punch is cold and dead
And we are in our tombs, sir,
May our Parish Clerk be a Hodkinson,
And sitting in this room, sir
        Chorus

Oh, Vicars come, and Vicars go,
Churchwardens are forgot sir,
Of Curates we have had eighteen,
Of organists a lot, sir.
But when our rockets reach the moon
And furthest outer space, sir,
May our Parish Clerk be a Hodkinson,
For none could take their place, sir!
        Chorus

Right: A line-up of clergy at the induction of Revd Raymond Harries in 1950. Left to right: Revd Kimber, ?, EL Shapley (churchwarden), Revd Harries, Revd McKew, Eddie Ridges (churchwarden), Revd Williams, Revd Tanqueray (Curate), Tom Hodkinson (Parish Clerk).
                    (BRIAN PASKINS)

Pre-Raphaelite styling, or the quieter tones of the recent memorial to his wife by former Chief Constable and PCC Secretary Alf Cullen – are all worth studying for their depiction of Bible scenes and themes.

Other brief recollections include: canasta drives in the old Edwardian Vicarage; one family wedding and three family funerals; former Vicar Revd John Boaden habitually grasping the scrolls on either side of the pulpit book rest when preaching; Curate Revd Peter Winstone's impassioned denunciation of the Soviet invasion of Hungary; visiting preachers contending with the summer sunshine streaming through the west window during evensong; stumbling through the churchyard on a dark and frosty night to photograph the newly floodlit tower and spire; my father's curtailed tenure as churchwarden; Bank Holiday Monday tennis on the courts beside the parish hall; the joy and privilege of being part of both the 100th and 150th anniversary celebrations.

Footnote: In October 2002 Bitterne Parish Church entered into an ecumenical partnership (see the article on Bitterne Methodist Church) with shared sites. The Parish Church became known as Holy Saviour and the Methodist Church became the Wesleyan Centre.

A letter from the Church Organ

From the Bitterne Parish Magazine, September 1948.

My dear friends,

Yes, you may call me old without giving offence. I came to Bitterne Church in 1875. Seventy-three years ago I was in my prime and a useful instrument. How well I recall the many Vicars and Organists I served under; especially the late Revd E.B.

Hill who composed a quantity of sacred music and the Revd B.S. Aldwell, still happily living in retirement. I recall too the beautiful rendering of violin solos by Miss Lister, now Mrs Bucknill, at organ recitals. Then I could maintain my part, but, alas, with the passing of the years, I have deteriorated. The tonal quality of my reeds leaves much to be desired, my action is worn and very unreliable. Among my organists I have a great affection for Mr W. Cross and also for Mr Frank Sara, who left me to serve his country in the war and is now living in London. I am deeply attached to my present 'master', Mr F.C. Gange, whom I first knew 50 years ago and when he returned in 1940, after an absence of 28 years, I felt ashamed to meet him, for I knew quite well I was not capable of doing what was required of me.

Now through the kindness of friends I am promised a new lease of life, all my pipes are to be re-voiced, my action is to be attended to, 150 new pipes will replace the old ones which are beyond repair. I am to have a sub and super swell action, new balanced swell pedal, new draw stops, my keys are to be re-ivoried, there is to be a new music desk and many exciting improvements.

I would like to thank you all in anticipation for the generous support which I know you will gladly give to meet the expense. I will not say goodbye for when I am out of the organ builders' hands I shall be ready to serve you for many years to come in the lovely services of worship and praise to God, which have always been associated with Bitterne Church.
Your old friend,
The Organ.

An organ renovation fund was being launched to raise the £1,015 required for the work. This same organ is now no longer in use, although still there, and is philosophically listening to his digital replacement, no doubt with tears in his pipes.

Top: Bitterne Parish Church organist Reginald Smith, c.1953. (BRIAN PASKINS)

Above: *By 2005 the church organ, which was bought second hand needed another renovation, but the cost was prohibitive so it is currently awaiting disposal.*

Bitterne Covenanters
Joy Bowyer

You will read elsewhere in this book of Alan and Gene John, but here their work with young people in the Covenanter and Girl Covenanter groups is related in more detail.

The strength of both groups was the pastoral care given by Alan and Gene and their leaders and in providing a strong Christian teaching along with lots of fun activities within the meeting and at other times. Local rallies with other Hampshire groups were organised, with competitions in the girls' group in cookery, netball, rag hockey (a violent indoor game using walking sticks and a sort of stuffed square 'ball' and the likelihood of cracked shins), table tennis and recitations from memory of Bible passages. The boys got away with Bible readings. Alison Hesketh brought fame to Bitterne by winning the Recitation,

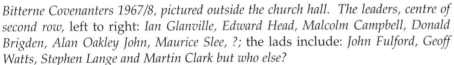

Bitterne Covenanters 1967/8, pictured outside the church hall. The leaders, centre of second row, left to right: Ian Glanville, Edward Head, Malcolm Campbell, Donald Brigden, Alan Oakley John, Maurice Slee, ?; the lads include: John Fulford, Geoff Watts, Stephen Lange and Martin Clark but who else?

Top: Covenanters' badge.
Above: The Girl Covenanters' badge.

The River Bure near St Benet's Abbey, 1998. The Bitternes Afloat fleet can be identified by their distinctive burgee, in this case showing the boat to be that of the Commodore.

The Girl Covenanters 1968/69, in the hall of 2 Chessel Avenue. Included are: Hilda Smith, Jane Sara, Angela Privett, Diane Frost, Margaret Campbell, Joy Bowyer, Janice Hutchinson, Angela Gear, Judy and Penny Clapham, Val Williams, Lynne Hitchcook and a young Catherine Johnson.

One of the first Bitternes Afloat cruises on the Norfolk Broads, c.1951.

Revd Raymond Harries walking the plank, the punishment for shooting the Commodore's burgee with a water pistol. In the dinghy, left to right: Malcolm Campbell, Alan Oakley John, John Williams.

and Janet Andrews was a winner at table tennis. When Gene John died in 2004, Alison Hesketh (now Saunders) recited her winning recitation at the memorial service in Bitterne Church. Alison recalls:

Looking back I now realise that being a Bitterne Covenanter has left a great imprint on my life. Each Sunday around 50 girls gathered in Dr and Mrs John's home to worship, learn and share our faiths. We sat on the floor, often squashed up against the wall. We sang, read and discussed issues with our peers and the leaders. Deep friendships were formed; everyone supported each other. Then there were the competitions: Bible reading, recitations, netball and crafts. The first rounds took place within the group and our proud winners then went to the regional final always held at Testwood School in Totton. Bitterne had an excellent reputation and often teams won the regional heats and so we went to London to meet other Covenanters in the national finals.

These were happy years; the rigour and enjoyment of learning with others as well as developing leadership skills. Older girls mentored younger girls; friends were made locally and nationally. The annual trip with the local boys' group to the Norfolk Broads was immensely popular and many young people growing up in Bitterne in the 1970s and 1980s will have good memories of friendship and fellowship.

As a headteacher of a large comprehensive school I now can appreciate just how much I learnt in my formative years. Covenanters for me was a community. Here I made good friends and we all accepted each other and learnt together, regardless of our abilities and backgrounds. It was a place of vision and values. Perhaps it is no surprise that I have ended up as a leader myself as I saw the best type of leadership modelled to me at Covenanters – that of selfless giving.

Another important part of the life of the group was the Duke of Edinburgh Award. Winners of the Gold Award would go up to Buckingham Palace to receive their certificates. Girls would have many months of work towards this, with service to the community included. The expeditions were like 'outward bound' ventures.

Gene John also arranged camping holidays in the New Forest and near Towyn in Wales and groups of girls went off to the CPAS house parties in August.

Valerie Marsh recalls:

I started on day one, and because my name began with a 'B' (Bowyer) mine was the first name on the list. We were then called 'The Bitterne Girls' Bible Class'. I think that on that first day there were probably about a dozen girls.

Because I was having music lessons, I was asked to play the piano, a duty I shared weekly with Margaret Shapley and Lorna Dunford. I still have my chorus book which I was given for playing the piano.

Through the Bible Class I helped out with some Sunday School teaching which I think was in Brook Road. Other teachers helped Mrs John with her work – Mrs Joyce Campbell, Alison Eldridge and another lady, I think called Miss Baker, who lived in a prefab. She later became quite ill, but we were all fond of her and visited her quite often after Bible Class.

The boys were taken every year by Dr John on a sailing holiday on the Norfolk Broads. We wanted to go as well but it was not until we joined the Epilogue many years later that girls were included. Great days!

Christmas parties joining with the boys were a regular feature, and they usually involved a theme, such as the 'Wild West'.

Sue Ward (née Golding) recalls:

I attended Covies in the 1960s. I remember meeting on Sunday mornings at 9.30 in various ground-floor rooms (sometimes we used the waiting-room of the surgery). A variety of chairs would be brought into the largest front room for a time of worship, which resulted in those girls who arrived early sitting on comfortable armchairs at the front, whilst those who were later arrivals had dining or folding chairs or even had to stand. We would divide into age groups for teaching sessions spreading round the house, or into the garden in the summer.

I have very fond memories of those days: we had a lot of fun, but also were given a very thorough grounding in the Bible, learning many Bible passages and choruses by heart. I am very grateful to Gene for all she taught me.

'Bitternes Afloat'
John Sturgess

The 'Bitternes Afloat' Christian Cruise is a week-long cruise, held during the Spring school holidays started in 1949 by Alan Oakley John and the Bible class leaders of Bitterne Church, for boys between the ages of 12 and 18. It was an adventure-type holiday on the Norfolk Broads aimed at promoting, through both sailing and study, the Gospel message of Jesus Christ.

It is still going strong today having, over the years, changed and refined itself to meet new challenges and needs by extending the same opportunities to the girls of the parish, and by attracting crew members from other churches where second and third generation Broads converts now reside. Cruise members and most skippers and leaders are drawn from our partner parishes. This ensures that churches, parents and members have recognised and known leaders to enable easy personal contact and follow-up. Partner parishes include Stopsley (Luton), Fareham, Buckingham, Rowledge (Farnham) and a few farther afield.

We use a fleet of yachts plus a day boat known as a 'half decker'. The boats are between 25ft and 31ft in length and are crewed by between five and seven people. Each boat has an experienced skipper and mate who supervise the cruise members, as they live and sleep on their Broads yachts. The boat crews are mixed during the days' sailing and reorganised for night-time accommodation. The half decker is skippered by a qualified sailing instructor and cruise members have the opportunity for more intensive training on this boat.

Our 'HMS Pinafore' shore crew provides a hot meal both morning and evening and is based in a local village hall where we gather to eat, worship and share fellowship.

The Methodist Church in Bitterne
Di Heathorn

Methodism began in Bitterne in 1806, only 15 years after the death of John Wesley, when a group of Wesleyans started to meet. This was initially in the home of John Sinnatt in Pound Street, then known as Pound Lane, at the rear of the Firs Inn. Bitterne had been linked to Southampton only since 1796 when the first Northam Bridge was constructed. Despite this, it really was a village and did not become part of the borough of Southampton until 1920.

Eric and Ken Gadd remove the foundation stone of the Methodist Church Hall in Dean Road, 100 years after their grandfather Esau William Gadd laid it.

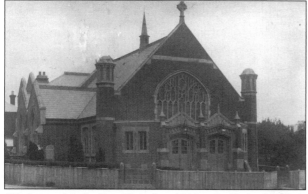

Wesleyan Methodist Church c.1910. Built in 1906, it stood on the corner of the High Street and Pound Street.

The first Wesleyan chapel was built in 1823 – in Chapel Street, renamed Dean Road in 1924. Bitterne village quickly grew during the 1850s. The railway came in 1856 and many people moved out from the town centre.

A larger Wesleyan chapel with ancillary rooms was erected on the corner of Pound Street and Bitterne Road, after the pound (last used for stray animalsBitte c.1955) had been moved slightly to the north. Its construction in 1906 cost about £3,000. Following the reconciliation of Wesleyan, Primitive and United Methodists in 1932, this was of course known as Bitterne Methodist Church. Worship continued during the Second World War and records show the names of many people known to present members who kept the society alive during those difficult days.

There was another large increase in the population of Bitterne during the 1950s and many houses were built in this suburb of Southampton.

In the mid-1960s Southampton Council planned a large-scale development of Bitterne's shopping centre and the Pound Street building was scheduled for demolition. At this time, talks were taking place nationally concerning union between the Methodist and Anglican Churches. This affected the decision made by the Trustees that they would buy part of the vicarage garden for a new Methodist church and community centre at a cost of over £30,000. These purpose-built premises were opened in 1969 and fulfilled their promise of serving the people of Bitterne.

During the 1970s the roads through Bitterne became more and more busy until the construction of a bypass became inevitable. The demolition of many properties began in 1983 and the dual carriageway was completed in 1986. The shopping centre became a pedestrian precinct and some long-term residents felt that the heart of the old village had gone. There is still, however, a strong sense of community in this part of the city.

The Whites Road building is very suitable for community use and huge numbers of adults and children still enjoy activities on the premises every week. One important change occurred inside the building in the autumn of 2002 when the main wooden doors to Wesley Chapel were replaced by beautiful glass ones. These enable all the users of the building to see that it is a Christian Church.

By the mid-1990s there was an increasing conviction that Christian witness in Bitterne would be strengthened if the two denominations with buildings so closely sited worked together. Talks began and initially the work with children and young people was combined. As time passed shared services became more frequent and the evolution into one church began. A 'Declaration of Intent' was signed in April 1998 and detailed planning continued. The Constitution, which dealt with the organisation of the Partnership, was finalised in May 2002. A Sharing

Agreement covered the entire site and premises. The Methodist building was to be known as the Wesley Centre and the Parish Church as the Church of the Holy Saviour – its proper name! An exciting service in October 2002 saw the inauguration of the new Local Ecumenical Partnership which has a common purse and a joint Council.

The Church at Bitterne is still very much part of the Southampton Methodist Circuit and there is a Methodist minister on the clergy team of the Partnership. Bitterne has changed beyond recognition since some Wesleyans met in John Sinnatt's house. However, the 'people called Methodists' are still bearing Christian witness here after 200 years.

Bitterne Congregational/ United Reformed Church
Margaret Sandell

The Congregationalists were known as Independents until a political party of that name was formed. In Southampton the Congregationalists were among the first dissenting bodies to be established after the Commonwealth ended in 1660.

By 1668 Above Bar Congregational Church was established and until its destruction during the blitz of 1940 was the leading dissenting church in the town. Isaac Watts, the famous hymn writer, attended the church where his father was a deacon.

Above: *Mrs E Sturgess, known as 'Gentle Annie' outside the Congregational Church that she joined in 1928. An active member of the ladies' sewing circle and helper at many church functions, she passed away in 1978.*

Left: *The old Congregational Church, decorated for their harvest festival, 1949.*

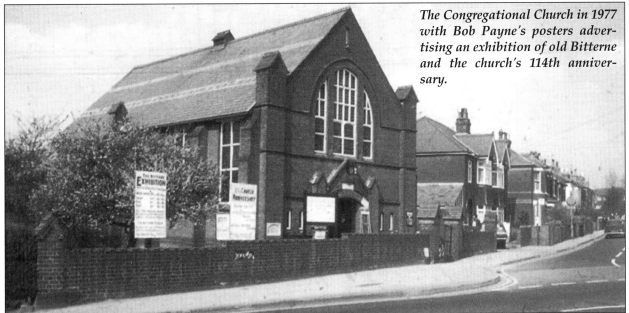

The Congregational Church in 1977 with Bob Payne's posters advertising an exhibition of old Bitterne and the church's 114th anniversary.

JOHN WESLEY 1703-1791

BITTERNE METHODIST CHURCH
AND COMMUNITY CENTRE

g. Abrahams
105 Bursledon Rd
Bitterne
Southampton
SO2-7LY

A commemorative envelope and franking to celebrate the opening of the new Methodist Church in September 1969.

Left: *The interior of the Wesleyan Methodist Church shortly before vacation in 1969.*

Right: *Inside the Methodist Church, Whites Road, now called the Wesley Chapel.*

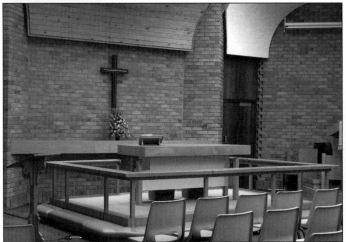

The Congregational Church Sunday School teachers in 1896, on the annual treat to Harefield, courtesy of Mr Edwin Jones. Left to right, standing: Messrs Brewer, Cowley, Mist, Borer, Stokes, Payne, Gould; sitting: Mrs Hague, Miss Abrey, Miss Matcham, Miss Osman, Miss Bracher.

Receipt and Expenditure – Annual School Treat.

Receipt; By Sale of Tickets . £1. 8. 9 . 160. Children and
By Donations _ 1 15.6 between 40 and
Received at Gate 0. 12. 3 80 Adults sat
3 16 6 down to Tea.

Expenditure. Mr Abrey Bill. 3 . 8. 6 . ½ 4. 14. 0 . ½
Band 0 . 10 . 0 ½ 3 16 6 ½
Mr Butcher 6 Expenditure ½

An extract from the Sunday School teacher's minute book for 1896, mentioning the treat at Harefield.

In the late 1700s Above Bar began to send out missionaries to the outlying villages and established a large number of small chapels from Hythe to Botley.

During the winter of 1850/51 a room was engaged in Bitterne where, on Tuesday evenings, a religious service was conducted by Revd R. Laishley of Pear Tree Chapel in connection with the Above Bar Home Missionary Association. In the spring of 1851 a Sunday School with nine teachers and 50 scholars was established and carried on under the auspices of Above Bar Sunday School Society. The room that was used, according to information that has been gathered, was in a coach house situated in Lion Place, High Street. In 1854 a new building was erected in Commercial Street on the site of the present Catholic Hall and in 1857 the Sunday School was formally recognised by the Sunday School Union. By 1860, 132 children had passed through the Sunday School.

The Bitterne Congregational Church came into being on 5 April 1863, led by a lay minister, Mr Brice. The building could be used as a sanctuary with the seats facing the communion table and when the seat backs were changed around the seats faced the other way to make a church hall.

By the 1890s the church had grown and a new building was planned to be built on land at the bottom of Chapel Street, now Dean Road; it was completed in 1897 at a cost of £1,277. Gradually the new building was itself modernised, with a second-hand pipe organ from the Isle of Wight being installed in 1916. In common with many churches, the congregation dwindled during the First World War when the young men left for the forces and many did not return after the war. Electric lighting, to replace the gas lamps, was not installed until 1934 following a new heating system with a coke-fired boiler in place of the old tortoise stoves.

The Revd Wilfred Wall was inducted to the church in February 1939 and in April of that year the Sunday School hall in Commercial Street was sold for £750 and plans were made to build a church hall at the rear of the church building. Building commenced in June and it was opened in October of that year just one month after the start of the Second World War. Shortly afterwards the hall was taken over by the Auxiliary Fire Service who ate and slept there. The Sunday School closed for a couple of years while most of the children were evacuated and started again in 1943 in the church vestry as the hall was still occupied. Revd Wall was a very popular preacher and the church was often full to overflowing during the war.

After the war the children's work in the church went ahead and in 1946 Mrs Gladys Snook started a Girls' Life Brigade Company and her husband Don a Boys' Brigade Company, both of which were very successful and are still in being today. When the Sunday School celebrated its centenary there were 22 staff and 182 children.

Shortly after the church was redecorated in 1959 Southampton Council announced plans for a Bitterne bypass that would pass just to the north of the church. After a site visit the planners realised that traffic noise would make worship impossible and it would be best to relocate the church on a new site. A compulsory purchase order was placed on the church and the Manse that was next door.

In 1963 the church celebrated 100 years of witness in Bitterne, expecting to be relocated in the near future. When Revd Arthur Nagle arrived in 1964 fund-raising was started for the inevitable expense of moving to a new site, although the new building would be paid for as a result of the compulsory purchase order. Life in the church carried on as usual, as did the fund-raising for years and years! In addition to the Brigades a popular Youth Club kept the teenagers happy and in 1969 a Junior Choir was started under the leadership of Margaret Lisby with a very talented group of youngsters.

In 1972 the Congregational Church joined with the Presbyterian Church of England to become the United Reformed Church – a name that people still find difficult to get right. In 1977 during a ministerial vacancy rehearsals were started for a religious musical entitled 'SPIRIT' and everyone in the church was invited to take part either on stage or backstage. In all about 70 people were involved of all ages from six to 60 and when the new minister, Revd Brian Coward, arrived he was invited to join in – which he did as a drummer and on stage as an angel! The musical was the start of a very successful run of musicals produced over the next 25 years with repeats of 'SPIRIT' always guaranteed to fill the church. The musicals were also taken to other churches in the area and as far away as Lymington! The cast included three generations of one family and several sets of parents sang alongside their offspring. The most recent musical produced by Margaret Lisby and her merry band was in 2002.

The demolition of the church building in Dean Road took place in 1982 and the new building above shops on the site of the old Bitterne School opened in 1985. A beautiful stained-glass window for the Sanctuary, paid for with donations given in memory of past members, was designed and made by the artist Mark Angus, who at that time was working from his studio in Bath. Members got used to directing people to the 'church above Iceland'. The church wanted to be 'in the market place' rather than away from the centre of Bitterne. The new premises were very much appreciated, especially as the congregation had been a mobile church worshipping at the Bitterne Junior School on Sunday mornings and in the chapel of Redcote Convent in the evenings (although the Sisters made members very welcome and enduring friendships were made at that time).

In recent years it has been very rewarding to work and worship with other Christians in Bitterne, something that our forebears would have found either amazing or perhaps even shocking, that we could all be comfortable taking part in worship in each other's churches!

Annie Sturgess (born in 1888) remembers:

In the summer we had our 'treat'. We met at the Sunday School and marched down Bitterne High Street (now Bitterne Road), up Chapel Street (now Dean Road), up to Inkerman Road (now Marne Road) and through to 'Harefield', kindly lent by Mr Edwin Jones, whose estate, farm, etc., extended from Inkerman Road to Westend Church. Mr Abrey did the catering and we took our own cups or 'mugs' as we called them and sat on the grass for tea.

We had various games before and after tea, also races with prizes for the winners. We used to love to see the peacocks in the private gardens, especially when they spread their lovely tails. After tea we all lined up with our teachers and walked up to the house where the family were in the drawing room with the french windows open. We sang and our superintendent thanked Mr Edwin Jones for the use of his field for our treat and he made a suitable reply... I never remember it raining when it was our Sunday School treat.

The Boys' Brigade in Bitterne – Early Days
Brian Lamerton

The first recording of a Boys' Brigade company (known as the Boys' Life Brigade until 1925) in Bitterne was in November 1923 when a company known as the 6th Southampton was formed at the Bitterne Methodist Church (at that time on the corner of Bitterne Road and Pound Street) under the captaincy of Major H.J. Furminger. The first meeting was attended by 12 boys namely H. Smith, J. Clark, T. Bunday, W. Eldridge, J. Shergold, E. Pomery, R. Perrin, H. Bunce, V. Scorey, A. Scorey, W. Harris and H. Winter.

The company flourished under successive captains R. Bollom, R. Pomeroy, H. Smith (founder member) and Fred Shergold who was still in charge when records cease in 1937. The company fully integrated itself into Battalion affairs, winning many trophies, taking part in civic events and attending camp at a variety of venues including Swanage, Poole, Christchurch and the Isle of Wight.

In late 1944 Donald and Gladys Snook together with daughters Pamela and Monica moved into the area having returned from their wartime home in Andover. The Snooks had previously been members of Baptist churches and had experience of working with the Boys' Brigade and Girls' Life Brigade movements, but for convenience, and having relatives

already as members, found themselves attending Bitterne Congregational (later United Reformed) Church then situated at the corner of Bitterne and Dean Roads. As early as November 1944 Gladys Snook was given the Church Deacons' approval to form a company of the Girls' Life Brigade. (It has been said that Gladys made this a condition of becoming a member of the church!) This action was shortly followed, in May 1945, by Donald Snook agreeing to form a Boys' Brigade company – to be known as the 2nd Southampton. Early records indicate that the only other officer at the commencement was Mr Reg Hunt (who immediately took charge of the football and cricket teams who were very successful in Battalion competitions for several seasons) although another officer, who appears at a very early date, was the Revd Gordon Mackay.

In June 1945 the Church made a £5 loan to each of the Brigades to help with initial expenses. The Brigades were very much an integral part of the Church from day one and continue to be, and whilst involvement with the Church was not a condition of Brigade membership, it was reported in September 1950 that nine out of ten young persons preparing for Church membership were also members of one of the Brigade companies.

Among founder/early members were Ken Trapp, Roy Haynes, Harold Roe, Keith Petty, Stewart Marshall, Brian Lamerton, Paddy Fulford, Roy Dommett, Charlie Weeks and 'Jack' Russell.

In the late 1940s/early '50s the Southampton Battalion of the Boys' Brigade was very strong and the 2nd played their full part in Battalion affairs and made many friends together with healthy rivalry on the sporting fields with such as 3rd (St Denys Methodists), 4th (Winchester Road Methodists), 7th (Brunswick Place Presbyterian), 15th (Bitterne Park Congregational) and the 18th (Bitterne Park Baptist). The Company also played its part in the annual Battalion displays at the Central Hall as well as offering their full support to events at their 'own' church with the presentation of pantomimes, and entertainment at Harvest Festival, New Year, etc.

The first camp was held in the summer of 1946 when both companies set off for Sandy Balls estate at Fordingbridge where the girls were to be accommodated within the timber-hutted camp by the river, whilst the boys were under canvas nearby. By midweek, however, the boys had invaded the girls' common room having been flooded out of their tents by a torrential storm. Transport to and from camp was by a mixture of hired bus, officers'/parents' vehicles and bicycle (this method favoured by most of the senior boys). Highlights of the week, away from the camp environment, were the Sunday Church parade into Fordingbridge and a visit to Bournemouth to watch a day's play in the cricket match between Hampshire and Yorkshire.

Above: *2nd Southampton Company (Bitterne Congregational Church) Boys' Brigade, c.1946.* Back row, left to right: *Jack Russell, ?, Brian Hunt, Charlie Weeks, ?, Roy Dommett, ?, Paddy Fulford;* middle row: *Stewart Marshall, Keith Petty, Roy Haynes, Revd Gordon McKay, Capt Donald Snook, Lt Reg Hunt, Harold Roe, Ken Trapp, Brian Lammerton;* front row: *?, ?, ?, ?, Joey Bloom, ?, ?, ?.*

Below: *15th Southampton Girls' Life Brigade, July 1947, including Revd Gordon MacKay, Mrs May Brown (president), Jean Brown, Margaret Foster, Dorothy Bridle, Jean Purver, Joan Bonner, Betty Booth, Joyce Wookey, Nancy Joyce, Margaret Hopkins, Pam and Monica Snook, Margaret Hare, Gwen Davies, Audrey Foster, Sheila Barnes, Valerie Waddington, Gladys Snook (captain), Lily Gurman, Amy Foster, Joyce and Pam Medway, Paddy Wilton, Sylvia Moody, Muriel Taylor, Pam and Pearl Derham, Edna Bunday, Sheila Bunker, Mary Roe, June Wells, Pauline Myers, Barbara Gubbins, Eileen Hopkins, Mary Cox, Janet Pratt, Joan Bulpit and Janet Brown. The building behind is The Winning Post pub in Peartree Avenue.*

Camp arrangements for 1947 and again in 1948 were much more adventurous when members of both Brigades travelled by Southern Rail ferry to Guernsey and to Morley Youth Hostel (a converted church building). The church was divided into two dormitories whilst the schoolroom was both the dining room and the centre of daytime activities. There were a few who were against the idea of the Guernsey visits on a matter of cost as this may have excluded some members from attending. The cost of a full week's food and accommodation, together with the ferry fare, was £5.

In March 1955 after a decade in charge Donald Snook relinquished his position with the Boys' Brigade and was succeeded by his son-in-law Ken Trapp. By this time Monica Trapp (née Snook) had also taken charge of the GLB. This was a period of change as around this time Mrs Walter Brown, founder leader of 'The Life Boys' (the Boys' junior section) also tendered her resignation and was succeeded by Brian Hunt.

The Girls' Life Brigade
Margaret Donaldson

Two months after the war finished in 1945, Mrs Gladys Snook started the 15th Southampton Girls' Life Brigade company. My mother, Amy Foster, became a lieutenant in the company and I joined the senior section as I was already 14 years old. My sister Audrey joined the junior section.

Mrs Snook was a very able Captain so we were a very active company. The minister at the time was Revd MacKay. He became Chaplain of the GLB and BB companies. His wife was a nurse. Each Monday evening the senior girls went into the Manse next door to train for our health badges (Home Nursing, First Aid and Baby Care). There were six of us.

I always enjoyed the maze marching and national dancing which were always on the programme. We had lots of helpers: Jean Brown, Miss Gurman, Mrs Stan Milnes and the Rowland sisters Dora and Gwen.

We took part in national and district displays. The national displays were held at the Royal Albert Hall. We went up for rehearsals in the afternoon and the actual display was in the evening. Afterwards we walked to the Underground station and spent the night on the hard bunks of the wartime shelters. The bunks were in two tiers all along the tunnel. As the event grew we had afternoon and evening displays.

The district displays were held at the Central Methodist Church in Southampton. The East and West Southampton Districts filled the hall to capacity.

Two years running we went to the Morley Youth Hostel on Guernsey for our annual camp. We took the overnight boat from Southampton and had to sleep rough on deck, arriving at the hostel in time for breakfast. We paraded to the local church, nearly everyone

falling asleep during the sermon!

The next two years we went to Sandy Balls camp near Fordingbridge. We had to walk about 1½ miles to church parade in Fordingbridge the next day. Again we had hard bunks to sleep in! We swam in the River Avon. It was very cold! We had primitive latrines – a trench with a canvas screen around it. Mrs Snook always had a toilet roll handy, hanging on a rope.

One year several of us senior girls went down to Woolston to be trained by the BB Captain for a gymnastic display in the Albert Hall. We did the display twice, afternoon and evening.

Besides health badges being compulsory, scripture badges were too. The scripture examination was held in Bitterne Junior School. We had to pass with 60 per cent and to gain honours we needed 80 per cent. We also took part in the GLB Divisional sports day at the sports ground in Southampton. I thoroughly enjoyed that.

We had annual inspections which were held in Bitterne Junior School yard or Middle Road Infants' School yard.

My time in the Girls' Brigade has stood me in good stead for 60 years!

Christ the King & St Colman's Roman Catholic Church
Sister Elizabeth

The parish originated in 1904 at Redcote Convent. The Sisters of Our Lady of Charity came from France when there were very few Catholics in Bitterne and no church. The sisters walked daily to Saint Joseph's, Southampton, or to Saint Patrick's, Woolston, for Mass. The convent oratory was later used for Mass when a chaplain had been appointed. In 1910 a corrugated-iron church was erected. It was built in six weeks, and comprised three sections – one for the parishioners, one for the residents and one for the sisters, which was the usual practice at that time in religious community chapels and churches. It was referred to affectionately as the 'tin church'. It had a life expectancy of ten years, but was in use until 1960 when Christ the King Church was built.

In 1939 a site was prepared for the new church and

The Roman Catholic Church of Christ the King, c.1961.

Above left: *Fr Walshe, priest to Redcote Convent from May 1943, then priest at the church until July 1991.*

Above right: *The blessing of the bells procession, 1959. At the front are John O'Brien? (processional cross bearer) and Joe Craen (altar boy on right); behind, left to right: Fr Joe Rea, Canon Desmond Close, Archbishop King, Fr Myles Christy.* (JEAN CRAEN)

the crypt was built. However, the outbreak of war put all plans on hold, and the crypt was used as the air-raid shelter for sisters and residents. Mass and prayers were said there on many occasions. The chaplain in the war years was Father Garcia, a Basque priest, who came to England during the Spanish Civil War. He left in 1943, when Father Denis Walshe was appointed by the Bishop of Portsmouth to develop the Bitterne parish; he was installed as parish priest at Saint Patrick's on 17 March 1944, as there were no Bitterne parish buildings at that time. He lived at Saint Patrick's in Woolston and worked from there. He resolved to build a church in Bitterne. Thornhill, West End and Hedge End were all part of the parish at that time. Redcote Chapel was used for Mass, baptisms and religious instruction. Much fund-raising went on – fêtes, bingo, bazaars, etc. – which was not easy because many people were evacuated so Mass attendance was quite low. Great efforts to find a suitable site for the church resulted in the present site and in 1958 an architect, E.M. Galloway, was engaged to design the church and presbytery. The church was officially opened on 3 September 1960. A former church belonging to another denomination was used as the church hall for many years and was replaced in 1987 by a new hall better suited to the needs of the growing parish. Father (later Canon) Walshe retired in the mid-1990s to his native Cork, and subsequently died on 1 January 1999. Father Sean Budden succeeded Canon Walshe as parish priest until 2004, when Father Richard Maniak was appointed. During Father Maniak's sabbatical, Father Eamon Walsh became the parish priest. Following Father Eamon's appointment, the neigh-

bouring parishes of West End and Hedge End were 'clustered' with Bitterne and put under his care. The current priest is Father James Carling.

On 15 July 2004 the parishes of Christ the King and Saint Colman, Thornhill, were formally joined as the Parish of Christ the King and Saint Colman's and the ceremony of re-naming took place. The declaration of this formal occasion was signed by Bishop Crispian Hollis, Father Sean Budden (parish priest) and David Hill (Chair of the Parish Council). This document is kept at the back of the church.

The sisters at Redcote have their daily Mass and other services in the convent chapel, which was also used by Bitterne United Reformed Church whilst their new church was being built.

The Corner Plot
Aubrey Robertson

On 24 March 1855, an Indenture of Conveyance was drawn up for the owner of the 'Plot', a Mr George Bone, to transfer ownership of the same to the Revd H. Usborne. It was described as:

All that piece of land in the parish of Bitterne, containing by measurement in width... ninety one feet and in the depth thereof seventy five feet... a little more or less... bounded on the north by a road known as Inkerman Road (now Marne Road) and on the south by land belonging to Mrs Othen and on the east by a road known as Commercial Street.

Should you wish to delve further back in time, you need only consult www.usbornefamilytree.com, to learn much concerning the interesting background of the Usborne family.

Henry Usborne, MA, was the first vicar of Bitterne Parish Church, (1853–87). He and his sisters were the main contributors toward its building cost. His Father, John Usborne, retired to Midanbury Lodge and it is believed that he, Henry and his sisters lived there until Henry built Redcote Vicarage in 1860.

To return to 'The Corner Plot': Henry, having purchased the ground, his sisters – Eliza and

The Gospel Hall in Commercial Street, before it was rebuilt in 1969. It was originally built in 1857 as the first infants' school.

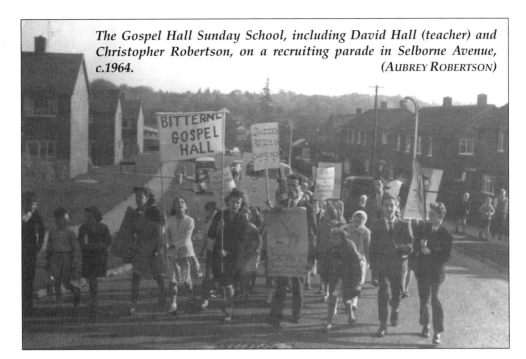

The Gospel Hall Sunday School, including David Hall (teacher) and Christopher Robertson, on a recruiting parade in Selborne Avenue, c.1964.
(AUBREY ROBERTSON)

Harriett (he had five sisters all told) – paid £400 for the erection of the Infants' School.

The building has been described as 'Neat and being of red bricks' (from one of our local brickyards, I wonder?). In 1857 the Inspector of Schools reported 'This is a new and very good building'. It is on record that Henry and his sisters took a great interest in the school and visited it often. The late R.C. (Bob) Payne remembered having to pay to attend school and transferring to the new school in the High Street in 1897.

The appointed teachers were Miss Hill (1857), then Mrs Byford (1865) and Miss Bennett (1893). For 40 years the younger boys and girls of Bitterne used the building to learn their 3Rs etc.

During this period the population of Bitterne increased and in 1897 a new Infants' School was built by the side of the existing Girls' School; Miss Bennett became headmistress of the new school building and, marrying the following year, became Mrs Prydderch.

With the exodus of the infants a new phase of service began for the community and the building became the Church Mission Hall, displaying a large board with the wording 'Good News Hall'.

From the church booklet *A Vista* (1853–1953):

A Friday evening meeting for children is held in the Mission Hall. The hall was usually well filled, and I would like to testify to the very happy times spent with the children there.

From the same source:

A Bitterne Girls' Club was formed under the Presidency of Mrs Aldwell with Mrs and Miss Chalmers and Miss Fry as leaders. As numbers

increased it moved from the Church Mission Hall to Itchen Secondary School.

In 40 years the Mission Hall was to have several owners. The Indentures, the earliest ones, beautifully handwritten in copperplate, make very interesting reading but give little clue as to the personalities of the 'Gentlemen' mentioned:

1895	*Edward Bance (17 days only)*
1895–1905	*Joseph S. Cockerton*
1905	*Alfred T. Thomas (three months only)*
1905–33	*John Richard St Barbe Baker*
1933–37	*John Doling*

Mr G. Brennan of the Bitterne Local History Society wrote:

In my young days (around 1918) the Mission was used every Saturday for a Magic Lantern show... there was only an oil lamp for the lantern and very poor gas lighting for the hall. This evening was called 'A Coffee Supper' with coffee and biscuits. Also the hall was used by the Bitterne 3rd Itchen Scouts of which I was a member. It was decided to have a Bugle and Drum Band. I well remember the din we made practising!

John R. St Barbe Baker, who was the owner of the Mission from 1905 to 1933, was born in 1860 and, like his father, was a keen evangelical Christian. At 18 years of age he hired the local village hall at West End on Sundays, preaching to packed congregations at morning and evening services. He also ran a large Sunday School.

As far as his involvement with 'The Corner Plot' is concerned, I have been unable to find any written matter at all, apart from the sale indenture, when, in his old age, John Doling took over.

It must have been around this time when 'outside' help became necessary to keep the work and witness going. Several names have been mentioned of persons who came voluntarily to help. There was Mr Neville, a retired naval officer who came to Bitterne from Portsmouth. He got Mr Leslie G. Harris interested and a friend of his, Mr Wild, joined him a little while later. They were both from the Church of Christ in Southampton (now Above Bar Church). There were also several who came, in turn, from Ebenezer Hall, Woolston, to help.

On Sunday there was a morning service, an afternoon Sunday School and an evening meeting. On Tuesdays there was a large women's meeting run by Mrs E. Woodley (a member of the Church of Christ) helped by Mrs Brown, Mrs Harris and Miss Iremonger who played the organ for all the services. On Wednesdays there was an evening Bible study class taken by Mr Charles Cannons. He was a colporteur who had a Bible shop in Carlton Crescent, Southampton.

There cannot be many folk living locally today that can remember the old building in detail, but Alf and Rita Gardiner have recorded their memories of it:

Our earliest memories must be approximately from 1928. There was a special children's campaign and the evangelist, a Mr Bloxal, had a horse-drawn caravan which was pulled up close to the hedge parallel to Commercial Street, the horse grazing in the field opposite. There was a row of sycamore trees in front of the building and a thick hedge on at least two sides consisting of a mixture of hawthorn, holly and privet. There were also many laurel shrubs in the grounds. The path to the door was flanked with these and in the winter time heavy snow weighed the branches on to the pathway. The privy at the back was somewhat shrouded with elderberry bushes (no flush toilets in those days). The coke for the 'tortoise' slow combustion stove was kept in a galvanised metal bunker outside, but some was kept under the floor in the old kitchen.

It was not until 1937, when the way forward with the owner seemed unclear, that Mr Buckle was asked if he could help. The outcome was that he, and four others who were all in fellowship at Ebenezer Hall, Woolston, a large fellowship at that time, decided to form a trust, and together purchase the Mission Hall.

The Conveyance for this was dated 22 June 1937. Part of the wording was: 'The Vendor has agreed with the Purchasers to sell the said property to them in fee simple... for the sum of four hundred and thirty seven pounds ten shillings.' The signatories to the Conveyance were: Charles John Buckle, 27 Little Lances Hill, Bitterne (shoe retailer and chiropodist); Herbert Cox, St Brelades, 4 Tranby Road, Itchen (motor mechanic); Reginald Cummins Thompson, Ivy Glen, Rosoman Road, Sholing (clerk); Benjamin

Edward Albert Trodd, 81 Middle Road, Sholing (electrician and crane driver); Stanley Ernest Williams, Fairview, Rosoman Road, Sholing (marine fitter).

In that same month application was made to the Registrar General certifying and registering places of religious worship that the building should be known as Bitterne Gospel Hall. Some years later the word 'Hall' was changed to 'Chapel' as many thought the latter was more appropriate to describe a place of worship.

With the coming of these brethren, their families and others who joined in the new fellowship, there was quite a nucleus to begin worshipping and witnessing together.

It was not until after the war years that I, having been demobbed from army service in the Middle East, was to have a more personal contact with the fellowship. The building was duly registered for 'solemnising marriages therein' (1937), and I was among the first half-dozen couples to be married there, my bride being the eldest daughter of Mr and Mrs Cox, now living at 'Holly Home' in Pound Street. She and the family were in fellowship there, her father being one of the first elders and Hon. Chapel Treasurer.

Having now a collection of reminiscences, leaflets, lists, registers, minute books, rebuilding plans, etc., plus copies of conveyances, trust deeds and other documents, as well as over 200 good photographs, I trust something of general interest will be preserved concerning the last 67 years of Bitterne Gospel Chapel's existence.

The National Spiritualist Church in Bitterne
Mary and Peter Clifford

In the mid-1940s the President of the Spiritualist Church in The Avenue suggested that Bitterne residents should consider establishing a church in their own area. Mr and Mrs W. Fowler, who lived at the top of Mousehole Lane invited like-minded people into their own home where they not only followed the teachings and principles of Spiritualism but also held money-raising activities for a future church. The group was able to rent the St John Ambulance Brigade hall in Dean Road at a cost of 10s. for Sunday, reduced to 7s.6d. if only the evening service was held. The church, known as the Bitterne and District National Spiritualist Church, held its opening service on 18 May 1947, and was affiliated to the Spiritualist National Union on 9 November, so celebrating its 60th anniversary in 2007.

It came to the attention of these pioneers that a plot of ground at the top of Lances Hill was for sale for £316.16s.6d. from Miss Dilys Jones, and a deposit of £30 was paid on 16 April 1951. The land had been used as tennis-courts by Messrs Frasers of St Mary

Street, and from a private drive it opened out and stretched back to the rear gardens of houses in Little Lances Hill and Grantham Road. There was a large wooden pavilion on the site that was sawn in half and converted to a useful shed.

The site acquired, work began with laying a base upon which block walls were erected to a height of about 3ft, on which a dismantled Nissen-type hut, purchased for £385, was erected. Along both sides were dormer-type wooden window frames and inside the lining was of fibreboard held in place by wires behind the panels. The assembly and fitting-out was done voluntarily by church members. Most of the heating was provided by paraffin heaters and for a long time the church paid for electricity on a 'horticultural tariff' allowing power all over the weekend, but only 6p.m. to 8a.m. on weekdays. The ladies' sewing circle could be found huddled round the oil heaters on a Wednesday afternoon with 6ft wide strips of coconut matting (which cost £49.3s.3d. in 1952) on the cold, concrete floor.

The building was officially opened as a church by Mrs Hart, a minister of the Spiritualists National Union, on 22 May 1952, when the collection amounted to £7.11s.5d. Fund-raising to meet costs and to contribute to the building fund came from fêtes, whist drives and social occasions, and the ledges on the walls inside the church held a 'trail of pennies'.

Southampton Council classified the building as temporary, renewing its certificate every five years until 1971 when they decreed that it must be demolished. The Committee chose to replace it with a single-storey concrete panel construction by the firm Compton, size about 70ft by 30ft and costing £1,720.1s.6d. A local Bitterne builder prepared the site and provided internal services, for the sum of £1,751, and volunteers undertook the interior decoration. The new building had been erected behind the old tin hut and was officially opened as a church on 26 September 1970. After the tin hut was demolished in 1972 the space became the car park.

The church has always been registered for weddings but the new building had to be re-registered on 22 July 1973. It was dedicated to the service of God and the Spirit World by the President of the SNU, Gordon Higginson, in January 1974.

Above: *Bitterne & District Spiritualist Church, 2006.*

Below: *The distinctive Nissen-hut shape of the original Spiritualist Church building with the old pavilion at this end, March 1969.*

The organisation is run democratically with an annually elected president, officers and committee. In 2005 they served a membership of approximately 120 with an average Sunday evening service attendance of about 55. Amongst past presidents has been Alderman George Dicks, who proclaimed his Spiritualist faith at his enrolment as Mayor of Southampton. As is usual at fêtes, local, well-known personalities have been invited to officiate and these have included Lord Maybray-King and Peter Clark of Southern Television fame.

Bitterne Infants' School, c.1926. The children had tiered seating, and here include Peggy Harding, Jack Hasler, Dora Streader, Sid? Spencer and Jim Hulbert.

John Abraham's certificate dated 23 October 1893, for passing his 3rd standard exams at Bitterne Boys' School.

As part of their early-twentieth-century education, boys at Bitterne School looked after allotments situated behind it. The boys here are pictured with headmaster, Henry 'Tubby' Cooke.

Right: Inside one of the Nissen-hut classrooms in the 1970s. Note the teacher's desk next to the stove!

Below: Some of the infants schoolchildren, including Jonathan Howard and Andrew Beale, in 1959.

Above: Bitterne Schools as many will remember them, the infants' on the left and the juniors' behind. Soon after joining Southampton Education Dept in 1957, Alan Leonard (now a BLHS Vice President) arranged for the erection of a 12ft chain-link fence to enable ball games to be played safely.

Chapter Five

Bitterne Schools
Rosaleen Wilkinson

Opening the musty covers of the old Bitterne School log-books was like stepping back into a different world.

As I turned the pages of the books, which may not have been opened for over a hundred years, I looked back into a simpler age, when it seemed that childhood was full of innocent rural pleasures. Children were unsophisticated. The promise of a 'treat' of tea and buns, or a concert of Christmas carols in the schoolroom, or the excitement of a magic lantern show, were eagerly anticipated. Even boyish misdemeanours seemed quite harmless. Yet the charming picture of Victorian schooldays was haunted by the spectre of extreme poverty for some pupils, and the ever-present threat of illness and death.

The log-books revealed a world where the church and the school were at the heart of everyone in the village – the vicar and the schoolmasters and mistresses were looked up to, and respected.

Many schools were established in mid-nineteenth century Victorian England. Bitterne's first school was built on land belonging to the Church in 1856. There were to be separate schools for boys and girls on the same site. The vicar, the Revd Henry Usborne, helped to finance the building, and the following year he also paid for an Infants' School in Commercial Street. The keeping of a log-book became compulsory in 1862 and these daily diaries have left us a fascinating picture of school life over a period of 140 years.

School attendance was always a problem in Victorian times because education was not compulsory, or free. Child labour was commonly used, especially in an agricultural area such as Bitterne, and children were kept away from school to help with haymaking, harvesting, gleaning, or fruit and vegetable picking. Whilst boys worked in the fields, girls were kept home to help their mothers with the new baby or to do the washing on Mondays. It was not until 1880 that education up to the age of ten was made compulsory, and the payment of school fees, albeit only pence, was not abolished until 1891.

Another problem was the weather. Winters were certainly much colder than those we enjoy today.

19 November 1875: *Inclement weather causes low attendance, several children have long walks from home along muddy or slippery roads and with insufficient clothing or boots.*

11 November 1886: *A heavy snow storm, more than half the children were absent. The schoolroom is intensely cold and draughty. The children have to stamp their feet and clap their hands to keep warm. They cannot write, their hands are so cold.'*

There were many entries recording epidemics of measles, scarlet fever, whooping cough, diphtheria and even smallpox in the village. Sometimes the school would be closed until the number of cases diminished, but all too often, sad little entries were made such as: **2 May 1870** *A lamb of the flock has been removed by death.* This shows the tragic outcome of these childhood illnesses. Poverty blighted the lives of many young pupils, some of whom were almost starving and had no shoes or proper clothes.

8 February 1895: *Still very cold weather, but attendance is good owing to the bread and cheese dinners provided to those whose fathers are out of work. I gave out six pairs of boots provided by Sir O'Bryan Hoare to needful girls.*

Bitterne in the nineteenth century was a fashionable place to live and there were numerous grand houses inhabited by wealthy families, usually known as 'the gentry'. Many of these ladies and gentlemen took a kindly and charitable interest in their poorer neighbours in the village, especially the children. Not only were they benefactors in financial terms, but they took an active part in the education of the pupils by visiting the school several times a week. Sometimes they listened to the children singing and reciting their set poems, or they would examine the handwriting or sewing. They would also actually teach lessons, despite being completely unqualified:

13 December 1866: *Lady Emily Macnaghten and another lady visited and expressed themselves pleased with the state of the school. They took the First Class in reading and spelling and examined the copy-books and slates. Lady Emily kindly invited the children to a Christmas party to be given at Bitterne Manor on December 27th. She distributed twenty cloaks and sixteen petticoats among those who had attended school most regularly during the year.*

Great events of history are noted in the log-books:

21 June 1887: *Her Majesty's Golden Jubilee Holiday.*
21 May 1900: *Holiday in honour of the relief of Mafeking.*
25 January 1901: *Practice for the annual entertainment stopped owing to the death of our revered Queen.*
11 November 1918: *News of the signing of the Armistice reached us at noon.*

There were many social changes after the First World War and the gentry no longer featured in the daily life of the school. Teaching became more professionalised and measures were taken to improve the health and welfare of pupils. Gradually Bitterne was being drawn into the life of the town of Southampton, and just as the village was no longer an enclosed community, the school too became part of the general education system.

No doubt the education provided was more up-to-date, but it meant the loss of some charmingly eccentric teachers. Henry 'Tubby' Cooke was headmaster from 1873 to 1918 and one of his pupils in the early 1900s described him:

On winter afternoons he would sometimes come and sit at the high desk beside the fire at the front of the class and read the Bible to us. He used to sit there reading away and scratching himself until he dozed off. Then, as the noise got louder and louder he'd suddenly wake up and start throwing bits of chalk at us.

The curriculum changed too. Girls had been taught housewifely skills such as knitting, sewing, darning and cookery, whilst boys were prepared for future employment in agriculture or manual jobs by taking woodwork and gardening classes. By the 1930s, however, pupils had higher expectations than working as domestic servants or farm labourers. Despite having few modern facilities, Bitterne School gradually gained a reputation for high standards and this was reflected in the number of scholarships which pupils won to the grammar schools. Teachers such as Miss Mist (1917–64) and Mr Wetton (1938–69) were outstanding.

During the 1930s the busy life of the school was overshadowed by fears of war, and on September 1 1939 the pupils were evacuated by train to the Bournemouth area. The early months of the Second World War did not bring the expected air raids; at this time it was a 'phoney war', and many parents brought their children home again. Arrangements had to be made for their education, whilst some Bitterne teachers remained with the evacuees. One girl who spent the war in West Parley remembered that Mr Wetton would have to return to Bitterne periodically and he would often bring back parcels or letters from parents. Some little evacuees never received anything, but he would say to them, 'Everything is all right at home and Mummy and Daddy are thinking about you.'

Back in Bitterne, the dreaded raids eventually came, and the school buildings were damaged by explosive and incendiary bombs on several occasions:

25 November 1940: *No school owing to a bomb which has blown out the windows and cracked the west wall.*
8 July 1941: *School roofs burned out with incendiary bombs. The day spent salvaging books and work.*
26 June 1944: *Attendance low owing to sirens which lasted from 8.40p.m. last night until 5.40a.m. this morning.*

Then at last there appears the entry:

8 May 1945: *School closed for two days on account of the ending of the war in Europe.*

When school broke up for the summer holidays later that year, it was the end of the old educational system and the start of a new era for Bitterne School. The 1944 Education Act established the principle of secondary education for all children after the age of 11, when they would leave junior school. Bitterne School had provided teaching for children from infant age up to the school-leaving age of 14, but now it was to become Bitterne Church of England Junior Mixed School and Bitterne Infants' School.

The austere postwar years brought long-term shortages of basic supplies:

21 February 1947: *We have completed another week of freezing weather. There has been a bitter north wind blowing since the middle of January and much snow. Owing to the national coal shortage we are not using electric light in school.*

Food rationing was even reflected in the poems I learned in school:

Teddy and I went shopping along the busy street,
Teddy had his Ration Book to buy himself some sweets.
Chocolates are lovely, but chocolates don't last,
So Teddy bought some toffee, that doesn't go so fast.

The postwar 'baby boom' brought large numbers of infants to the school and new accommodation had to be built for them. The old Queen Victoria Infant Schoolroom, opened in 1897, was totally inadequate. Three Nissen huts were also installed in the playground.

The wedding of Princess Elizabeth and Prince Philip in November 1947 brought national celebrations and a holiday from school. Then, on 7 February 1952 King George VI died and the school gathered around their new radio in the canteen to hear the proclamation of Queen Elizabeth II. Coronation tea parties were held at school in 1953 and all the children were presented with blue commemorative mugs. I still have mine.

As the standard of living in society as a whole improved, the school buildings came in for criticism. They were out-of-date, dark and cold, and the Nissen huts leaked. In January 1970 the managers discussed proposals for a new school on the Brownlow site. Meanwhile, following revised educational policy, in September 1970 the Junior School became a Middle School catering for children from eight to 12 years. However, the national economic situation was dire, and funds were unavailable for new premises. Successive plans were put forward and shelved until 1976. Then at last, in 1977, the headmaster, Mr D.V. Wright, wrote in the log-book:

As we come to the end of the school year my feelings are mixed. With all its disadvantages the old school has withstood the ravages of time and has an individual character of its own. Naturally we are looking forward to the eventual transfer to the new building and being housed in brighter and warmer conditions, but I doubt very much if the new building will withstand the 135 years service of this present building.

The new school was to be the last of the SCOLA buildings in Southampton; it was a semi-permanent structure built in ready-made sections. The Queen's silver jubilee was fast approaching, but a proposal to change the name of the school to the Queen Elizabeth II School was defeated. The Silver Jubilee Pageant in June 1977 was a huge success, with scenes of a Viking raid, King Canute, the departure of the Pilgrim Fathers for America, the granting of City status, and the presentation of the 1976 FA Cup, being re-enacted in the playground. It was to be the last big event on the old school site as children were moved to the new accommodation in March 1978, as sections became ready. There was no opening ceremony.

The 1980s were momentous years for the village as its centre was ripped apart for the construction of the new bypass, and the gracious old school buildings were completely swept away. In 1985 Mr Ian Herring became headteacher. He was to preside over many educational changes – the introduction of the National Curriculum and testing of pupils at various ages, computer technology, and the re-organisation of age groups, which meant that the school became a Junior School once again in 1994.

The year 2006 marks the 150th anniversary of Bitterne School. It has seen so much over the past century and a half. There have been two world wars, six Kings and Queens have reigned – Victoria,

Edward VII, George V, Edward VIII, George VI and Elizabeth II – and men have walked on the moon. Technology, and society itself, have changed beyond imagination, yet the school has moved with the times. It has educated generation after generation of village children, and it continues its role in a modern world.

Footnote: In *A Vista*, published in 1953 to mark the centenary of the Parish Church, Mr C. Watson, headteacher of the Mixed School wrote:

The old infants' school building in Commercial Street was condemned and a new infants' school was built by the side of the girls' school. This building was opened on 20 September 1897 by Mrs Prydderch, the head teacher, and the former infants' school (in Commercial Street) became a mission hall.

End of an Eyesore, Birth of a School
Eric Wyeth Gadd, headmaster, 1953-66

Often, on a sunny Sunday morning in those far-off days before the First World War, a small boy set out with his dad from their Bitterne Park home to visit his grandma in Bitterne village. Their favourite route began by way of Midanbury Lane, followed by Monks' Path. This ran between Bitterne Grove (now St Mary's College) and the edge of Glenfield Farm, where Jersey cows peacefully grazed. They then crossed a stream by a neat little plank bridge. (During holidays, the lad and his mates often visited this stream with jam jars in search of tadpoles). A stile, which stood at the foot of the narrow, tree-lined Lances Hill, was reached by a well-trodden footpath. To the left of this footpath was a hedge of hawthorn ('bread and cheese') and to the right lay an untidy overgrown area which had once been a brickfield, but had become an eyesore.

Years passed and the fields were sold to developers. The stile, stream and plank bridge vanished, and the footpath became part of a new road, Glenfield Avenue. Other roads followed, and many houses were built. As more children came to the area, so the

Cows grazing, c.1925, approximately where Beechwood School was built.

need for a school increased. Existing schools in the district had become overcrowded and the need for a new school could no longer be ignored. The Council spotted the former brickfield and acquired it in 1948 for precisely £1.

The disreputable spot was cleared of its weeds and the accumulation of litter dumped there over the years. Work in preparation for the new school began in April 1950, but soon ran into difficulties. From higher ground nearby rainwater had for years drained into the low-lying site, and so the foundations demanded greater attention and expenditure that had been anticipated. In consequence the building was not ready for occupation until 5 January 1953. The name Beechwood Junior School was chosen for its association with neighbouring Beechwood House and the Beechwood housing estate. Such are the whirligigs of time that the first headmaster at the school was that little boy who 40 years before had crossed the stream by the plank bridge with his dad.

Beechwood Junior School
Ronald Fry, headmaster, 1966–84

Beechwood Junior School was built on a former brickfield. The site was compulsorily purchased for £1 but possession was not obtained until May 1948.

The site of 2½ acres presented many difficulties, one of which was drainage. In addition, the low-lying position caused the original proposal for the Infants' School to be changed owing to the lack of natural lighting.

Building began on 16 April 1950. Originally, 15 classrooms for 450 children were optimistically intended. I know that in 1959 one classroom contained 50 children whilst each of the other 14 classrooms had over 40 children in them.

Beechwood Middle School Staff, summer 1979. Standing, left to right: *Audrey Cleverley, Neil Reynolds, Beryl Cross, Audrey Please, Ken Palmer, Joan Harrison, Colin Marshall, Joy Donaldson, Phil Hemmingway, David George;* sitting: *Gill Charnley, Rosie White, Sue Hankey, Ron Fry, Annette Brook, Sylvia Meyrick, Daphne Dann.*

The school opened on 5 January 1953, whilst the official opening by Sir Martin Roseveare, from Her Majesty's Inspectorate, and the Mayor of Southampton, Alderman E. Burrow, took place on 20 January 1953.

When I became Beechwood's headteacher there were 12 classrooms in use for 405 children. The number on roll grew steadily with all the 15 classrooms being used. In 1970 the status of the school was changed from 'Junior' to 'Middle' School. This resulted in children arriving from the Infants' School, now 'First School', a year later and similarly children leaving Beechwood a year later at 12 plus. Today, the titles 'Infant' and 'Junior' have returned, with the original age ranges.

The growth of the school in the early 1970s necessitated further classroom space. It was fortunate that one more room was organised on the first floor and three more on the ground floor, plus an excellent room for science.

Two more classrooms had to be found and the only solution was reluctantly to install two large huts in the lower playground. The teaching accommodation at this stage included 21 classrooms and a room for science. The number on roll in 1972 peaked at 625 pupils. This still allowed the large hall and the dining-room to be freed for their original use. With the kitchen supplying meals for some other schools as well as for Beechwood, the catering staff was daily preparing 1,000 meals.

In my 18 years at Beechwood, there were many features that spring to mind but I should like to include just two.

In 1970 a party of 47 children accompanied by six members of staff spent the whole of the summer term's half-term break in Dinard, France. Having our own coach enabled us to visit several places of interest and enjoy the sandy beaches in the area. This venture was completely new for the school and in our preparations we feared that we might have omitted some essential element. However, our anxiety was not merited, as the holiday was most successful, thanks in no small measure to the children's behaviour and the part played by the staff.

The other event was the installation of the swimming-pool. A member of the Local Education Authority's Physical Education staff visited the school and offered £1,000 towards the cost of the swimming-pool if the school could raise a further £1,000 – sums of money which, in 1970, were substantial.

A committee of parents was formed for the sole purpose of fund-raising. The interest generated was both amazing and spontaneous. Many ingenious methods of raising the money followed on the part of many parents, members of staff and children. Unbelievably, thanks to this tremendous team effort the sum of £1,000 was raised in just five months! The fund-raising continued unabated, resulting in not only an excellent swimming-pool but also in a substantial building, changing room, heating and lighting.

Once the main goal had been reached, the Friends of Beechwood School evolved and many parents continue to support the school in a variety of ways.

Merry Oak School
Eddie Croxson

Most people will have happy memories of their schooldays and, even if they go on to university and only return home occasionally to visit their parents, they will recognise the place of their early schooling as their home town.

Several thousand boys and a few hundred older girls will remember their days at Merry Oak School and many will feel sad that it had to close in 1985.

Merry Oak was opened in 1936 in the centre of the new housing estate. At first it was for both boys and girls over 11 years old.

For those who were born in the early 1930s the memory of the wartime evacuation will be prominent. How was it possible to move so many children away from the danger areas in one day and have them settled in time for bed? It was almost like the magic of Dr Who and his time machine. If it had to happen at all no one could have fixed the date for the evacuation any better than the end of the long summer holidays and even the weather was perfect for the move.

The effect of the evacuation and early return of so many youngsters made life difficult for Southampton schools. At Merry Oak the teaching staff were new to one another as well as the pupils who were themselves from different schools. Some had been transferred from Sholing School and others from Ludlow Road. No sooner did the school become one family than the tranquillity was upset and the school was closed as a result of the evacuation, but by

Merry Oak Former Pupils' Association membership card for 1949 belonging to Miss Jean Brown.

Christmas so many children had been brought home that the school was reopened and most of the teachers were brought back. The strength of character of the first head teacher, Mr F. Permain, and the teaching staff that had been assembled ensured that the school had a good start.

A small number of pupils from local junior schools passed the scholarship and had gone to grammar schools but the majority in the senior schools were given lessons which would prepare them for work as manual workers in the docks and shipbuilding yards as well as with the local aircraft makers.

The girls were expected to become housewives and they studied domestic subjects such as cooking and sewing while the boys were taught woodwork, metalwork and gardening. Merry Oak School was purpose-built to cover the relevant subjects. There was a cookery room (later to be called a domestic science room) and separate rooms for woodworking and metalwork.

There were many differences between schooling in the early days of Merry Oak and the schooling of today.

A study of the school magazine *Oak Leaves*, which was published monthly during the whole time of the school's existence reveals that, as well as the normal lessons that one would expect in a senior school, there were a total of more than 50 out-of-school activities including both a successful football club and a cricket club that played in the inter-school leagues. Other activities included athletics, boxing, canoe building and a music society but what seems difficult to believe is that a mathematics class was popular and well attended in out-of-school time.

The most ambitious out-of-school activity that took place then and which could not possibly have been entertained today was the collection and assembly of the school organ. A number of boys were taken to a

Merry Oak School's athletics teams, 1939. Boys, left to right: F. King, L. Stickland, C. Whiting, D. Willcocks, R. Brading (capt), E. Ember, E. Taylor, N. Myatt, J. Medley; girls: K. Lyon, T. Martin, E. Ferguson, J. Appleton (captain), M. Simpson, R. Swain, H. Eades.

Rehearsals for a Coronation Day display at Merry Oak School, May 1937, with quite an audience!

83

Left: *Guest of Honour, The Rt Hon Horace King, pays tribute to Merry Oak headmasters F. Permain (1935–47) and H. Haslam (1947–58), at a commemoration on 25 February 1967 when the Permain organ and Haslam Library were named. On the right are Alderman Mitchell (the Mayor), Mrs Mitchell and Ted Ford (headmaster).*

Below: *Merry Oak lads learning the practical way by building a large Wendy house at Sholing Infants' School, in 1958.*

The spirit of Merry Oak School, c.1967: the lads pose in various sports kits with their dinghies, canoes, ski and raquets. The staff include Messrs Edwards, Pursch, Dommett, Saunders, Masters, Parris and Southwell.

disused church in Bristol where they stayed locally in a hostel for five days and during that time they dismantled the church organ and prepared it for shipment to Merry Oak. They reassembled it under professional supervision and it was used for 15 years before the school closed. Another project that engaged the boys both academically and in their trade skills was the building of a wooden hut at Sholing School which was used by the infant children there as a 'Wendy House'.

A cycling club was very popular among the boys and many members continued to ride with the club after they had left the school. The season for cycling lasted from January to October and they would have travelled a total of more than 1,000 miles in a single year. Two masters used to accompany the boys and occasionally they would stay overnight in a hostel somewhere and return home the next day. At one time the teacher who taught metalwork in the school gave lessons in motor repairs using old cars for demonstration purposes and afterwards he gave driving lessons in the playground.

From the time of the opening of the school until the end of the war in 1945 the school was a senior mixed, but when the new girls' school in Sholing opened the girls moved into their new school and Merry Oak became a senior boys' school.

With the decline of school numbers in the early 1980s a decision had to be made – either Woolston School or Merry Oak School had to be closed.

It is not easy to understand why Merry Oak was chosen for closure. The building was away from the busy traffic routes and it was in close proximity to the large recreational open space, the Veracity Ground. Woolston stands today at a busy road junction and has had to be enlarged to take the number of pupils requiring places.

Itchen – From School to College
Joan Rolfe

Itchen College, formerly Itchen Grammar School, which in turn was formerly Itchen Secondary School is, today, an attractive red-brick building standing in its own spacious playing-fields. It had its origins in the early 1900s.

In 1906 the then Director of Education reported that he had made arrangements for the hire of a room at the Oddfellows Hall, Bridge Road, Woolston, at a rental of 14s. a week. The building would house a pupil-teachers' centre. Pupils would enter at the age of 13 and, after a two-year course, take the Cambridge Junior Local Examination. It was to be co-educational and, if successful, the boy or girl would be indentured as a pupil-teacher, spending two days at the centre and the remaining three days in elementary schools, learning to be a teacher. Miss Edith North, a woman of character and determina-

Itchen was a teacher training college, and these five ladies were students c.1916. Left to right: Dorothy Gould, Dorothy Price, Selina Oram, Flossie Hinton, Lotty Forder.

ITCHEN SECONDARY SCHOOL.

This is to Certify that, to the best of my knowledge and belief,

.... is free from any infectious complaint, and that he has not been exposed to any infection during the three weeks preceding his return to School.

Signature of Parent or Guardian,

Date 192

II. MEDICAL CERTIFICATE (in case of infectious disease).

I Certify that I have recently attended ....
professionally in a case of* .... and believe him now fit to return to School without risk to himself or to his schoolfellows.

Signed ....

Address 192

This Health Certificate must be brought by the Pupil on his return, or forwarded to the Head Master so as to reach him before the Pupil rejoins School.

["A.L." Medical Inspection Series, No. M33.] * Specify Disease.

In the 1920s a medical certificate had to be completed before a pupil could return to school.

tion, 'a real tyrant' according to one of her pupils, was appointed headmistress.

During the First World War, Miss North retired and the centre, with its new head, Miss Cook, moved to the first floor of the Porchester Road School, Woolston. Later Mr F. Hemmings, BSc, took over as the first headmaster and the school began its existence on a grammar school basis. After the First World War plans for temporary premises to accom-

Above: *Girls' physical training at Itchen Secondary School.*

Left: *An English lesson at Itchen Secondary School.*

Below left: *Itchen Secondary School fooball team, 1922–23, with headmaster F. Hemmings on the left, and George Dumbleton at the right end of the front row.*

Bottom left: *An aerial view of Itchen School in 1956, showing the wooden huts used as classrooms.*

Below: *Mr Pearson's Spanish class, 1951. Left to right, standing: Christine Rogers, Elizabeth Veal, Valerie Bowyer, Raymond Coombes, Peter Judd, Mr Pearson, Jennifer Gaskell, Pauline Trew, John Vickers, Pauline Kerr; middle row: Joy Calloway, Anne Phillipe, Marlene Hockridge, Lilian Hargreaves; front row: Pamela Faulkner, Pat O'Hara, Joyce Wilkins, ?.*

modate 160 pupils were brought forward. The site chosen for the new school was in Middle Road, Sholing, an area of rough, unfenced land, with an abundance of gorse, blackberry bushes and bracken.

Southampton accepted responsibility for the school in November 1920. Temporary premises – called bungalows, but more often known by the common name of 'huts', were erected. When completed they would accommodate 160 pupils, but as there were 250 on roll, makeshift arrangements were made. Pupils had to travel between Middle Road and Porchester Road Schools for different lessons.

When Mr Hemmings left Itchen, it then fell to a new headmaster, Mr E.C. Coteman, MA (Cantab.) to take charge in January 1925. He presided over the ceremony of the laying of the foundation-stone in December 1925, in preparation for the construction of permanent buildings. On that occasion, the Mayor said that the Council did not expect every child to benefit by secondary education, nor did they provide for everyone. But they did believe that if children, whether of rich or poor parents, had the capacity for higher education, then the town would make every provision for them. The building progressed slowly and in 1927 the front was two-storey, while the left wing was single-storey. Temporary buildings were still used for laboratories, practical rooms, an assembly hall and staff room.

On the night of 8 December 1930 the assembly hall caught fire – 'a huge conflagration which startled the inhabitants of Whites Road.' Future school assemblies took place in the school corridor, with Mr Coteman standing on a box to address the pupils. The hall was replaced by yet another temporary building. Not until 1939 was a second storey erected to include a gymnasium and dining-hall.

En Avant was chosen as the school motto and a house system introduced – houses were named Argonauts, Crusaders, Venturers and Vikings. A prefect system was established. The prefects were given considerable responsibility and we young children viewed them as minor staff. School uniform was strictly enforced (Joan Holt was once given detention for being seen in public without wearing the uniform hat). In the winter the girls wore gymslips with white blouses and the school tie, and in the summer they wore fawn dresses, and long stockings and maroon blazers on all occasions. The boys wore suits, school tie and maroon cap – at one time these caps had a round white stripe, so each boy appeared to be wearing a halo.

I was a scholarship pupil at the school from 1931 and still endured PE lessons in a wooden hut with very limited facilities. In spite of this handicap, the school gained an excellent sports and athletic record. Mr Coteman was headmaster during my years at the school, with Miss Sampson as senior mistress and Mr Scott as senior master. One never-to-be-forgotten

member of staff was the formidable French teacher – Mademoiselle Beauregard – commonly known as 'Mammy'. Few of her pupils failed the School Certificate – they wouldn't have dared!

I left school in 1937 and so missed the completion of the buildings. The school was evacuated to Andover in 1939 and joined Andover Grammar School. Throughout September staff and senior boys of both schools dug air-raid shelters. The schools attempted to provide normal education in difficult circumstances. One school worked in the morning, the other from 1.30p.m. to 5.30p.m. with alternate Saturday afternoons at school. An effort was made to keep school games going.

Meanwhile, in Southampton, the school buildings were serving a very different purpose. ARP Medical Services immediately set up a casualty station and later the Medical Officer of Health took over the gymnasium as a clinic. The Ministry of Food established a British Restaurant in the dining-hall. I served as a part-time ambulance driver and slept at night (when the Luftwaffe permitted) on a makeshift stretcher in one of my former classrooms.

In June 1940 French troops evacuated from across the Channel were given food and accommodation for several nights before returning to France. During the nights of the blitz on Southampton the school corridors were lined with casualties and unfortunately there were several fatalities. The buildings themselves escaped major damage; although one bomb fell through the dining-room, luckily it failed to explode. The only real 'casualty' was the groundsman's hut and equipment which was destroyed by fire from an incendiary bomb.

At the end of the war the buildings were returned to school use. At the start of the spring term only three boys and one girl had studied at the school before evacuation. Numbers of pupils increased rapidly. The Butler Education Act abolished fees in grammar schools and provided secondary education for all, which created great problems in school organisation. The school field was in poor condition and the railings had been removed for scrap during the war. In November 1949 the war memorial was dedicated by the Rt Revd Spencer Leeson. Many of the names inscribed on the board are familiar – the boys were at school with me only a few years before.

In 1950 Mr Coteman retired owing to ill health and was replaced by Mr S.C. Thompson. From 1967 he was faced, with the great challenge of the school's development to a Sixth Form College. The open-access policy of the school, now a college, meant that there was an interesting mix of students with different interests and abilities. The wearing of uniform was abandoned, pupils were known as students and the headmaster became the 'principal'. A tutor-group system was formed, mixing students of different abilities for pastoral and humane studies. Provision of a students' common room allowed the development of a student social life.

The college continued to grow in size. The roll in September 1979, when 433 students entered the college, rose to over 720. On the retirement of Mr Thompson, Mr P.H. Vennis took over as principal, c.1970. The college went from strength to strength and Mr Vennis could congratulate himself as well as the students for disciplined work, good results and a good 18-plus entry to higher education.

When Mr P. Church, BSc, was appointed as principal, further additions were made to college buildings. A large, well-equipped sports hall was added and the college provided for further education and leisure activities for adults during the evenings. College roll continued to increase and specialist classrooms were added, such as for art and performance studies.

On the retirement of Mr P. Church, Mr Barry Hicks became principal in 2003. In July 2005 the roll stood at 1,200 and the college has credit for the highest academic achievements amongst colleges in the Southampton area. Itchen has both an international and national reputation for offering a unique and successful combination of opportunities for success.

There have been so many changes in the 100 years of the school's existence, both as a grammar school and now as a flourishing sixth-form college. It has certainly lived up to its motto – *En Avant* – Go Forward!

Valerie Marsh remembers:

When I first went to Itchen in September 1947, the fourth form was called the Shell Form. But that changed when Mr Thompson replaced Mr Coteman as headmaster, and the fourth form became lower and the Shell became upper.

I am now 69. Sometimes if I cannot sleep at night, I try to remember the names of everyone in my class. I went into Form 2A in September 1947 and we had 31 in the class and I can recall 30! It would be interesting to hear about anybody in Class 2A in 1947.

The uniform when I started was a navy-blue gymslip with a slit up both sides which, when seated, revealed the mechanism for keeping up the brown lisle stockings which were the order of the day. How we all hated them because, although socks were allowed the first summer, the dreaded lisle stockings were obligatory thereafter, even in the street before and after school. With the new head came a relaxing of some of the rules, and the uniform changed to a grey skirt and maroon blazer with green edging. And goodbye to the velour hat! The summer dress changed from cream (such a handy colour for a girl who liked to climb trees) to a maroon stripe.

I have worked recently in a girls' grammar school in Plymouth which is architecturally very similar, but the changes in education and discipline, too numerous

to mention, are considerable. I had fun at school, but would never have stepped out of line. Punishment at school was followed by punishment at home! I achieved moderate results and, as was expected of me, learned office skills which have stood me in good stead all my working life. Today, greater opportunities abound for all.

St Mary's College
John Edgar Mann

One of the first things to impress parents of potential pupils when they visit St Mary's College is its beautiful surroundings, set off by one of the last 'gentry' houses left in the Southampton area. As Bitterne Grove, which also features in the chapter on the homes of the gentry, it was the home of a Georgian squire, a retired East India Company surgeon named James Dott. Midanbury Lane was at one time dubbed 'Dott's Lane'

In 1910 a Roman Catholic teaching order, the de la Mennais Brothers of Christian Instruction, who had been chased out of France by anti-clerical laws in 1903, bought the fine old mansion and 18 acres of land. Initially it was a 'house of formation' where young French men with a vocation for the religious life would spend three or four years in spiritual or professional training.

They left St Mary's House, as it was then called, to teach in France where they had to avoid any indication that they were members of a religious order. Discovery could mean a fine or prison.

On 15 September 1922 the school which became St Mary's College opened with a small group of 30 pupils. It wasn't long before its reputation spread, numbers reaching the 200 mark in 1939.

At that time there were between 30 and 40 boarders, some of them coming from as far afield as South America. St Mary's had something of an international feel then. The first head was a Frenchman who had been a missionary in Tahiti and his successors included an American and a Frenchman from St Malo (this was Brother Maurice, who eventually reached the age of 100).

St Mary's College in 1964.

Top: *St Mary's College sports day presentations, June 1929.*

Above: *An early picture of St Mary's College brethren and pupils.*

Left: *The boarders' dining room at St Mary's College.*

The war years helped St Mary's to expand because it was the only school that was not evacuated (the boarders joined the pupils at the order's boarding-school in Shropshire). By 1945 there were 400 boys at the college.

Time brought changes. In 1947 the order bought Charlton House, a large dwelling in Midanbury Lane, and converted it to a school for preparatory and junior boys. Many years later, in 1991, a new Charlton was built on what was formerly the community's vegetable garden and orchard.

The old Charlton was bought by Hampshire County Council who set up a school for autistic children there.

The college continued to develop after the war. The playing-fields were levelled, a new science block was built and, among other developments, a sixth-form block with an assembly hall/gym and reception area came into being. The mid-1970s were the best for numbers – as high as 729.

In 1982 the college marked its diamond jubilee with a dinner dance. In the 1990s a computer room was set up and the school went on the internet. But history was really made when, in 1991, girls were introduced to Charlton. In 2000 they were admitted to the senior school.

To mark the college's 80-year anniversary there was a dinner and later a ball.

St Mary's has some distinguished old boys, notably the theatre director Patrick Garland and the author Philip Hoare (whose real name is Patrick Moore – no wonder he changed it for literary purposes!)

Finally, I must thank Brother John for allowing me to dip into his brief history in the school magazine he edits.

Washday Blues!
Notes taken from an exercise book belonging to Joyce Robertson, a pupil at Ludlow Road School, dated 14 January 1930

Instructions given to girls concerning washing day:

Order of wash:
  1. Light the fire and put on the kettle
  2. Prepare the soap jelly for use
  3. Collect and arrange all utensils
Order of work in a family wash:
  1. Wash the silks and woollens
  2. Coloured cottons and prints
  3. Table linens, bed linen and handkerchiefs
Washing of white wash:
  1. Collect the clothes
  2. Sort and do any necessary mending
  3. Remove stains
  4. Steep
  5. Wring the clothes out of steeping water
  6. Wash in hot soda water
  7. Boil for 20 minutes
  8. Prepare the rinsing water, Blue and starch
  9. Take the clothes out of the boiler and rinse
  10. Blue
  11. Wring
  12. Hang to dry
Rules for drying:
  1. Peg by strongest part
  2. Turn inside out
  3. Hang with bag toward the wind
  4. When dry, roll down and put in basket
Rules for ironing:
  1. Prepare the table
  2. Put the irons to get hot
  3. Test and clean the irons

A typical 1930s kitchen shown in 'Houses of Distinction', a sales brochure for houses in Glenfield Avenue being built by local builders W.M. Hinton.

Chapter Six

Hum Hole Memories
Pat Wilson

I grew up in Peartree Gardens (now Angel Crescent) and like most of my friends in the 1930s went to school and church, and spent most of my leisure time in Bitterne where I had lived since the day I was seven years old.

I spent a lot of time on Freemantle Common, which was allowed, but Hum Hole was definitely out of bounds, possibly because it was a large uncultivated area, very wooded and not many paths. In the low-lying parts there were natural ponds. My friend, also named Pat, and I roamed all over Hum Hole. There was a main path which went past fields where horses were kept. It was a lovely place to play.

Unfortunately, a lot of rubbish was disposed of at Hum Hole – no local authority tips in those days – and on the edge of one of the ponds was a small galvanised bath of a size to suit a child. We discussed going across the water in this but decided it would only take one at a time. My friend would go round to the other side and come back in it. As I recall, the pond would have been about 12–15ft across. I got in and all was fine until about 5ft out when I realised water was coming in fast. I scrambled out quickly and luckily the water was not very deep, just above my knees. Unfortunately I was wearing a new pair of knee-high fawn socks commonly worn by both boys and girls at that time and these and my shoes were soaked.

We wandered round for ages hoping I would dry out a bit, but I didn't, so we went home and I quietly wore the wet socks for the rest of the day, saying nothing!

It was not until I was married and left home that I told my mother and all she said was 'I wondered why your socks were so wet.'

In that not so 'throw away' age how could I have thought that the bath would be watertight?

We secretly went back to Hum Hole many times and even though it was 'off limits' I am sure my mother knew where we were all the time.

It was obviously a foretaste of many happy years spent on boats after I was married.

Pat Wilson, aged 10.

The Ritz, Built by Braziers
Bill White

The year 1999 marked the 200th anniversary of a business whose building work has done much to shape the skylines around Southampton; the firm of Brazier & Son Ltd. A century ago building, decorating and contracting activities came to the fore, and today the Brazier family presides over a number of business activities. Key to their expansion were contracts to build several super cinemas for Associated British Cinemas Ltd, including the 2,000-seat Forum in Above Bar. Braziers also won contracts for many smaller cinemas in the £10,000 range, including the Savoy at Swaythling, the Classic in Above Bar and the Ritz at Bitterne.

The Ritz was built on the corner of the High Street and Maytree Road, the site of Bitterne House, a private school in the late 1800s. In the garden was a magnificent may tree, hence the road's name. The 800-seat Ritz opened on 28 September 1936 with *Jack of all Trades* and *Men of Action*, but with

Cinemas used to print monthly programmes. This is the cover for the June 1961 edition, the last for The Ritz.

The Ritz Cinema, October 1936. (BRAZIERS)

no special ceremony. The manager was James Herbert Ransome-Burbage, a local man who had served in the Royal Hampshire Regiment in the First World War. He had managed many cinemas before the Ritz, and was a popular figure, living with his wife and twin daughters in West End Road. A slightly rotund gentleman, he made sure that teenagers behaved themselves in the cinema he managed for about 20 years. He was 75 when he passed away in 1957.

It was hoped that a cinema showing family-orientated films would do well in the suburbs, and initially the Ritz was successful. Up to 700 regularly attended the children's Saturday morning film show at 6d. admission. Among the patrons was Rosemary Rogers who helped in her father's butcher's shop at the top of Lances Hill. Mr Ransome-Burbage was a customer and would regularly invite her to see a 'U' film as long as her dad approved it as suitable. She would always be given a bar of chocolate to enjoy, which of course was very welcome, as sweets were still on ration.

The Ritz was taken over in around 1957 by Harry Mears Theatres Ltd, who spent a lot of money refurbishing and re-equipping the interior, but unfortunately it failed to attract enough patrons to keep it going. Its last manager, Mr Paton, remembers that they tried all types of films to get a full audience, but the curtain fell for the last time on 1 July 1961 after *Mutiny* and *The Last Command*. The last Saturday morning show saw 600 children turn up, to be joined by Sandra, Mr Paton's Great Dane and a great favourite of the children. Among the staff was Arthur Smith, the doorman (who joined the cinema just after its opening) a commissionaire and a pageboy (the pageboys would usually expect to graduate up to the projection room). The building

was subsequently demolished to make way for shops and the bowling alley.

John Fanstone, who lived in the High Street, was allowed to leave Bitterne School just before his fourteenth birthday to get a job at the Ritz. He recalls the story in the book *Dream Palaces*:

The headmaster came to me one day and said there's this vacancy going at the Ritz and he knew the circumstances... it was a bit of a struggle, and in those days my wages were the best of any industry, we're talking about '36, '37 and I started with my bike, taking the newsreel from the Ritz at Bitterne to the Woolston cinema and from Woolston back to Bitterne, for each programme, and I used to get twelve and six, and half a crown for my bike, fifteen bob a week. In those days there were many, many men who weren't earning that.

After serving in the Royal Navy in the Second World War, John returned to the Ritz, moving to Woolston's Picture House in 1957. Jimmy Mead recalls being in the Ritz when an air raid started:

I completely forget what the picture was. I know it was quite an interesting one. By that time of course, things were getting more and more hectic and it was quite a treat to go to the cinema anyway. But during the performance we were conscious of the fact that something was happening, although there hadn't been an alarm given. There was a few ominous noises and eventually the manager made an announcement that the film would be stopped for a short period, when anybody who wished to could leave the cinema, as there was an air raid in progress. So they cut the film for a few minutes. I said to my wife, 'What we going to do?' We'd got interested in the film so we stayed, but gradually the noises began to get more and more until eventually there was a tremendous crunch and the building seemed to lift up and come down again. We decided it perhaps was time to go then! So we left. Well, actually I'd played football that afternoon, and had my bicycle with me, so my wife sat on the bar and off we pedalled to get from Bitterne to Sholing, but on at least three occasions on that journey we dropped the bike and dived for the nearest wall.

The Ritz wasn't Brazier's first interest in Bitterne. In 1914 building work was increasing, so the company acquired the Redcote Brickworks (now Sunningdale Gardens) assuring them of a supply of bricks. They also bought the Thornhill Brickworks, on the opposite side of Bitterne Road, from George Honey in about 1930. Braziers also constructed several notable buildings in the area: the Target Inn in Butts Road (1936, but demolished in 2006) St Patrick's R.C. Church, Woolston (1938), Sainsbury's in Bitterne (1963), Southern TV studios at Northam (1967) and a geriatric unit at Moorgreen Hospital (1983).

Amusement at the Fox & Hounds
Hiram Spencer

When my grandfather Frank Reeves took me into the Fox & Hounds at Bitterne for my first pint of beer, I was exceedingly amused at the spectacle in front of me: elderly men shuffling dominoes, and their strange

eccentricities were really comic. This was in the autumn of 1938. Eli Diaper, who at 79 was still working, was telling his memories of the Itchen Ferry vicinity. Freddie King, in his bowler hat, was so small but could certainly drink! Then there was a sprightly middle-aged man who wore a Cycling Association badge on the lapel of his coat and wore huge cycling clips, although he could not ride a bicycle and nor was he in any cycling association. My grandfather, too, appeared a strange man: corduroy trousers, a check cap and spotted red muffler, and to match these odd clothes he wore hobnailed boots. Then he too became absorbed in the game of dominoes. 'Now when I lived in Itchen Ferry…' continued old Eli dreamily, and he became lost in his thoughts.

A Bit About Pubs
David Haisman

Commercial Street had three pubs which were well patronised in the 1950s: the Percy Arms, the John Barleycorn and the Commercial. The Commercial was a Mew Langtons (Isle of Wight brewery) pub and a somewhat acquired taste was necessary for their amber liquid. The landlord, Sam Arrowsmith, was a most likeable man and was well known for his pigeon-fancying. I remember Sam never used a till when serving, but had coins of all denominations lined up in rows on a shelf with notes stuffed into a jug. No doubt at all

High Street in 1908 with The Angel on the right, built in the 1840s with a dummy second floor, and demolished in 1972. A few buildings along on the corner of Maytree Road, is The Carpenter's Arms, dating from the 1830s, from where John Rockett later started a carrier service.

The Fox & Hounds was originally called The Cooper's Arms, but landlord John Taplin, a hunt follower, changed it in the 1880s. Both Harefield and Mersham estates had kennels.

The Firs Inn, Pound Street, in the 1960s. Once owned by John Sinnatt who founded the Wesleyan Chapel in the house at the rear in 1806, the building became a pub, c.1872, and was demolished in 1974.

Mr William Sly the landlord outside the original Bitterne Brewery, now The Big Cheese. The building was destroyed by bombing on 22 June 1942, and Mr Sly was fatally injured. In 1902 it was one of the first pubs to commission its own matchboxes, using them to advertise whisky at 14s.9d. (73p) a gallon!

The Red Lion c.1895. Built in the 1860s in front of the original building, this was an important staging post (where horses could be changed) on the hilly road to Portsmouth.

that he delivered one of the speediest transactions ever when serving a pint to a customer!

Up on West End Road, the Bitterne Brewery had been rebuilt after being bombed, and was considered to be a little more upmarket than the normal pub; it was our local watering hole with Vic Sly as the landlord and Percy Bush, everyone's favourite barman. This pub boasted a cocktail bar and a regular pianist in the lounge bar and a very busy public bar along with a 'bottle and jug'.

Anyone for Tennis?

Glebian Tennis Club, Bitterne
Rene Russell

The Glebian Tennis Club was formed in 1923, founded by Mr and Mrs P.S. Small and Mr and Mrs W.T. Bailey. They played on land belonging to the Bitterne Glebe Lands Committee, glebe land being land owned by the Church of England, in this case land alongside Bitterne Church in Bursledon Road. They entered teams in the local leagues and after four years were promoted to the first division of the Apsley League.

On 1 October 1933 the club moved to land on the Harefield estate in West End Road, where they had three shale courts, eventually resurfaced as all-weather courts. The club was affiliated to the Apsley League in the summer and the Hampshire & Isle of Wight League in the winter. The teams did very well in the matches and won the leagues on many occasions during the years. Table tennis was also played in the clubhouse.

Tragedy befell the club on the night of 26 July 2000, when the original wooden clubhouse was burned down during the night. The disaster was eventually proved to have been caused by an electrical fault. However, play continued even without a clubhouse until the new brick one was completed and offically opened by BBC weather presenter Dorcas Henry on 20 June 2001.

Junior members have always been encouraged at Glebians. The club continues to flourish under the chairmanship of Mr John Farley, having added croquet to its facilities.

Bitterne Church Tennis Club
Colin and Irene Hesketh

Our memories of the club started as a young married couple in the mid-1950s coming to Bitterne Church and socialising with other church members (mainly 'Young Wives') as a 'Rabbits Club'. Later the club progressed to include other young couples and developed into a very active social group. We enjoyed theatre trips, treasure hunts, beach trips and dinner dances.

With the inevitable arrival of children, various sizes

Above: *The winners of a Glebian Tennis Club's tournament week in the 1960s. Left to right: Jean Dix, Bertha Small, Hugh Lyons, Terry Martin, ?, Mel Voller, Pauline Garrett, John Farley, Sue Bradfield, John Saunders, Doris Bone, Arthur Ventham, Philip Smith, Wendy Martin, Pamela Mansfield, Betty Martin.*

Below: *A ticket for the Glebian Tennis Club's annual dinner, November 1933.*

Glebian Tennis Club, Bitterne, Southampton.

The members of the above Club request the pleasure of your Company on the occasion of their

SEVENTH ANNUAL DINNER
AND SOCIAL EVENING

to be held at the Church Institute, Bursledon Road, Bitterne, on Wednesday, November 22nd, 1933, at 7 p.m. prompt.

To_____

Tickets 3/- inclusive.

R.S.V.P. by
NOV. 15th to (Mrs.) B. A. SMALL (Hon. Sec.)
65 West End Road, Bitterne.

of prams began to appear by the courts and some people will remember the building of the tennis hut. Bank Holidays were a highlight of the season as, due to lack of transport, it was much easier to come to Bitterne and have a great day out with the children playing tennis and have meals in the church hall provided by us all.

Children's Sports Day at Farley Mount was not to be missed. A great day was organised by the Ridges family and members enjoyed the ice-cream from the handy ice-cream van nearby.

By now we were into 'League Tennis' for which we received no prizes but gained the reputation of the 'best tennis teas in the area' (all home-made of course!)

After playing for many, many years and enjoying the friendship of all members we were saddened when it eventually dissolved, but it has left us with many happy memories.

The Maytree Players
Eric Speller

The Maytree Players were formed as part of the Parent/Teacher Association at Bitterne C. of E. School, which was located between the Parish Church and Maytree Road, hence the name. This road is now a pedestrian route between Bitterne Bowl and Sainsbury's supermarket. The idea was put forward by the then headmaster, Mr D. Wright, and the first meeting was held in the school during the early part of 1973, which 17 attended.

Having sorted out who would be actors, workers on back stage, lighting and sound, set construction, costumes, make-up, etc., scenery was constructed, lighting was hired and rehearsals got underway for the first production, *Blithe Spirit*, produced by Betty and Ray Lloyd, to go on stage in June 1973, in Bitterne Church Hall, by kind permission of Revd Michael Perry. A further five productions were staged in the hall: comedy, farce, thriller, romance, etc., until June 1978, when our membership was then up to 26.

In July 1978 the group had the great news that the new school would be opening soon with a purpose-built hall, including stage lighting and a sound system, but no stage. A portable stage was designed and constructed from chipboard using an 'egg box' construction where each part of the base slotted into another part and surrounded by timber edges with the decking fixed on top. Curtains and extra scenery were made and old scenery was adapted to fit the stage. Several new members joined the group ready

for its first production in the new venue. This was *A Murder Has Been Arranged*. It was on stage from 29 November to 2 December.

The Players were also asked by Mr Robson to help with school concerts, with Eric Speller setting up the stage and lighting system.

From 1978 to 1985 a further 12 productions were performed and in July 1982 a special Farewell Concert was staged on the occasion of the retirement of Mr R.E. Matthews (February 1948–July 1982).

November 1984 saw the retirement of the headmaster, Mr D.V. Wright, and during the interval of the production of *My Giddy Aunt*, on 8 November, the Players presented a gift to Mr Wright for all the co-operation and assistance he had given them since 1973.

Sadly in May 1985 the Players were asked to leave Bitterne School by the new headmaster, due to school commitments. However, they found a new venue not far away at All Hallows Church Hall, situated on Witts Hill, Midanbury.

Here they had a small permanent stage, but no lighting or sound system. However, Eric soon fixed up an extension to the stage, using the same construction as before, together with lighting, a sound system and side curtains. Scenery was modified to fit ready for their first production in their new venuw, *No Time for Fig Leaves* on 5–7 December, 1985.

The Maytree Players went on to stage a further 29 plays until May 2002, when, unfortunately, the number of members was declining. Despite advertising for more, the group was unable to continue, so sadly the curtain dropped for the last time.

A Public Mischief, a light comedy by Kenneth Horne, performed at All Hallows' Church hall, November 1989. Left to right:Heather Chamberlain, Richard Bird, Liz Hunt, Ron Pople, Muff Baker; standing: Iris MacNish. (ERIC SPELLER)

The Escaped Bear

On Tuesday morning a young bear that had been exhibited outside a caravan at the fair made his escape and gained the Portsmouth Road. On his absence being noted, pursuit immediately took place and, in consequence of intelligence from the various affrightened persons he met in his way, he was found on Bitterne Common in a tree, and secured.

Hampshire Chronicle, 14 May 1856

The only casualty in this escapade seems to have been a large dog that was unfortunately shot several times, though not fatally, in mistake for the bear. Of course in those days the well-being of most animals was of little importance, and as common folk were highly unlikely to see wild animals in their natural habitat, they proved highly popular at fairs and touring shows.

Riverside Park Miniature Railway
Molly Giles

The connection with Riverside Park of the Southampton Society of Model Engineers Ltd dates back to 1958/59 when the then Southampton and District Society of Model Engineers approached the City Council with the purpose of building a miniature railway in the city. The Society also ran boats on the ornamental lake on the Common.

The Society had found an area known as Cobden Meadows that was very suitable for their purpose and talks began with the Council's 'open spaces' offi-

One of many humorous postcards that could be overprinted with the name of a particular place.

What, Come Home ? Not likely when I'm at Bitterne, near Southampton.

Bert Trussler was an active supporter of the railway and is seen here driving a working steam model of the Southern Railway locomotive Maid of Kent *that he built himself.*

The Conservative & Unionist Association committee organised sports fêtes, this one at Brownlow in August 1913. These included running races (ladies in long skirts), children's skipping races, and a greasy pole competition.

cers. Permission was eventually granted in 1960 for the building of the track and work started in earnest on raising the funds required for construction to begin. The building of the track took some 15 months. It is one-fifth of a mile in length and enabled, when completed, the running of three-quarter and one inch to the foot scale models. This original track was officially opened on 14 April 1962.

The locomotives that use the track are privately owned by the members of the Society. Their construction and working are based on the same principles as those of the main line. It is interesting to note that the Society's archives record that a total of 10,694 passengers were carried in the first year at the cost of 6d. (2½p) per ride. Public liability cost the princely sum of £1.7s.0d. (£1.35). The 'ticket office' and the members' hut were erected during the winter of 1962 and are still in use, although the ticket office has moved to accommodate the ground-level track. The members' hut facilities have been increased as the Society has grown.

In September 1993 the Society, by now called the Southampton Society of Model Engineers Ltd applied for and was granted the right to build a 1½-inch to the foot ground-level track around the perimeter of the original track. The official opening of the ground-level track took place on 12 April 1997 by Mr Jeremy Hill of the recreation, parks and open spaces unit of Southampton City Council. This track, from cutting the first sod to its opening, had taken three years, some 3¼ tons of rail, 3,600 sleepers and 14,000 screws. Its concrete base contains some 85 tons of ballast, 12 tons of sand and 4 tons of cement.

The Society celebrated its ninetieth year in 2002 which coincided with the fortieth year of the first track at Riverside Park. During this period the Society has given approximately 400,000 rides to members of the public since its inauguration.

Bitterne Conservative & Unionist Club
Norman Ballard

Between 1902 and 1913 two local Bitterne businessmen, a Mr Haynes and a Mr Bradfield, each put up £100 to purchase Cloudesley, a large house in its own grounds on the corner of what was then called Chapel Street (now Dean Road) and Inkerman Road (now Marne Road). From this beginning Bitterne Conservative Club was born, Mr Haynes being the secretary.

The district was part of South Stoneham District Council. Just down the road from the club can be seen one of the original drain grids marked SSDC, believed to be the only one still in existence.

The club joined the Association of Conservative Clubs on 16 April 1913, registration number 1794. The first reference to the house being used as a club is in *Kelly's Directory* of 1916, with H. Maddison being listed as the Hon. Secretary of the Bitterne Conservative and Unionist Club. In 1932 the subscription to the ACC was 21s.0d. (£1.05). The club had 100 members and paid a liquor tax of £8.12s.0d. The capacity of the club was given as 50 seats and the main recreation was billiards and whist.

Left: *BLHS Vice President Ivy White of Wellington Avenue, in her robes as Mayor of Southampton, 1987/88.* Centre: *BLHS member Edwina Cooke was the 783rd Mayor of Southampton in 2005/06.She is best known as having been Bitterne's Postmistress for many years.* Right: *John Martin of Dean Road, was Sheriff of Southampton in 1992/3 and Mayor of Southampton for 1993/94.*

During the Second World War the club suffered in the blitz and was severely damaged on 29 November 1940. All the club record books and minutes were destroyed. In the snooker room there are two very short billiard cues on display with the following inscriptions:

RIP. In memory of the period November 1941 to June 1946 when owing to alterations to our premises by Herr Hitler we were compelled to use these instruments of torture causing unavoidable quotations in old English.

These were the actual cues used when the billiard table was accommodated in the lounge, the only habitable room after the premises were destroyed by enemy action November 14th 1941. Presented by the President A.E. Gash to the club December 20th 1946. Chairman R.G. Haynes.

On 1 October 1954 the Club President, Albert Edward Gash, laid a foundation-stone to commence the rebuilding. On 6 May 1948 local businessman Tom Misselbrook was accepted for membership and he duly paid his dues two days later – 5s. (25p) a quarter (a yearly payment was not accepted). Tom was elected President in 1960, a post he still holds at the time of writing. In the 1970s, when the club had financial difficulties, Tom Misselbrook did a lot to increase interest and held evening bread and cheese meetings which were also open to ladies, to raise funds.

An associate member, Mrs Ivy White, daughter of Mr Tom Dunning Mason, a chairman of the club, was Sheriff of Southampton in 1986/7 and Mayor in 1987/88. She recalls that after the war women could only be associate members and the Bitterne Conservative Club Ladies' Branch meeting could only be held upstairs, but due to the large numbers attending they were eventually allowed to hold meetings downstairs.

Members of No.6 Company, Hampshire 1st Volunteer Brigade, Royal Artillery, outside the barbers' tent at camp at Sandown, c.1900. This unit met at the Drill Hall in Red Lion Cut (one wall of which remains), from c.1880 until 1939 when it moved to Margam Avenue.

"A WELCOME HOME"
TO BITTERNE MEN

HEROES OF THE GREAT WAR
(LAND, SEA AND AIR.)
1914 - 1919.

The MAYOR OF SOUTHAMPTON

Alderman S. G. Kimber, Esq.

PRESIDING.

SUPPORTED BY

Surg-Lieut. H. W. COOKE, R.N.

Nov. 18th, 1919.

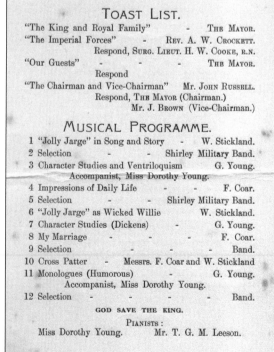

TOAST LIST.

"The King and Royal Family"   -   THE MAYOR.
"The Imperial Forces"   -   REV. A. W. CROCKETT.
    Respond, SURG. LIEUT. H. W. COOKE, R.N.
"Our Guests"   -   -   -   THE MAYOR.
    Respond
"The Chairman and Vice-Chairman"   MR. JOHN RUSSELL.
    Respond, THE MAYOR (Chairman.)
    MR. J. BROWN (Vice-Chairman.)

MUSICAL PROGRAMME.

1 "Jolly Jarge" in Song and Story   -   W. Stickland.
2 Selection   -   -   Shirley Military Band.
3 Character Studies and Ventriloquism   G. Young.
    Accompanist, Miss Dorothy Young.
4 Impressions of Daily Life   -   -   F. Coar.
5 Selection   -   -   Shirley Military Band.
6 "Jolly Jarge" as Wicked Willie   W. Stickland.
7 Character Studies (Dickens)   -   G. Young.
8 My Marriage   -   -   -   F. Coar.
9 Selection   -   -   -   Band.
10 Cross Patter   -   Messrs. F. Coar and W. Stickland.
11 Monologues (Humorous)   -   G. Young.
    Accompanist, Miss Dorothy Young.
12 Selection   -   -   -   Band.

GOD SAVE THE KING.

PIANISTS :
Miss Dorothy Young.   Mr. T. G. M. Leeson.

Above, left and right: *Servicemen from Bitterne were invited to 'A Welcome Home' dinner and entertainment on 18 November 1919, probably held at the Church Institute.*

Left: *A war-time concert party, Fairway Follies organised by Billy Williams. Left to right: Queenie Underhill, Eddie Udall, Colin Aspe, Joy Hoare, Ted ?, John Lintott, Vi Tucker and Freda Young.*

Chapter Seven

The Effects of Wars

Over the centuries wars have affected Bitterne in differing ways. The French invasion of Southampton in October 1338 and skirmishes before and since left a legacy of fear of invasion such that Bonaparte was seen as a real threat to all living near the coast. A consequence of the Crimean War (1854–55) was the huge demand for bricks from the area's brickyards for the construction of the Royal Victoria Hospital, Netley. The war was recorded in the names of roads constructed about that time: Balaclava, Alma and Inkerman. The Boer War (1899–1902) seems to have little affected village life, although hospital trains passed through the station on route for the RVH.

The First World War had more impact. Bitterne's proximity to Southampton Docks led to it providing many troops with shelter on their last night before embarkation: they slept in the Wesleyan Chapel, the Angel Inn and the school, whilst horses were grazed on The Sandpit and Freemantle Common. The occasional Graf Zeppelin airship was seen overhead and hospital trains again passed through. Many young men of the district joined the armed services and some are recorded in The National Roll of the Great War, though this is not a comprehensive list. It hints at the exploits of 188 Bitterne people, including Dick Heard, a blacksmith living at the bottom of Bath Road who, at over 6ft tall, looked older than 17, and like so many lads put his age up to enlist:

Heard, A.R. (MM) A/Sergt, 2nd Hampshire Regiment. Volunteering in September 1914 he was sent to France in the same year and later drafted to the Dardanelles. Whilst on the way out he was on the Prince Edward *when she was sunk in August 1915. He was rescued and took part in heavy fighting on the Gallipoli Peninsula. After the evacuation of this theatre of war, he returned to the Western Front and served with distinction in many important engagements. He was wounded and gassed in action, and on March 25th 1918 was killed at Passchendale. He had been awarded the Military Medal for conspicuous bravery and devotion to duty in the field, and was also entitled to the 1914–15 Star, and the General Service and Victory Medals.*

The Bitterne Roll of Honour lists 449 men who were in the services between August 1914 and November 1918, including captains and a major amongst the numerous stokers, drivers and privates. More poignant is the war memorial, unveiled in the Parish Church in 1920, which records the names of the 62 who 'gave their lives for God and Country'.

The German Air Force brought the Second World War to the doorstep of Bitterne residents; Southampton docks, again a main supply route, became a strategic target, as did the Supermarine works at Woolston, and shipyards on the River Itchen, along with bridges and railway sidings.

But the war had started quietly, becoming known as the 'phoney war'. On a day in August 1939 three very long trains passed through the station, carrying part of the British Expeditionary Force from the RVH to the docks for embarkation: the first train was for 'other ranks', the next carried nurses and the third carried officers. On 1 September Bitterne schoolchildren were evacuated to Bournemouth, but by 5 December so many had returned home that the schools reopened until the next summer when they were evacuated again. Identity cards and gas masks were issued to everyone, signposts (such as the Bitterne Parade that adorned the roof of the shops in the High Street) were removed, as were metal gates, railings, etc., and the letters SWS (Static Water-Supply) appeared on concrete basins holding 500 gallons of water. Corporation bus drivers were encouraged to take their buses (with their family, if they wished) out of town at night to reduce their loss to bombing. On 9 January 1940 sugar, bacon and butter became rationed.

Air-raid shelters were constructed. Corrugated-iron Anderson shelters were built in gardens (many of which were sold off after the war as garden sheds), steel and wire mesh Morrison shelters were for indoor use, and public trench shelters were put into use, such as the one on The Sandpit that held 150 people. In 1940 the Luftwaffe started its bombing and created two new pastimes: collecting shrapnel (from bomb casings, etc.) and logging air raids. The logs of Walter Kingston, John Holt, Harold Blackmore and Bob Payne detail the extent of the bombing; these are a few extracts:

26 September, 3p.m. to 5.30p.m.: *... direct hits on Supermarine, seven hits on White's Yard... gasworks hit... bombs in Peartree Avenue. Homes demolished in Marne and Balaclava Roads. Bombs in convent grounds...*

17 November, 6.35p.m. to 7.45p.m.: ... *a stick of bombs fell... Milbury Crescent... gardens of 103 Chatsworth Road / 40 Bursledon Road... 10 Chatsworth Road demolished and the entire family killed... residents of 34 Chatsworth Road were caught in their house and afterwards... found that their Anderson shelter had taken a direct hit...*

23 November, 6.15p.m. to 11.30p.m.: ... *450 HE bombs fell on the eastern side of the river... 250 planes... bombs in Chessel Crescent, Bitterne Way, Acacia Road, Spring Road... Mrs Haynes was killed when her house, 103 Bursledon Road, was completely destroyed.*

1a–2a Heath Road, completely destroyed by bombing. *(SO'TON CITY ARCHIVES)*

30 November: *A bomb landed in front of 11 Edwina Close but did not explode and had to be dealt with by the Bomb Disposal Squad... Mr Harris was almost buried in his Anderson shelter at 22 Bitterne Crescent; a bomb went through the shelter... it exploded 24 hours later shaking 9, 11 and 13 Edwina Close off their foundations... hardly any windows broken but they had to be demolished.*

14 March 1941: *At 11.20p.m. many incendiary bombs dropped in Whites Road area. Bitterne Church Institute destroyed by fire. Two incendiary bombs through the church roof... HEs at Butts Road*

10 April 1941: *Air-raid warning 9.08p.m.... 12 parachute mines dropped on Southampton, many estimated as over one ton... mines dropped in Howards Timber Yard (Bitterne Manor), Cleveland Road, Norwich Road and Bitterne Road. Considering the scale of this attack casualties were remarkably light: one dead, four seriously injured and five slightly injured. The damage to property was much more serious: 41 houses totally destroyed, 320 houses severely damaged to warrant demolition, 1,190 houses badly damaged but capable of repair, and 3,503 houses slightly damaged.*

17 April 1941: *Bombs in Chessel Crescent, Garfield, Athelstan, Rampart Roads.*

8 July 1941: *Heavy raid on Southampton at 12.30a.m. 5000 incendiaries and 150 high explosive bombs dropped, many on the Bitterne and Peartree areas. The railway between Bitterne and Woolston*

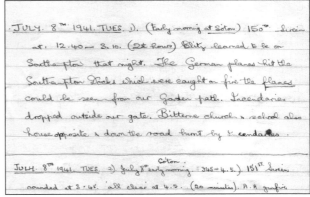

The entry in Bob Payne's diary of air raids for 8 July 1941.

received a direct hit, St Patrick's Church in Woolston was destroyed and Bitterne Church damaged by fire bombs. 38 people were killed and about 100 injured. 400 properties were destroyed or needed demolition; about 4,000 houses were damaged and needed repair.

22 June 1942, 12.45a.m. to 2.05a.m.: *Very heavy raid, flares, incendiaries and HE bombs... Brook Road, Bitterne Brewery, West End Road, top of Lances Hill, Peartree Avenue, Mousehole Lane... raid by 50 aircraft, 14 killed.*

At 1.04a.m. on 12 July 1944 the first V1 flying bomb (or 'doodle-bug') to land on Southampton fell in Sholing, injuring nine people with about 50 needing accommodation at rest centres. The effect was described as similar to a parachute mine. Another V1 fell at 4.38a.m. three days later on a military camp north of the Bursledon Road/Sedgewick Road junction, injuring half a dozen people and damaging 153 properties. Mr Kingston calculated that by 27 June 1944 Southampton had endued 1,678 hours of bombing.

Blackouts were enforced by the ARP (Air Raid Precautions); Mr E. Ventham was Head Warden of Bitterne & Sholing District, whilst G.J. Powell was in charge of Bitterne & Peartree District, each district then being divided into about a dozen posts each covering a few roads. No. 18 Platoon of the Home Guard was formed at Bitterne under Lt Franklusen, and became a last line of defence; they used St Mary's College for training. Civilians joined these organisations and assisted in vital tasks such as fire watch, recording the fall of bombs, manning road blocks, first aid and casualty evacuation. After the war many civilians were awarded the KC (King's Commendation) and RCC (Regional Commissioner's Commendation). Others were less fortunate: ARP senior warden E.A. Newman, wardens George Hannant, Soren Busk, Mrs N.E. Sothcott, A.G. Preston and H.G. Thwaites, ARP messenger Master A.G. Stannier, and W.G. Rollett of the Home Guard were killed during air raids. The 43 servicemen of Bitterne who gave their lives during the Second World War are

Above: *Bitterne Platoon, Home Guard march up Mousehole Lane to a church parade at Bitterne Park. Leading the platoon* (second from left) *is Major Percy Stannard, followed by Major Collins and Captain Jack Wheatle. The platoon contains John Hampton, Doug Prudden, Lionel Topp, Percy Sutton, Jack Hasler, Lt W.M. Newman and Sgt Ron Hawkesworth.* (MRS HAMPTON)

Below: *The Whites Road children's victory party at the pavilion at Itchen School, including Tony and Maureen Scane, Allan and Brian Hunt, Gerald Thorn, David and Michael Dymott, Cyril Potter, Derek Childs, Leslie Street, Sheila Lymburn, Wendy Shergold, John Russel, Clare Moody, Thora Clements, June and Joyce Buckle, Ann Sumner, Mary Hamnet and Sylvia Weaver.*

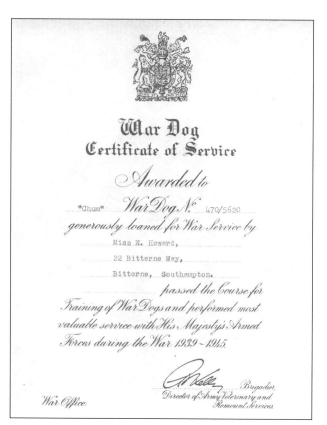

Pets also saw war service, as shown by this Certificate of Service to Miss Howard's dog, Chum.

recorded in a beautifully illuminated Roll of Honour held in an oak stand in Bitterne Church. The civilians who died are listed in a Roll of Honour compiled by the Imperial War Graves commission; this records the many local tragedies such as the death from her injuries of Doris Martin (aged 32) at the Royal South Hants Hospital, nine days after the bombing of her home 89 Chessel Avenue, in which her eight-year-old daughter Fay was killed.

The war in Europe ended on 8 May 1945 and was celebrated as VE Day with street parties. Church bells were rung to celebrate the surrender of Japan on 15 August (VJ Day) and Dr Horace King led a crowd of 500 in community singing and dancing at Bitterne Park Triangle.

Memories of The Blitz
Alec Wardell

'The blitz' started when we were living in 22 Harcourt Road and I remember men coming to dig out and fit an Anderson shelter. My father couldn't do it himself as he had a broken back at that time. Due to ground water being present, the men found that as they dug the hole it filled with water, so before they could fit the shelter they had to line the hole with concrete. Gradually, however, water seeped up through the concrete and it could become quite deep. My father eventually had to dig a sump hole in the floor so that as the water came in we were able to bale it out.

Unfortunately the shelter suffered badly from condensation which my father managed to reduce by lining the inside of the steel with cork.

I can remember more than one instance of being dragged from a warm bed in the middle of the night, made to run like hell, still half asleep and with bombs falling, down the garden path and jumping into the shelter and up to my knees in ice-cold dirty water.

When the first raid took place there were flashes and bangs going off and my father stated categorically that he wasn't going to the shelter or anywhere else until he had found his trousers. He was just starting to eat his dinner one evening when an air raid began and my mother grabbed his plate and ran to the shelter with it. He was the last one in and then leaned out of the entrance finishing his meal and watching the raid taking place in the near distance.

Another memory of the blitz was that one day I decided to go and see a friend of mine, Maurice Budd, who lived in Bullar Road. As I walked down it was completely deserted. I arrived at his house and found all the doors wide open. I went inside but nobody was in. I went out into his garden but all his chickens and rabbits were also missing. I wandered back up Bullar Road towards my home in Harcourt Road and was stopped by a policeman who asked me where the hell had I just come from. When I told him he said that I should not have been down there as there was unexploded bomb in that road. The warning sign was at the top and bottom of Bullar Road but I entered from the middle.

A stick of bombs dropped and destroyed a number of houses between Bullar Road and MacNaghten Road and the gap that was left remained for years. On the bomb site masses of buddleia grew and as kids we used to go there and catch butterflies which seemed to be everywhere in those days.

On a bomb site in Bullar Road they built a large concrete tank to hold water. This was used as a reserve for fire-fighting should the water main be broken.

3 Cobden Avenue, almost completely destroyed in the blitz.
(So'ton City Archives)

Painted on it was SWS for Static Water Supply. When we asked the workmen what it meant they told us it stood for Scotch Whisky and Soda.

We moved from No. 22 to No. 10 Harcourt Road as the blitz continued. I remember there were two warnings to go to the shelter. One was the general siren and the other was the docks whistle which meant that the bombers were actually coming our way. We tended to wait for the docks whistle to blow before going to the shelter, but one night we left it a bit too late and the bombs had started falling and exploding. My mother told me to run on in front of them to the shelter, which I did. Because we had left it too late my mother, father and sister had to stay indoors. As I was running along the pathway some incendiary bombs fell in the garden which set fire to some dried plants. I dived into the shelter and found that I was all alone except for our dog and a neighbour's dog who was already in there taking refuge. I remember the three of us lying in the dark together just shivering – with fear I suppose.

Another night Gladys and I had been put to bed in the kitchen under the table as usual when a raid started suddenly and an incendiary bomb hit and set fire to the back bedroom of our house which was above the kitchen where we were sleeping. My father rushed out with a hose pipe but it was useless so he had to leave it to burn and get us down the shelter. The bedroom was destroyed by the fire. I still have the top of the incendiary bomb which started the fire.

The Lances Hill Plane Crash
Keith Marsh

In 1939 the RAF commandeered the playing field of St Mary's College (then half of its present size) for mooring a barrage balloon. These large hydrogen-filled balloons were tethered by cables and were winched up and down, to a maximum height of about 10,000ft. Their purpose was to force enemy aircraft to fly higher, thus reducing the accuracy of their bombing whilst lengthening the time that they were in the sights of anti-aircraft guns. The cables were difficult to see and, due to the force of the wind, did not lie directly under the balloon, thus posing a threat to all aircraft.

The *Walrus* flying-boat was another of Spitfire designer R.J. Mitchell's brilliant designs for Supermarine: with a range of 500 miles and a cruising speed of 80 knots, they played a vital role in air-sea rescue, and were produced in vast numbers. *Walrus* No. K8556 was with 754 Squadron Fleet Air Arm, based at Lee-on-Solent, and it was just before 3.00p.m. on Tuesday 12 December 1939 that it struck the cable mooring the barrage balloon over St Mary's College, and crashed on to Lances Hill.

The accident was witnessed by George Lockyer on Peartree Green, and by Tony White at Witt's Hill, who later described it:

I was at home in Midanbury one afternoon when I heard the unmistakable sound of a Walrus *amphibian passing by. I looked out of the window to watch it and was horrified to see it come to an abrupt halt as it struck a barrage balloon cable and spin down to destruction.*

Miss Stott, who had been doing her hair in the back bedroom of No. 8 Little Lances Hill, thought the plane was coming straight for her, so ran downstairs and out of the front door, whilst a woman and child had to run for their lives when they saw the plane about to crash on top of them. In fact it hit a small car travelling down Lances Hill and bounced into the garden of No. 340 Bitterne Road, an empty house on the corner with Little Lances Hill. The plane was enveloped in flames and several loud explosions were heard. Blazing petrol poured down the road from the wreckage, catching hedges alight and scorching nearby houses, causing considerable alarm to people in them. Would-be rescuers had little chance to extricate the four occupants of the plane, who all died.

Men of the Balloon Barrage Squadron came running, and the fire brigade attended to put out the fire. The driver of the car, Mr Mouland of Southsea, escaped with his trousers on fire, which he extinguished by rolling on the ground; he was treated in hospital for burns before returning home by train. Dr Roberts, a police surgeon, attended the scene at 4.30p.m., and the Royal Navy put a guard on the site overnight, residents keeping them supplied with hot drinks and food.

Three of the aircrew were buried in the cemetery at the RN Haslar Hospital: Lt Richard Herriott-Hill, RN, aged 24, Leading Airman Michael McLoughlin, RN, aged 25, and Pilot Officer Michael Fortnum, RAF, aged 19. The fourth crew member was Air Mechanic Louis Moorhead, RN, aged 19, who was buried in Hartlepool.

At the subsequent inquest, the coroner heard evidence that the plane was air-worthy from Lt-Cmdr Esmonde of the Fleet Air Arm, whilst Flight-Lt Sherwood of the RAF described the visibility as variable to a distance of about two miles. He also described how he had seen the plane hit the cable with its port wing and a piece of wood fall away. The inquest closed with condolences to the bereaved.

This was not the only friendly plane brought down in the area by a barrage balloon. On 26 August 1940 a Bristol Blenheim bomber L8870, returning from a night-time sortie over St Malo, collided with the cable tethering a balloon over Southampton Common, and crashed at West End, killing its crew of three.

In 1940 St Mary's College classrooms were taken over by the ARP as a decontamination centre, and the Home Guard took over the gym and carried out manoeuvres in the grounds. Then on 1 December 1940 it became a Luftwaffe target, nine bombs exploding in the grounds. A further raid occurred in June 1942.

On 23 October 1940 an Avro Anson crashed in the back garden of 61 Cobbett Road. The details were suppressed and the RAF requisitioned the property for the duration of the war. Letters in the *Southern Daily Echo* recently suggested that another plane crashed in Hum Hole c.1945.

Bitterne Manor House showing the affect of Second World War bombing. (SO'TON CITY ARCHIVES)

John Arlott, OBE, and *Clausentum*

John Arlott, 1914–91. (SOUTHERN DAILY ECHO)

Leslie Thomas John Arlott was many things: poet, author, wine connoisseur and cricket commentator. He was born in Basingstoke in 1914 and was brought up in humble surroundings in a cemetery superintendent's lodge. Amongst his early jobs was that of diet clerk at the local psychiatric hospital.

In 1934 he joined the Southampton Police Force with whom he served during the Second World War, rising to the rank of detective sergeant. Cricket had always been one of John's passions and the police force gave him the opportunity to play competitively. It was whilst in the police that he became a published poet with *Of Period and Place* in 1944, and his poetic works brought him to the attention of John Betjeman. The police also gave John the opportunity for his first broadcast: on VE Day, as a police representative. Betjeman became his mentor and in 1945 John left the police to succeed George Orwell as the BBC Literary Programmes Producer.

The following year he wrote a sequence of sonnets inspired by the wartime destruction of Bitterne Manor House. Together with seven full-page drawings by Michael Ayrton, these were published by Johnathan Cape in a book entitled *Clausentum*. The book's preface captures the atmosphere of the immediate postwar period and, if possible should be read imagining John's celebrated Hampshire dialect:

Clausentum is clenched in a twist of the tidal River Itchen at Southampton, its southern boundary now the main Southampton-Portsmouth road instead of the old fosse. There is good reason to believe that it has been in human occupation for over two thousand years, that it was the site of an ancient British encampment and, later, a Roman landing-station and the galley fleet headquarters of the usurper-emperor Carausius, Count of the Saxon Shore.

The house at Clausentum, Bitterne Manor, has been damaged by fire and bomb-blast during the past seven years and now stands empty, probably for the first time for over one thousand years. In its present state of dilapidation the house shows, in startling depth, its

medieval, Elizabethan, Georgian and Victorian stages of building and extension.

When we saw Clausentum for the first time we felt an air of peace and isolation almost incredible in a place pent in by the industries of a modern port. We went there again, many times; once late on a still summer night. Every visit brought some fresh revelation. Out of our visits came this book – not a book of poems with illustrations, nor of pictures with commentary, but of sonnets and drawings that are complementary, the outcome of shared and similar impacts on two men working in different media.

Part of the grounds has been made into allotments, the front of the house has been used as a rifle-range and hooligans have defaced the walls and torn away the

One of Michael Ayrton's eight drawings from the book Clausentum.

woodwork. Even in the few weeks that covered our visits to Clausentum we saw tragic and irreparable damage done to the house. Without exception we record the hope that some steps may be taken to preserve this parcel of land, its trees, its buildings and that rare character which became our familiar.

JA and MA

Alongside his literary job for the BBC, John began commentating on cricket in 1946, covering India's visit to England that summer. His passion for the sport was much evident in his poetic descriptions presented in the unique Hampshire burr that was to become known as 'the voice of summer'. In 1949 John published *Concerning Cricket*, his first book on the sport and one of over 80 books he wrote, co-wrote or edited. In 1950 he became a full-time journalist and broadcaster, writing in the *Guardian* and commentating for the BBC. John's final broadcast was in 1980, and following his last Test Match commentary during the Lord's Centenary that year, the players on both sides joined the crowd in turning to the commentary box to applaud him. John died at his home on Alderney in 1991.

By Night

The south-west wind goes down before the night
And soundlessly the river southers by:
The crumbling walls are chalked in moonbeam-white
On trees pinned out with stars across the sky.
A still and sharply-lined grey figure fills
The glassless window of a floorless room,
And creeper on a smashed door-pillar spills
Across the hallway's shuttered trap of gloom.
Now with the mask of midnight on its face,

The faithful river mutely toils to force
The bank that bars the long-dry fosse and race
Once more along the old remembered course,
To make again the old full-circle sweep
And, with its body, guard Clausentum's sleep.

John Arlott

The Cold War in Bitterne
Keith Marsh

In the 1980s, a plot of land on the corner of Somerset Avenue and Bitterne Road was put up for sale by the Council. Mr and Mrs Major (living at 6 Somerset Avenue) and their neighbours at No. 4 were offered the land to stop potential development at the bottom of their gardens. This they bought, and the dental surgery was built on the remaining piece of land. Upon clearing the undergrowth the neighbours found a street lamp in their plot, but Mr and Mrs Major found what at first seemed to be an air-raid shelter, but was much larger. Demolition of this structure did not seem an option as an attempt would probably do more damage to their bungalow's foundations than to the structure, so there it remained. But what was it?

To comply with postwar Home Office directives, Southampton needed one control centre for use in the event of a nuclear war, and this was situated in Bassett. However the Civil Defence Committee of the Council felt that this was inadequate, perhaps conscious of the way the River Itchen divided the borough, so it was decided that a sub-control centre should be built on land adjacent to the junction of Somerset Avenue and Bitterne Road. When planned the site was just 250ft inside the borough boundary, was partially wooded and was protected to the south by a steep earth bank.

The outside of the sub-control centre in the back garden of 6 Somerset Avenue, as seen in 2001.

Planning permission was granted on 8 December 1953 and the centre was officially opened on 1 September 1955 by Councillor A.J. Guard, Chairman of the Civil Defence Committee. As with the Bassett control centre, the Bitterne sub-control was retained on a 'care and maintenance basis' after the stand-down of Civil Defence in 1968, until the land was sold as a result of 'the peace dividend'. The centre did not go entirely unused though; in the 1960s it was apparently used as a polling station at elections!

I was shown around the centre by Mr Major in 2001, which was fortunate because in the spring of 2006, 4 Somerset Avenue and the bungalow at No. 6 (used as a show bungalow by Somerset Gardens Estaes) were demolished for redevelopment. The following observations were made during that visit.

The building itself consisted of a custom-built surface blockhouse, and was in amazingly good condition in 2001. Passing through the entrance, the passage turned right into an airlock; on the outer door were the words 'Air lock doors to be kept shut when ventilating plant is working'. Passing through the inner door, the passage turned left into a corridor. The first room on the right was the plant room and, inside, the ventilation plant was still there, although the standby generator had been removed. The corridor turned right to a small pantry containing an electric stove, sink, water heater, large kettle, teapot and a cupboard containing a large quantity of 1950s crockery. Next to the pantry were men's and women's dormitories; in the former was a ladder leading to an emergency

Mr Major in the corridor of the centre.

The Operations Room showing the large-scale map of Southampton.
(NICK CATFORD / SUBTERRANEA BRITANNICA)

escape hatch in the roof. Adjacent were the toilets, each with two cubicles, basin and water heater.

The first room on the left-hand side of the corridor had 'Communications' on the door. It had switchboard operators' booths located along two walls and two hatches for passing messages through, one into the corridor, the other to the next room. This had 'Operations' on the door and inside was a large 12ins to 1 mile map of Southampton on one wall, though in a dilapidated state. This was flanked by blackboards, one headed 'Locations Board', the other 'Resources Board'. There were several tables, and a small door in the far wall marked 'Emergency Exit' that led to another ladder to the roof. In both rooms there were three lights, red, amber and green, for indicating the state of alert. But alas no more! In 2006 the shelter was demolished to make way for further development of housing.

The other more audible reminders of the Cold War threat were the early warning sirens, which were regularly tested until the 1970s. Following use as air-raid sirens during the Second World War, they were retained postwar as part of a countrywide network to give the 'four-minute warning'. They were sited on buildings such as police stations or, if none existed, on high poles like that at the junction of Castle Road and Dell Road. But the nuclear threat receded, the sirens were became obsolete and in 1992 the Home Secretary reduced the funding for maintenance. So by March 1993 all were withdrawn from service, with most being scrapped, although some are now used as industrial sirens.

Chapter Eight

The Diapers of Bitterne
Ann Galbraith

The family name Diaper is intrinsically linked to Southampton and Itchen Ferry, and indeed has been since the 1500s; some say their forebears arrived with William the Conqueror and this certainly would not be their only royal connection. As you would expect, some of the family drifted up the road to Bitterne and secured their place in local folklore.

John Unwin Diaper was born in Itchen Ferry in 1833, the second of the three sons of Henry and Mary. In 1876 he, his wife Elizabeth and their five children moved to Ivy Cottages in Pound Street, Bitterne. Like many of the Itchen Ferry Diapers he was a mariner, but in this case not a fisherman or ferryman but the Captain of the Royal Yacht *Victoria and Albert*, first serving Queen Victoria and later King Edward VII. By 1881 Elizabeth had turned the front room of the cottage into a 'Cocoa Room' by extending the front and having a large window put in. Cocoa Rooms were fashionable at the time as the drink was considered wholesome and satisfying, and Elizabeth's became a popular meeting place for villagers. And it was in the cocoa room that Captain Diaper entertained King Edward VII, when he paid him a private and unexpected visit.

Captain Diaper was suffering from an attack of gout and was sat with his legs stretched out on a stool in front of him, his grandson Claude (then about six years old) sitting at his feet listening to stories of life at sea. The door opened and the

Captain John Unwin Diaper, 1833-1915.

Captain's daughter Mary called out, 'Father, you've got a visitor.'

'Well let him in then,' replied the Captain, and into the room strode an impressive figure wearing a long black coat and Homburg hat.

'Well, what's the matter with you, John?' questioned the King.

'I've got gout, Ted' replied the Captain.

'Been at the bottle again then?' said the King and then, noticing the little lad sitting on the floor, he asked Claude his name. 'Come and sit on my lap' ordered his Majesty, and took the bemused little boy on his knee. As the two men chatted over a glass of wine, the little boy grew restive. 'Don't fidget' commanded the King.

When news of the King's visit to Ivy Cottage leaked out a few days later, young Claude was called out at school assembly and was asked to recount all that the King had said to him. From that time on, the schoolmaster, Mr Charles Watson, nicknamed Claude 'Fidget', even at a crowded sports meeting years after he was married! Some have queried the use of Christian names between King and subject, but Claude explained it thus:

You have to remember that my grandfather was the first one to teach the young Prince of Wales to sail. They used to have races round the Isle of Wight. As the young Prince grew up an understandable camaraderie developed between them, when they were on their own. I know from my own father of the democracy that exists between men at sea, when they must all co-operate against the might of the ocean.

Ivy Cottage, Pound Street, once home to Captain John Diaper and visited by King Edward VII, derelict prior to demolition for the bypass.

The pound in its final location in the 1960s, with Christopher Robertson gazing in.

Captain Diaper owned a large area of land alongside Pound Street stretching as far as the corner with the High Street. In 1906 he sold the corner plot so that the Wesleyan chapel could be built but this meant that the pound had to be re-sited, so he decided to give it to the parish, along with ten golden sovereigns for its upkeep. When the Wesleyan Chapel was demolished in 1969 to make way for Sperring's new shop, Claude Diaper was horrified to see that preparations were being made to build on the pound as well. Protesting that they had no claim to this little piece of land, he engaged solicitors to search for the title, but alas, the deeds were never found. Nor was there any indication of what had happened to the ten gold sovereigns!

Claude Diaper was campaigning again in the early 1980s when the long-proposed bypass finally reached the planning stage, but this time it was directed at the City Council for allowing homes to be blighted by the plans. He was successful in that he proved that his home, 11 Dean Road, did not have to be sacrificed to the bulldozers. He and his wife Marie had moved there as live-in housekeepers for Freddy McQueen, and inherited the house from him when he died in the early 1960s. So until July 2002 the home that he and Marie shared stood as a legacy to his arguments, sandwiched forlornly between the bypass and the leisure centre. It was not until the widowed Marie died that the bulldozers won; and the white cottage, despite an attempt by the BLHS to save it, was replaced with a block of flats: Cairn Court.

Above: *Christmas 1957 at 11 Dean Road. Left to right: Mrs Spratt (Marie's mother), Freddy McQueen, Marie and Claude Diaper.*
Below: *11 Dean Road, saved from the bulldozers when the bypass was built but, like too many of the village buildings, now replaced by flats despite attempts by the BLHS to save it.*

Bitterne's Blue Plaque
Keith Marsh

For nearly 140 years blue plaques have been a familiar feature of the London townscape, with over 760 now adorning the façades of buildings. Some are grand, others not so, but all were once the home of a famous or remarkable person: actors, authors, politicians, reformers and scientists are so honoured. Strict criteria have to be met before a blue plaque is agreed, such as the person having been dead for over 20 years, being considered eminent by their own profession, and their name recognised by the well-informed passer-by. Since 1986 the scheme has been run by English Heritage, who ran a pilot scheme in four areas including Southampton, before deciding to roll out the scheme nationally from 2004.

The house at 38 Chessel Avenue received one of the first blue plaques in Southampton, and the only one in Bitterne. Its famous resident in 1922–29 was aircraft designer Roy Chadwick, CBE, MSc, FRSA, FRAeS.

Born in Farnworth, Lancashire in 1893, Roy was the fourth in a generation of mechanical engineers, so it is not surprising that he continued the tradition. As a lad he built model aircraft, flying them at night for fear of ridicule. At 14 years old he started work as a trainee draughtsman for the British Westinghouse Co. in Manchester, whilst studying mathematics and engine design at the Manchester College of Technology for three evenings a week. In 1911 he changed jobs, and became a draughtsman and personal assistant to Alliott Vernon-Roe at the newly formed A.V. Roe & Co. Ltd, then based in the cellar of Alliott's brother's mill in Ancoates, Manchester. His job involved taking notes from his employer, making sketches and then transferring these to the drawing-board. Designs included five versions of the Avro D, the Avro F (which in 1912 became the world's first monoplane and flew to a height of 1,000ft), the Avro 500 and the Avro 504 (of which over 7,000 were built during and after the First World War). The Avro 504 was used by the RAF as a trainer for many years, and indeed King George VI learnt to fly it. In 1915 Roy designed his first aircraft, the Avro Pike, the first plane to have internal stowage for bombs and a gun turret behind the wings.

The large order book meant insufficient floor space at the Manchester works, so in 1917 A.V. Roe opened an assembly works and testing station at Hamble. With his office relocated from Manchester, Roy moved to the area, though he frequently visited the A.V. Roe works at Manchester, and also the Admiralty and Air Ministry in London. In 1918 Roy officially became A.V. Roe's chief designer and during the next 30 years he was responsible for over 200 aircraft designs. These included the Avro Baby, the Aldershot (the world's biggest single-engine

English Heritage's Blue Plaque.

Roy Chadwick's home for seven years, 38 Chessel Avenue.

Left: The staff of Henry Bell, solicitors of Woolston, in 1927, with Mr Bell in the back row. Front row, left to right: C.A. Fudge, May Chadwick (Roy's sister), Les Payne and Irene Dible (Hampshire's first lady solicitor). The picture was taken by Norman Gardiner, a prolific local photographer.

Below, inset: Avro Lancaster No. R5868 at the Bomber Command Museum, Hendon, 1985. Famous for its use in The Dambuster's Raid, the Lancaster was the RAF Bomber Command's main weapon in the Second World War.

Avro Vulcan B2 No.XH558, delivered to the RAF in June 1960, was the last Vulcan in service when retired in March 1993, and is now being restored.

bomber), the Andover air ambulance, the Manchester and Lancaster (Roy was proud to be a Lancastrian and Mancunian), the Tutor, the Cadet, the York and the Vulcan. Seven variants of the Baby were produced, the last being the Antarctic Baby, with floats and folding wings, used by Sir Ernest Shackleton's expedition in 1921. The Avian was another particularly successful aircraft, being used by Roy's friend and A.V. Roe colleague Bert Hinkler for many of his record flights. The role of the 7,300 Lancaster bombers in the Second World War is legendary, as is that of the Anson of which 11,000 were built for transport and crew training (two squadrons of Coastal Command were stationed at RAF Southampton). In 1928 A.V. Roe was sold to industrialist Sir John Siddeley, who owned several companies including aircraft makers Hawkers, and shortly after Roy moved back to the Manchester works.

Roy was known to start his designs as doodles on graph paper and often had several projects under-way concurrently. The Vulcan was conceived this way, though Roy did not live long enough to see it, nor his Shackleton, fly. He was killed in a crash during a test flight of his Tudor II airliner at Woodford in 1947; a crash that happened as a result of a mistake in servicing. But many of the results of his doodles fly on.

My Son Chris Packham,
Rita Packham

It was a sunny day in May 1961 when Christopher was born. His father Colin and I met in our teens in a cycling club, and married after a seven-year courtship. We then lived in London whilst Colin sailed the seas with Royal Mail Lines as an engineer officer and I worked as a secretary. Colin's father was a sailor; my own was a soldier in India, who returned home to Southampton to start a coal business, and met my mother who was one of the few women in Southampton at that time to become a dressmaker. Four years after we married we returned to Southampton and decided Christopher would be welcome: we were certainly glad when he was born because life was never the same afterwards.

When Christopher was nearly two we moved from Peartree to Bitterne Park; Colin worked in a local industry and four years later Christopher's sister Jenny arrived. By this time his energies and interests were already heading towards wildlife: there were snakes, frogs, insects, mice, ants, a tortoise, budgie, lizards, goldfish and beetles in the house, garden and shed. Christopher liked school and the home was always alive and busy.

As Chris and Jenny grew older we spent days rambling in the New Forest or along the beaches

surrounding Southampton. In the holidays we visited museums and art galleries wherever we were; London, Edinburgh, Winchester, etc. At one time we had a fox which Chris used to take for walks like a dog! Our poodle, Max, was so nature-orientated that we noticed that when the blackbird nesting in the garden gave the alarm call (such as blackbirds do) that there was a cat in the garden, Max ran slipping all over the kitchen floor growling and barking as loud as possible, but the cat was gone! There were quite a few cats in the neighbourhood chased away by Max, and nests of blackbirds resulted.

So whilst President Kennedy was shot, Wilson and Heath battled for power, Dickie Valentine sang *The Twelfth of Never*, the Beatles enjoyed the screaming, and Southampton recovered from the Second World War, Chris grew up, watching *Captain Scarlet*, *Thunderbirds*, and David Attenborough. He and Jenny enjoyed a 'learning' life together: they were always interested in finding out, and talking about their interests. We always had a collection of books for their ages, Chris would search for new wildlife and wondered at its delicacy or strength, whilst Jenny loved drawing, painting, music and dancing, all of which Chris shared with her (except the dancing!) He became a very clever artist, painting birds and animals.

To our horror, at the age of 12 he grew his hair shoulder length. Then when he reached college he became a punk! He bought a guitar and with a group of others set about forming a music band.

It was with his bleached punk hair-do that Chris started his first job in television, co-present-ing the BBC's new children's wildlife programme, the *Really Wild Show* with Terry Nutkins and Nicola Davies. Chris worked on the show from 1986 until 1995 during which time it

By the age of 15 Chris had such a reputation that he was asked to care for and release four fledgling Barn Owls, which he flew at Frog's Copse.

Punk rock gave Chris an outlet for his ferocious teenage energy. The noise he made was...appalling!

won three BAFTA tv awards for best children's programme, and the immensely popular programme is still running. More recent programmes have included BBC2's *Nature Calendar* and *Hands on Nature*, and BBC1's *X-Creatures* (investigating mythological creatures such as the Yeti), BBC2's *Watch out* (on British wildlife), BBC1's *Countryfile* and currently BBC South's *Inside Out* investigative programme. Wild Watch was a recent British wildlife series which he wrote, presented and produced, using his own production company, Head over Heels Production. He is now working on another BBC2 series, *The UK's Top 40 Wildlife Spectacles*.

Stills photography is also a passion, and he has been awarded three category winners in the Wildlife Photography of the Year competition. And if filming isn't enough to occupy him, Chris also acts as an ornithological tour guide overseas, has written several books and is involved with numerous conservation organisations.

Chris Packham

I was fortunate that my parents were very tolerant of my obsessive interests. At times our house in Midanbury was quite a zoo and my bedroom a brightly lit snake pit! This personal contact with animals was incredibly important to continue my fascination and excite a curiosity that is still vigorous today. It has fuelled a life packed with experiences in all corners of the earth but I remain grateful for those who gave me so much help.

John Buckley, my secondary school biology teacher, turned my egg-collecting hobby into some serious science, which gave me a great advantage over my fellow students at an early age. Stephen Bolwell, a freelance wildlife cameraman, took me on as an assistant, paid me from his own pocket and his generosity knows no bounds. I enjoyed some great tutoring at all my schools, college and university, and Alec Falconer and Rory Putman were notably encouraging.

But I believe that I was able to embrace their advice because of a ferocious early sense of competitiveness which matured into an equally vigorous desire to achieve perfection in all fields. Of course I've never done that! But I'm still trying, whether its film-making, writing or taking photographs: it gets me up early and keeps me working late.

I liked Bitterne Park where I grew up. It seemed a friendly place, with corner shops, local pubs and plenty of rich characters on its streets. There were also plenty of scraps of 'wasteland' for me to explore. But these have gone – the corner shops and those over-grown patches where lizards lounged, butterflies flew and hedgehogs rustled. Now infilling with new houses means that wildlife is in shorter supply, a sad fact for those kids who might be more interested in real life than the internet. This neighbourhood is like so many others, we've thrown away the simple things that create a healthy community, shops where people knew our names and habitats which give a break to the creatures which can in turn give us a higher quality of life. There are less trees. People cut them down because they can't be bothered, because they are misinformed about their 'dangers'. I would like to see urban planting schemes to 're-green' suburbia and I'm no fan of faceless supermarkets. But whatever, the benefit of hindsight and nostalgia are evil demons at times and I know that growing up in Bitterne Park and Midanbury is still preferable to virtually every other place on earth and those '60s and '70s kicking foot-balls, watching foxes and running to and from schools were something to remember with great fondness.

Favourite moment? Well, its tricky... the morning John Buckley came to see me flying my kestrel in the field in front of Frogs Copse, I can see now as a defining moment. By then I was incubating defiance, recognising my independence, channelling my energies and learning to love – but I was still a Midanbury 'moosh' with a bird on his arm!

Dan Parker and the *Flying Enterprise*
Keith Marsh, with acknowledgement to John Avery

A small metal plaque on the arched entrance to Bitterne Parish Church reads:

The porch light was installed by Edith Parker, to the glory of God and in loving memory of her husband, Captain Dan Parker, Master of the Ocean Rescue Tug Turmoil, *who died at sea as the result of an accident, 8th August 1955.*

Quite an insignificant plaque for a Chessel Crescent resident who was centre stage in one of the most dramatic sea rescues ever!

The 6,711-ton cargo ship SS *Cape Kumukaki* was built during 1944 at Wilmington, Delaware, for the US Maritime Commission who sold her in 1947 to the Isbrandtsen Shipping Co. Ltd of New York, who renamed her *Flying Enterprise*. On 21 December 1951 she sailed from Hamburg bound for the United States, under the command of Captain Henrik Kurt Carlsen, and with a crew of 45. She carried a cargo of 2,500 tons of pig iron, over 900 tons of coffee, and ten passengers.

By 26 December she was 300 miles south-west of Ireland, and the weather conditions were described as atrocious. At about 07:00hrs *Flying Enterprise* was hit on the starboard side by a wave estimated at 60ft high, causing her cargo to shift so that she listed heavily to port. She also suffered structural damage, the most serious being two cracks several centimetres wide across her weather deck which the crew tried to lash with wire hawsers. The crack resulted in number three hold flooding so the ship reduced speed and turned into the wind. At about midday all power was lost, the engines stopped and all lighting went out; engineers managed to restart the engines around 14:00hrs and kept them going for another four hours, but then they stopped for good. The ship by this time listed at 25 to 40 degrees.

On 28 December, with heavy seas still breaking over the deck, and a 45 degree list, *Flying Enterprise* transmitted her first SOS, which was acknowledged by SS *Southland*, and by the next day she and five other ships were standing by. With the rapidly deteriorating situation, Captain Carlsen gave the order to abandon ship, but the passengers refused to the extent that some threatened to tie themselves to the ship. Eventually they agreed, but the sea's heavy swell combined with the ship's list prevented lifeboats from the other ships getting alongside. So each passenger was allocated two crew members and, with one each side, they all jumped into the sea, to be picked up by lifeboats from the other ships. Just one life was lost. The captain, however, refused to leave his ship.

The next two days Carlsen spent alone on the badly damaged, drifting and badly listing *Flying Enterprise*. By now he had not slept for five days and his plight was headline news around the world. The 1,136-ton Bustler-class salvage tug *Turmoil* of the Overseas Towing & Salvage Co. Ltd radioed that it would give assistance after it had delivered another damaged ship, and at 04:30hrs on 2 January it left Falmouth under the command of Captain Dan Parker. The *Turmoil* arrived on the scene the next day but, with the *Flying Enterprise* now listing at 60 degrees, Carlsen found it impossible to attach the tow line single-handed: he needed one hand to hold on to the ship. By 5 January the storm that had driven the *Flying Enterprise* 200 miles closer to England, had moderated, turning to fog and light rain. Then, as the *Turmoil* rode up beneath the stern of the *Flying Enterprise*, Ken Dancy, the *Turmoil's* Mate, made a spontaneous decision to jump on to the stricken ship. Carlsen welcomed him aboard with the words 'Well hello, welcome aboard. Make yourself comfortable!' After half an hour they had attached a wire hawser from the *Turmoil*; the tired crew of the tug cheered when they heard Carlsen's voice call 'Everything is clear!' Another tug, the French *Abeille 25*, had now arrived but the idea of a twin tow was rejected because the risk of the *Flying Enterprise* rolling to a greater degree of list was too great. And so began the long and painfully slow tow towards Falmouth.

Although the weather was improving, her list made the *Flying Enterprise* veer wildly from side to side, and the tow line parted several times. Both men on her were utterly exhausted with little food, no heat, nowhere to sleep, and being constantly wet. On 6 January the captain of the USS *Willard Keith* sent a telegram to Carlsen's wife in New Jersey reporting

that Carlsen and Dancy were exuberant at a job well done, the tow progressing at 3 knots in a moderate sea. However, on 8 January the weather deteriorated again, and in gale-force winds with only 60 miles to go, both *Turmoil* and *Flying Enterprise* were forced to heave to. The latter was now rolling through 80 degrees and, when the tow line parted again, was once more adrift. On 10 January, 15 days after the wave struck and only 40 miles from Falmouth, the ship was almost on her beam ends and there were signs that she was beginning to break up. Dancy walked along the now horizontal funnel and stepped into the sea followed by Carlsen; they were picked up after only 4½ minutes in the water. The *Flying Enterprise* sank shortly after, at 16:10hrs.

Carlsen received a tremendous welcome when the *Turmoil* arrived in Falmouth the next day, but there was sadness that the fight had been lost so close to port. Press coverage made Carlsen and Dancy famous, though Carlsen was adamant that he only did what any seaman would do. He was awarded the Lloyds Silver Medal and his next command was the *Flying Enterprise II*. He died in October 1989 and his ashes were scattered where the *Flying Enterprise* sank.

In August 1955 Captain Dan Parker suffered a heart attack climbing the *Turmoil's* bridge ladder, and was badly injured as he fell to the deck. He died aged 63 and his ashes were also scattered at sea. Some years later Edith Parker, Dan's widow, suffered serious leg and head injuries in a collision with a motorcycle in Little Lances Hill, and a report in the *Southern Daily Echo* included a photograph of Dan, Edith and their daughter with Captain Carlsen and his family.

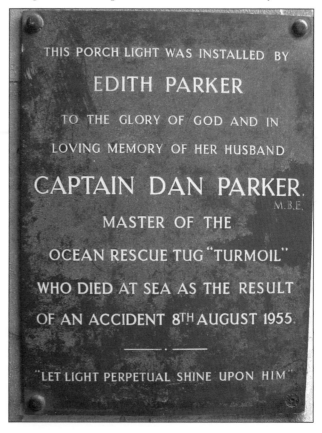

Dr Alan Oakley John (left) *in Sudan, 1977–82.*

Celebrating the 50th anniversary of the first Bitternes Afloat, 1999. Left to right: *Don Brigden, Alan and Gene John, John Sturgess, Elisabeth Linfield, Jack Earl.*

A Couple Who Wanted to Serve
Joy Bowyer

Alan Oakley John was born in Highbury Terrace in London. He was always proud that he was a true Cockney and born within the sound of Bow Bells (if the wind was in the right direction!) His mother was also a Londoner and his father was from Swansea. His great-great uncle was a pioneer missionary in China, known as Griffith John of Hankow. Alan went to the City of London School where he joined the rugger team and Christian Union. Here he met Gene's brother Rob and eventually Gene herself.

After training at St Bartholomew's Hospital as a doctor he worked in the Mildmay Mission Hospital during the London blitz. In 1941 he became a Medical Officer in the Royal Navy, sailing to the Indian Ocean with the battleship HMS *Resolution*. On his return to Plymouth he became engaged to Gene and they were safely married in April 1944, in spite of all leave being stopped.

On D-Day Alan was on board a landing-craft which brought casualties back to England from the French beaches. He later served in the Northern Approaches Escort Group and North Russia. He was amazed and relieved to find himself on VE Day surrounded by packs of surrendering U-boats.

In 1948 he and Gene, with their first child, came to live at 2 Chessel Avenue, Bitterne, where he started work in a very busy Christian general practice. He found himself often on call for 24-hour days and most of each week. He was senior partner for many years and was heavily involved in local medical matters. Most of his life was spent treating patients and he loved it.

Elsewhere in this book is an account of Alan's Christian service with young people, but another interest for him was that of the training and work of the St John Ambulance Brigade, where he became County Surgeon for Hampshire. He also became chairman of Governors for Bitterne School, involving himself in the development of the new school,

and served Bitterne Church as a churchwarden and reader.

He was very pleased when he followed his grandfather's footsteps and became a Freeman of the City of London. He delighted in telling everyone that he could now drive his sheep over London Bridge. The family grew and Alan and Gene had six daughters, now all married and there are many grandchildren.

Having retired, in 1978 Alan and Gene were called to serve abroad with the Church Mission Society and spent five years in Sudan. By their return, the practice had moved to 4 Chessel Avenue and they lived in one half of 2 Chessel Avenue before moving to Marne Road.

Alan had a great many hobbies where he enjoyed using his hands. One of them was candle-making. He poured liquid candle wax down the kitchen sink one day. It took two engineering graduates to unblock it! Many Bitterne folk have their own special memories. When Gene and Alan became engaged someone said to Gene, 'My dear, I don't think you will ever have a dull moment.'

Gene (whose name was Gertrude Imogen) also has her special place in Bitterne memories. As well as her work with young people, Gene was also very active in other church groups, in between bringing up six daughters. In retirement she and Alan would do temporary fostering of children. When she had to give up driving she could be seen trudging around

2 Chessel Avenue, the home of Alan and Gene John and their six daughters, and the Girl Covenanters' meeting place. Two of Chessel House's four stone gate pillars are shown; the telephone kiosk is now a thing of the past.

Bitterne with a wicker basket on wheels filled with things for people.

Her father, Revd Sinton, was a China Inland Missionary and Gene was born and went to school in China. When Alan died in 2000, Gene could not manage on her own and went to a CIM Retirement home in Tunbridge Wells, where she died in 2004. I now live in what was their last home together in Marne Road.

Joe Harriott
Keith Marsh

Parker? There's them over here can play a few aces too...

So reads the inscription on a modest, red granite headstone in Bitterne churchyard, the final resting place of Joe Harriott, nick-named 'Mojo', alto-saxophonist and one of the greatest jazz musicians.

Joe was born into poverty in Kingston, Jamaica on 15 July 1928. He was the eldest of 'Rafael' Garfield Harriott's and Theresa Scarlett's three children, born at two-year intervals, but after his brother Ivanhoe's birth, his father died. His mother had a second daughter, Velma, with her new partner, then died of a fever three weeks later. The two girls were brought up by Joe's aunt, whilst Joe and his brother were eventually taken in by the Sisters of Mercy, a Catholic order of nuns, and were brought up at the renowned Alpha Orphanage, Kingston's unofficial music college, where Joe's talent was soon recognised and nurtured.

The late 1940s was a time of high unemployment in Jamaica, whilst Britain seemed to offer work and a higher standard of living, especially to talented jazz musicians. Joe played with fellow Jamaicans, trumpeter Dizzy Reece and tenor saxophonist Wilton Gayner, before coming to England in 1951 with the Ossie da Costa Band. A distant cousin, Chester Harriott, was already in London playing piano and singing, having won a scholarship to study music at Trinity College, but his and Joe's paths rarely crossed (Chester was father to a star of the future – TV chef Ainsley Harriott). Joe was an extremely proud man, preferring to form his own group than to join any particular band just for popularity. This led to fellow musicians describing him as a bit of a loner. Even so

he earned a high reputation in international jazz circles, and played alongside stars including Ronnie Scott and John Dankworth. Joe's first record was an EP 'Cool Jazz with Joe', released in 1954 by the Joe Harriott Quartet.

Joe Harriott, from the cover of the aptly named Genius CD.
(JAZZ ACADEMY RECORDS)

Dozens of records followed, some with his own quartet or quintet, others in collaboration with other great jazz musicians of the day: Chris Barber, Michael Garrick, John Mayer, Shake Keane and others. In February 1958, a few weeks before forming his quintet, Joe performed at the Concorde Club (then at The Bassett Hotel) and as the *Southern Evening Echo* reported: 'there was logic and an odd sort of rough beauty about everything he did.'

Originally a bop-orientated player, Joe envisaged a new method of improvisation during a stay in hospital in 1958. He ignored the usual chorus/bridge-passage/chorus occupying a set number of bars, instead using a simple theme to develop a mood within which the musicians shared their ideas to build a musical picture. This idea was used for Joe's 1960 album 'Free Form', followed a year later by 'Abstract'. Joe went on to build a reputation as a great musical innovator, famed for pioneering the fusion of Indian music with jazz. This was illustrated on his 1967 albums with John Mayer, 'Indo-Jazz Suite 1' and '2'. His profile, however, remained modest.

During the second half of the 1960s jazz music was being usurped in Britain by pop, and in the clubs by rhythm and blues. By the early 1970s, Joe's career was in decline, leaving him demoralised and in poor health; he was a very heavy smoker, and even managed to attach a cigarette to his saxophone. Whilst staying with local bandleader Teddy Layton and his wife Marilyn, Joe was taken ill, and tests revealed tuberculosis and cancer of the spine. He spent five months in hospital, alternating between the Wessex Radiotherapy Unit at the Royal South Hants, and the Isolation (now the Western) Hospital. Following appeals on Radio Solent's jazz programme a few fellow musicians visited him, but found him extremely frail. He died on 2 January 1973 at the Wessex Radiotherapy Unit.

Joe's funeral was held at Bitterne Parish Church a week later and the service included musical tributes from colleagues. Marilyn Layton recalled one nice touch: a lone West Indian lady attended the funeral and when asked if she had known Joe answered, no, she had read of his death and attended because she wanted 'a black face there for him in all these white people'. With no known family Joe had asked Teddy Layton (who died in 2002) to be his 'next of kin', and he inherited Joe's saxophone. A fund was started to raise £250 for a suitable headstone; many individuals and jazz clubs contributed, including

A simple memorial to a great musician.

Ronnie Scott's Club, which held a benefit evening. The words on the memorial represent a characteristic quote from Joe, 'Parker' referring to the great American alto-saxophonist, Charlie 'Bird' Parker. At the time of his death Joe was being pursued for paternity liabilities, and since his passing four children have emerged, none known to the others: Pauline (in Jamaica), Theresa, Christopher and Amber.

Jazz bassist Gary Crosby described Joe:

A passionate musician yet a lonely, troubled soul, emotionally detached, longing to be accepted as a serious artist, he found himself worn down by a system that refused to accommodate him.

Yet despite it being over 30 years since his death, concerts are still held in his honour, revisiting some of Joe's brilliant original music.

The Revd Michael Perry
Beatrice Perry

Michael Perry arrived in Bitterne as Curate to the parish church in the summer of 1968 with his wife Beatrice. Their children Helen and Simon were born in 1969 and 1973. Following the departure of the incumbent (Revd Arthur Geary Stevens) Michael was inducted as Vicar of Holy Saviour Church, Bitterne in 1972.

Michael's main aim in life was to make Christianity and church life relevant and accessible to as many people as possible. As Vicar of Bitterne he set about this task in many and various ways.

Michael Perry with Catherine Bainbridge, his last baptism in Bitterne, 1981.

He took the church to where people were. Partly because Bitterne parish was divided by the major Southampton to Portsmouth road and also because many younger families were not accustomed to going into church buildings, he decided that a system of 'area churches' held in schools and halls would help to solve these problems. These took the form of Sunday Schools and Family Services held in five places: Thornhill (in the Scout Hut); Glenfield (in the school); Moorlands (in the school); Deacon (in Itchen College); Brook (in The Gordon Hall). They were run by lay people with Michael visiting and encouraging them.

Michael also held services that would appeal to young families and held festivals that would attract a wide spectrum of people. These events were held in the autumn for about a week. Michael chose topics which it was hoped would interest the general public in Bitterne. The first was called 'A Bend in the River' (the literal meaning of 'Bitterne'). It was an audio-visual presentation of the history of Bitterne from Roman times to the present day and Michael persuaded John Arlott, the well-known cricket commentator, to record the script on tape for it. Another production was an adaptation of *Pilgrim's Progress*. Another year an exhibition of beautiful religious 'tapestries' was hung in the church.

Shortly after moving into the vicarage, Michael and his family bought a donkey, hoping he – named Bossy – would save the time and effort needed to keep the large vicarage lawn trimmed! Michael soon found that Bossy could also be used as a means of outreach – to the children of the parish. A club was run during the August holidays for children and their mums to come to the vicarage garden for games and Bossy rides, the idea being to recruit children for the Sunday School. Bossy did his own outreach. On one occasion he was apprehended as he gazed through the (fortunately closed) door of the local Sainsbury's.

Besides his gifts and energies used for reaching out to people, Michael also possessed a great gift for writing words and music. He used Bitterne congregations to try out new forms of services and hymns. Working with a team of musicians and writers, a modern hymn book, *Hymns for Today's Church*, was published in 1982 and a service book, *Church Family Worship*, followed in 1986.

Joy Bowyer remembers:

As I was a bit of a pianist, Michael used me sometimes when he wanted to publicise Psalm Praise, a modern interpretation of the Psalms. On one occasion we were going to somewhere in the Millbrook or Redbridge area. It was at a time when many new roads were being built. Michael was confident that he knew where we were going on a dark and stormy winter's night. We bowled along happily for a while when abruptly the road ended, unfinished, filled with dumped rubbish and furniture. With renewed navigation we made it in the end.

Although Michael left Bitterne in 1981, his books were very much the fruits of his experiences and experiments at Bitterne. One composition which he brought to Bitterne was a carol for which he wrote both the words and music while at Oak Hill Theological College. This carol, now in many books and sung world-wide at Christmas time, is called *The Calypso Carol*, the tune being a West-Indian-type rhythm, which children love; the words tell the Nativity story, with a chorus expressing personal longing for us to be part of that story:

O now carry me to Bethlehem
To see the Lord appear to men:
Just as poor as was the stable then,
The Prince of Glory when He came.

Following Michael's death in 1997, I received this letter:

Dear Mrs Perry,
I hope you won't feel this presumptious but I thought you might like a copy of the enclosed photograph of your husband with our daughter.

Catherine was the last baby to be christened by Michael in June 1981, shortly before you moved on to pastures new.

Catherine is very involved with the youth groups here at Bitterne and I hope it is a comfort to you, knowing that Michael lives on through the people touched by both his ministry and music.

Yours sincerely, Barbara Bainbridge.

Lord Maybray-King's Way
Keith Marsh

Horace King in his robes as Speaker of the House of Commons.

It is now Southampton City Council policy to name main roads in the city after local 'servants of the city' so it was entirely fitting that in 1983, the new Bitterne bypass was named after the local MP who continued to live locally, even after his elevation to 'the other place.'

Horace Maybray King was born on 25 May 1901 in Stapylton Street, Grangetown, his father being a Bolckow Vaughan steel worker and a lay preacher. Horace later recalled, 'The blast furnaces worked all night and when you were in bed you would often see a mighty flare in the sky as a furnace tipped out its molten metal.' Lay-offs meant pawning your Sunday best, and going barefoot in summer to save your boots for the cold winter.

Despite their poverty Horace's parents found the sixpence to pay for his piano lessons and this later enabled Horace to play in a dance band to help fund his studies at King's College, London. Even so, times were extremely tough, and he was forced to teach at weekends and to live in a tent, existing on cheap scraps of food bought at markets. But the hardship paid off and with a first-class degree in English and his nick-name 'Doc' King, he started teaching at Taunton's Grammar School, where he was to become Head of English for 17 years; it is said, though, that he only came to the town upon the toss of a coin! In 1938 he and wife Victoria 'Queenie' moved to 37

Manor Farm Road, his home for nearly 50 years.

A duodenal ulcer resulting from the hardships of his university years, kept him out of the armed forces during the war, so, besides teaching in a greatly understaffed school, he contributed to the war effort by entertaining servicemen. His V Concert Party ('V' being for victory) proved exceedingly popular, Doc playing the piano and accordion, and singing (often bawdy) songs.

In 1947 Doc was appointed headmaster of Regent's Park Boys' School, but he was keen to enter Parliament, politics being a major pursuit of both him and Queenie (who, as a long-serving Labour councillor, was to become a Mayor of Southampton). His first attempt to get elected was doomed to defeat: he was adopted as Labour Party candidate for the New Forest in the 1945 General Election. It did, however, give him valuable experience including that of ridicule, his war service being challenged. In 1950 he successfully entered Parliament as the MP for Southampton Test. Doc remained an MP for 20 years (though he did switch to Southampton Itchen constituency in 1955) and for the final six years he was Speaker of the House of Commons, Labour's first Speaker. He once confessed to a feeling of awe when faced with 600 MPs eager to speak. Indeed, he became an Independent in order to remain non-partisan and this created a feeling of ill-will with some Labour MPs. He remembered, 'I was not allowed to eat in the dining-room, or drink in the bar and couldn't be seen to show any favouritism to any person or party.' Doc always took politics seriously, fighting hard for the deprived and ensuring fairness, skills learnt during years of teaching. Hansard records that Chris Chope MP recalled this in the Commons:

Maybray-King was still alive when I was elected in 1983. I remember him impressing upon a group of my Young Conservatives the important role of the Speaker in defending our rights under the constitution. He had been a Labour man originally, but was then an independent because he had assumed a new role. To reinforce his independence, we even passed a special Act of Parliament to provide a pension, not only for his first wife, but for his last wife: he certainly enjoyed the company of women. When he visited my Young Conservatives he was given a lift by the lady president and his first question to her was whether her husband was still alive. His reputation was such that he commanded tremendous respect as an independent upholder of the traditions of the House.

On 2 March 1971 Doc was made a life baron, and became Deputy Speaker of the House of Lords; he took the title Lord Maybray-King as there was already a Lord King in the House. He became an honorary graduate of Loughborough University the

Above: *Horace King's home for nearly 50 years, 37 Manor Farm Road.*

Top right: *In 1983 the road that changed Bitterne forever, the bypass, was named after the MP.*

Right and below: *During the Second World War Taunton's School was evacuated to Bournemouth, and there Doc King wrote 'The Hampshire Spitfire Song', which was sold to raise funds for the Hampshire Spitfire Fund.*

same year. The Lords proved to be quieter and easier to control than the Commons, and he commented that the debates were of a higher standard too. Meanwhile Southampton Itchen was now represented by one of his former Taunton's School pupils, Bob Mitchell. Doc's strong chapel upbringing led to him being asked to write the introduction to *Isaac Watts Remembered 1674–1748*, a biography of another Sotonian, Isaac Watts, written by David Fountain.

After Queenie's death in 1954 Doc remarried but was widowed again, and his third marriage ended in divorce. He then wed a long-time friend Sheila Atkinson but alas died soon after on 3 September 1986.

Bitterne's 'Artful Dodger'
Yvonne Devereux

As the new millennium arrived a new comet was hurtling across the skies – Artful Dodger was heading Top of the Pops on television and winning awards for their records and songwriting. One half of this successful duo was Peter Devereux, a member of the Parish Church choir as a small boy and later leader of the young people's music group. He also began to learn the violin with Mr Harvey at Bitterne Middle School and, more to his liking, the piano with Mrs Gwen Batchelor.

His violin playing gained him a place in the Southampton Youth Orchestra. His increasing ability on the piano led to him having lessons with David Edwards who was also responsible for setting up the church orchestra in which Peter also played, but on the keyboard.

Artful Dodgers, Mark Hill (left) *and Pete Devereux.*

When the young people's music group was formed Peter was the rock around which it flowed with much success and appreciation. It was a short step then to playing for the Parish Pantomime with style and humour. Bitterne Park School enjoyed his playing at a school concert and as the accompanist to the school's production of *You're a good man Charlie Brown*.

So how did he make the transition from church musician to the world of pop music? He got some experience DJ-ing whilst at college in London, but a difference of opinion with his mother about whether the words or the music should be written first was probably the start of his composing career. Although they wrote a couple of songs for church Peter was growing more interested in popular music and began DJ-ing in Southampton clubs.

In 1997 he linked up with Mark Hill, another classically trained musician, and they began working together as 'Artful Dodger'. A year or so later they both happened to be DJ-ing in a club in Southampton when a young, chubby-faced kid asked if he could sing over their set. The kid was Craig David and if ever there was a career-defining moment, then that was it.

The rest as they say, is history. Their quirky record 'Rewind' was only kept off the number one spot by Cliff Richard, but stayed in the charts long enough for their particular brand of music, called 'UK Garage', to reach a wider audience. Further hit records with various artists earned them many TV appearances, live performances and won them several awards, including the coveted Ivor Novello award for songwriting. However, all this proved to be a punishing schedule and after a couple of years the duo split up.

Since that time the world of popular music has changed considerably. The availability of music to be downloaded from the internet and the ongoing online price war has also meant that Peter has had to move with the times and come up with new ways of working.

Subsequently, Peter has set up a music production company called The Bomb Factory and is working with a new team writing, re-mixing, and recording with established artists both here and in America. Their sample album and website (http://thebomb-factory.co.uk) have received very favourable comments and led to increasing recognition of their talents and new opportunities.

A Spy In Our Midst
Keith Marsh

That was the headline in the *Daily Echo* on 19 September 1999 as it told the story of Melita Norwood, an 87-year old woman living in Bexley Heath, London. The previous week she had been exposed as having been a Soviet spy for over 40

Above: *Thornhill Road, now Upper Deacon Road, c.1910, with Thornhill Cottage just visible through the trees.*

Left: *Melita attended St James' School, West End, and is seen here in the middle row, fifth from right.*
(WEST END LOCAL HISTORY SOCIETY)

years, becoming the KGB's most important woman British agent; she could have advanced the Soviet nuclear bomb programme by as much as five years. So what was her local connection?

Born in Pokesdown in 1912, she had a Latvian father, Alexander Sirnis, and an English mother, Gertrude, plus a sister, also Gertrude, and a half-brother. The family moved to West End, and have been described as 'self-sufficient and industrious'. Melita and her sister attended St James's School, but were kept out of religious assemblies because of their parents' socialist sympathies. In fact her father had fiercely left-wing views and was a pioneer of the British communist movement, translating the works of Lenin and Trotsky that had to be smuggled out of Russia. From 1922 until 1932 Gertrude and the children lived in Thornhill Cottage, Deacon Road, Bitterne, where they lived with Henri Valois. This large cottage stood in 1½ acres of land where High Meadow is now located. Melita attended Southampton Grammar School for Girls, where she became head girl, then spent a year at Southampton University studying Latin and logic.

In 1937 Melita got a job in Euston, London, as a secretary in the general office of the British Non-Ferrous Metals Association, a trade organisation co-ordinating research for atomic weapons. After five years she had been promoted to personal assistant to a director. As a highly trusted employee, sensitive documents crossed her desk daily. This was despite concerns over her links to communist groups: she had secretly joined the Communist party in the 1930s. About this time she agreed to work for the KGB with the code-name Hola, but always refused payment saying that she was working for the ideology not financial reward. In 1945 she passed vital information about Britain's atom bomb to Soviet agents via clandestine meetings, enabling the Soviet Union to build an exact replica within a year. She maintained that with the super powers equalling each other, nuclear war was less likely;

her critics say she contributed to the 'arms race'.

Eventually, after further enquiries and fears about her sympathies, Hola's access to secrets was blocked in 1949, and her vetting clearance was revoked in 1951. In 1962 her clearance was again rejected and three years later MI5 identified her as a spy, yet chose not to interview or arrest her as this would have jeopardised other counter-intelligence activities. In fact Hola continued passing information to the KGB until she retired in 1972, and was awarded the KGB's highest decoration, the Order of the Red Banner; she last visited Russia in 1979.

In 1992 former KGB archivist Vasili Mitrokhin defected, handing MI6 six trunks of information about Russian agents. This included proof of Hola's activities, though MI6 decided it was not enough to prosecute her. However, in 1996 the Foreign Secretary decided to make the archives public, and journalists found the story, resulting in the BBC interviewing Hola, and her alleged confession being considered as evidence against her. She was exposed as a spy on 11 September 1999 but the Solicitor General decided she would not be prosecuted.

So after 40 years of spying she was still living in the same spartan house bought 50 years earlier with her teacher husband Hilary, the only person who had known of her activities, although he disapproved. She died on 28 June 2005.

Captain Haddock and a *Titanic* Connection
Keith Marsh

The first captain of RMS *Titanic* was Herbert James Haddock, CBE, RNR (who lived at 4 Bitterne Way for over 20 years) although he was Master for just one week, from 25 March 1912 until her delivery to White Star Line on 1 April. On that date he retook command of the *Titanic's* sister, RMS *Olympic*, from Captain Smith, who took over the *Titanic*. The *Olympic*, captained by Haddock, was on route from

A rare photograph of a camera-shy Captain Haddock (with coat) outside the Titanic Court of Enquiry.
(SO'TON CITY MUSEUMS, BURROUGH HILL COLLECTION)

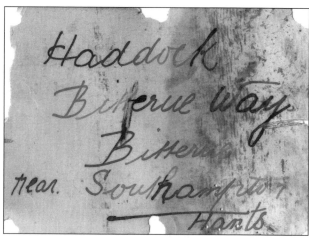

A handwritten luggage label for Captain Haddock's home in Bitterne, written on a breakfast menu card from the RMS Olympic *dated 2 November 1914.*   (BRIAN TICEHURST)

New York to Southampton when the *Titanic* was sunk. She was 500 miles away and set course for the *Titanic*, but resumed her passage when informed there was nothing more that could be done; she did, however, assist with communications. When the *Olympic* arrived in Southampton she was fitted with more lifeboats, but some of the crew, still concerned by the lack of lifesaving equipment, went on strike; non-union firemen were brought in, resulting in a mutiny and the arrest of 53 men.

Captain Haddock was a very modest man yet made the news again seven weeks after the *Titanic* disaster, when he nearly ran the *Olympic* on to rocks near Land's End due to a navigational error. The previous September the *Olympic* (then under the command of Captain Smith) had been in a collision in the Solent with the cruiser HMS *Hawke*, which suffered severe damage to its bow. The subsequent investigation aroused much interest due to the theory that the large amount of water displaced by the *Olympic* led to suction, which drew the Hawke off course. It also spawned a conspiracy theory that the identities of *Titanic* and *Olympic* were switched for insurance purposes, due to the damage received by the *Olympic*.

In October 1914 Captain Haddock and the *Olympic* rescued 600 men from the sinking super-dreadnought HMS *Audacious*, which had struck a mine leaving Loch Swilly; a tow was also attempted but failed, and *Audacious* eventually sank. As the ship was only 14 months old the story was hushed up!

The *Olympic* was converted to a troop ship during the First World War and Captain Haddock was put in command of a dummy fleet of wooden dreadnoughts and battle cruisers at Belfast. Despite requests, the Admiralty would not release him to command the *Britannic*, which had been converted to a hospital ship, and it seems he did not rejoin the White Star Line. He died on 5 October 1946.

Sports Personalities
Ken Prior

The Bitterne area has a rich and varied sporting history with figures of national importance intertwined with local sporting personalities.

Terry Paine, MBE, Southampton and England, was a resident of Bitterne and was frequently seen around. A speedy right-wing football player, he signed for 'Saints' in 1957, playing 763 matches and scoring 160 goals. In 1966 he was influential in the club reaching Division One for the first time. His debut for England was in 1963, in his second international he scored a hat-trick, and in the 1966 World Cup he was in the side that beat Mexico 2–0. From 1966 to the late 1970s he was living at 72 Glenfield Crescent, a house named Garrincha after the Brazilian international footballer; can you imagine an England star living in Bitterne today? Terry was a fine winger for Southampton and playing on the other wing in the same team was John Sydenham, brought up in West End Road. John was a paper boy for the Sperring's news agency and attended St Mary's College.

Don Roper, who played for ten years with Arsenal, helping them win two league championships, as well as playing for Southampton, started his football career as a 16 year-old playing for Bitterne Nomads alongside locals Percy Foot, Stan Bunday, Tom Sperring, Norman Catlin and Ron Hinton.

Darren Anderton, the Portsmouth, Tottenham and England footballer was brought up in Bitterne, attending Bitterne Park School. He played football as a boy for Albion at Riverside Park. It is also known that Darren, along with brothers Ryan and Scott, were frequent visitors to the local pitch and putt course.

Riverside Park was also home to many local evening league cricket teams which curiously included Martin Chivers, the Southampton, Tottenham and England footballer. Kevin Keegan,

Successful competitive cyclist Tommy Salter in 1920. His cycle, which looks extremely basic by today's standards, had wooden wheel rims.

BLHS member Cecil Bailey of Kathleen Road was a speedway star, riding for Southampton Saints Speedway Team 1948–51.

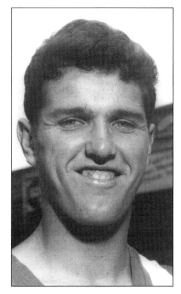

Terry Paine, 1966 Football World Cup star who lived in Glenfield Crescent.

On 2 May 1976 the F.A. Cup came to Bitterne, when the winning Southampton FC team from the previous day paraded round the city. Team member Nick Homes attended St Mary's College. This picture was taken from the roof of the bowling alley by Eric Thompson.

most famously known as England manager and footballer, also played evening league cricket at Riverside whilst on Southampton's books. On the other side of the coin Bob Cottam, the Hampshire and England cricketer, played football at Riverside Park on occasions during the 1960s.

Peter Sainsbury, a leading cricketer and coach with Hampshire CCC, captained Bitterne Park School at football and cricket. The great all-rounder Arthur Holt, prominent as a player and coach with Hampshire CCC, as well as playing football for the 'Saints', started his football playing in the Church League for Bitterne Congregationals.

Ted Drake started his football days as a boy at the Veracity Ground in the late 1920s, before going on to play for Arsenal, then managing Chelsea from 1952 to 1961, followed by a spell at Barcelona as assistant manager. The Veracity Ground was the starting point for many local lads. It included an enclosed football ground with a stand before 1925, hosting Hampshire and Southern League teams like Bitterne Guild, Woolston and Thornycroft's.

Other Bitterne schoolboy footballers include Ian Baird, Pat Earles and Nick Holmes who all attended St Mary's College before going on to play for Southampton.

Bill Dodgin, manager of Fulham, Queen's Park Rangers, Northampton and Brentford, started his playing days at St Mary's College.

George Horsfall, Southampton FC trainer throughout the 1960s and 1970s, lived in Glenfield Avenue.

Aaron Flahavon, Portsmouth goalkeeper, tragically killed at the peak of his career in a car crash, and his brother Daryl, still playing in goal for Southend, were both brought up on the Bitterne housing estate of Harefield.

Sholing Sports played at Birch Lawn in North East Road until the early 1990s. The site has now been built on with roads such as Vokes Close.

During the 1980s a strong Sholing Sports team attracted hundreds of spectators to watch local stars such as Ian Bampton, Steve Barnes, Mark Barber and Dave Poole. Sholing honours included Hampshire Senior Cup, Hampshire League Championships, and Russell Cotes Cup. Graham Roberts, at one time manager of Scottish club Clyde, started at Sholing Sports and went on to play for Tottenham and England.

Dave Munks, former Sheffield United and Portsmouth footballer of the 1960s and early 1970s, who famously beat George Best in a poll for 'Best Looking Footballer', was manager at Bitterne Leisure Centre after retiring from football.

Bitterne Leisure Centre was also the venue that set Helen Troke on the road to badminton fame. She developed into Britain's leading player, winning Commonwealth gold medals in 1982 and 1986.

Cecil Bailey, local resident who still lives in Sholing, was a leading rider with Southampton Speedway teams. He rode in many different countries, including Italy, racing in the Milan Stadium to let the Italians know what speedway was all about. Riding in Amsterdam, Cecil managed to fall into a canal. In Edinburgh he survived a crash, narrowly avoiding a neck injury, and at Plymouth he was a fifth of a second away from breaking the track record. His happiest times were racing alongside Frank Goulden, Alf Kaines, Tom Oakley, Jim Squibb, Alf Bottoms, George Bason, Tony Buxey, Alf Boyce and Bill Thatcher.

The Sad Tale of Richard Parker
Jim Brown

A modest tombstone in Peartree Churchyard bears the inscription:

Sacred to the memory of Richard Parker, aged 17, who died at sea July 25th 1884, after nineteen days dreadful suffering in an open boat in the tropics, having been wrecked in the yacht Mignonette. *'Though He slay me yet will I trust in him', Job XIII.5. 'Lord lay not this sin to their charge', Acts VII.60.*

The yacht *Mignonette* was built at Brightlingsea, Essex, in 1867, a 33 ton yawl-rigged vessel, 52ft long with a 7ft 5in draught and 12ft 5in beam. In 1883 she was bought by wealthy Australian lawyer and politician, John Henry Want, who employed Tom Dudley, an experienced sailing master, to sail it to Australia. The terms were £100 in advance, with another £100 on delivery to Sydney, a worthwhile commission despite the fact that this included payment for crew and provisions.

Thomas Riley Dudley was born in April 1853 at Tollesbury, Essex, the youngest son of a local customs officer. His mother died when Tom was six years old; three years later he signed on as a boy on a fishing smack, progressing from ordinary seaman to first mate on various ships, eventually becoming a sailing master. He was short, stocky, with reddish hair and a beard, teetotal, and described as 'sober, steady, respectable and God-fearing'.

On 5 May 1884 Dudley, with brothers Jim and William Frost, sailed the *Mignonette* from Tollesbury to Southampton in preparation for her voyage to Australia, but as the short trip (during a severe thunderstorm) revealed defects, she was taken to J.G. Fay & Co. at Northam, for repairs. The Frost brothers decided against continuing, so Dudley engaged James Haynes, a master mariner from Devon, as mate, but he departed the following morning; probably he too was unhappy about the yacht's condition. A new crew was found: 37-year old Edwin Stephens as mate for £8 a month, 38-year old Edmund (Ned) Brooks, as able seaman for £5.10s. a month, and 17-year-old Richard Parker, as ordinary seaman for £1.15s a month.

Stephens was born in Southampton, married with five children living in Northumberland Road, Newtown. Brooks was born in Brightlingsea, but had moved to Southampton for summer work on yachts and winter on Union Line ships; he lodged at the County Tavern. At the last minute Brooks tried to withdraw from the trip having been told by friends that it was foolhardy, but Dudley persuaded him to stay.

Richard Parker was born on 31 March 1867 in Itchen Ferry, the youngest son of Daniel 'Old Chick' Parker, a yacht skipper and well-known cricketer on Peartree Green. Richard's mother Mary died in April 1874, and his father in May 1881, leaving Richard, three elder brothers, Daniel, Stephen and William, and younger sister Edith. Richard was cared for by a yacht skipper, Captain Jack Mathews and his wife, who tried to prevent him sailing on the *Mignonette*, fearing the vessel unsuitable for such a trip, but on 15 May 'Dickey' signed on without telling them; actually, being illiterate, he 'made his mark'.

Just after 5.00p.m. on 19 May 1884, having been towed down the River Itchen by the tug *Meryphic*, *Mignonette* set sail, passing the Needles at midnight. Making steady progress, averaging about 100 miles a day, they reached Madeira at midnight on 1 June. Although staying there only 12 hours taking on water and fresh provisions, Richard sent his first letter to Captain and Mrs Mathews, probably copying a draft written by Dudley. He wrote: 'I am happy and comfortable and all on board are well. We have had a fine and pleasant voyage all the way.' The weather had been beautiful, and it is known that Dudley, a devout Anglican, had taken his prayer books and held a service on board every Sunday.

A fortnight after leaving Madeira they were seen by the *Bride of Lorne*, outwardbound from Liverpool, this being the last recorded sighting of the *Mignonette*. On 17 June she crossed the equator; in 14 days the wind having strengthened into a substantial gale with heavy seas, the captain decided, on 3 July, to shorten sail and ride out the storm but the pounding sea damaged timbers of the yacht's hull, causing a leak with which her small-capacity bilge pumps were unable to cope. At 4.30p.m. on 5 July, hundreds of miles south-east of Trinidad, she was struck by a particularly heavy wave, breaching her stern.

Dudley gave orders to launch the ship's dinghy and abandon ship. The mahogany dinghy was only 13ft long, with a 4ft beam and depth of just 20ins. Acting on instructions, Richard threw a cask of water into the sea rather than into the dinghy, which would have holed the bottom of the ¼-inch thick timber, anticipating that it would float and be recoverable. With the *Mignonette* awash the crew climbed into the dinghy whilst Dudley grabbed his sextant, the binnacle compass and a few tins but, after frantic shouts that the vessel was going down, he fell into the dinghy losing all but two of them. The dinghy was just a short distance away when the *Mignonette* sank.

Baling out in a turbulent sea they were fully occupied, quickly tracing and plugging a leak, and

This pictorial record of the events appeared in the Illustrated Police News *on 20 September 1884.*

making a sea anchor using wood from the binnacle and a grating that had floated clear.

After the storm, soaking wet, cold and dejected, the four encountered further ordeals when a large shark bumped their small boat, the cask of water had disappeared and the two tins of food were one-pound tins of turnip! One tin lasted for two days; later a turtle came close enough to be caught, cut into strips and eaten raw, together with the remaining turnip. Sheer necessity forced them to overcome the initial repugnance of drinking their own urine in a desperate attempt to stay alive.

By the fifteenth day, rainwater, gathered during sporadic storms, had just kept them alive, with no turnip or turtle or further supplies in sight. The young Richard fared the worst; trying to satisfy his raging thirst by drinking seawater he was racked with pain, barely conscious and delirious. For five days they continued suffering torturous blistering heat by day and freezing cold at night, the agony of parched throats becoming unbearable.

Thus, nearly three weeks after the *Mignonette* sank, the fateful decision was made, detailed in Dudley's subsequent personal narrative:

We went from the 15th day to the 20th day without any food at all, or drink, and by that time we had begun to look each other in the face, very black. The boy, who had drunk some seawater, had said 'We shall all die', and I remarked 'We shall have to draw lots boys'. This was ignored by all and they said 'We had better die together', to which I replied 'So let it be, but it is hard for four to die when perhaps one might save the rest.'

On either the 19th or 20th day the boy was lying in the bottom of the boat, gasping for breath and nearly dead. At about three o'clock in the morning I said to the Mate 'What is to be done? I believe the boy is dying. You have a wife and five children; I have a wife and three children.' I said that human flesh had been eaten before. Brooks said he could not do it and Stephens said we would see a ship the next day. We arranged if nothing was in sight by sunrise and no rain came, to put the poor lad Parker out of his misery. At about 8.00a.m. I had a last look round to see if there was anything in sight, but there was nothing. I offered up a prayer most fervently that God above might forgive us for such an act, and then I knelt down by the boy and said 'Now, Dick my boy, your time has come'. He murmured 'What, me Sir?' I put the penknife into his throat and he was dead instantly.

The survivors' maddest craving being drink, Dudley caught and divided the gushing blood. Brooks, who had retreated and covered his face, also had some. They cut out the liver and heart, devouring them hot, and continued eating the body until 29 July when Brooks sighted the German barque *Moctezuma*.

After 90 minutes of hope, fear, prayer and feeble rowing, they were eventually seen, rescued and taken on board.

Dudley knew that he had acted correctly to save the lives of Stephens, Brooks and himself, telling his rescuers the whole truth and accounting for the boy's mutilated remains of a rib and a few fragments of flesh, which were thrown into the sea. The dinghy was taken on board as evidence but the three emaciated men were treated very kindly on the ship during the voyage to Falmouth.

In an excerpt from the full story of this heartrending tale, it is sadly not possible to recount in detail the happenings after the *Moctezuma* berthed on 6 September 1884; suffice to say that the unfortunate mariners were arrested, much to their surprise, and subsequently charged with 'willfully, feloniously and malice aforethought' killing Richard Parker on the high seas. Brooks was later discharged but Dudley and Stephens were sent for trial in November. The case was referred to the High Court when, on 4 December, the two accused appeared before the Lord Chief Justice of England (Lord Coleridge) and four judges of the Queen's Bench Division. Following much lengthy and prolonged legal argument they were found guilty of murder and sentenced to death by hanging, though the Lord Chief Justice made a recommendation for mercy. Six days later the Home Secretary advised Queen Victoria to suspend the death sentence and their sentence was commuted to six months' imprisonment.

Released from Holloway Prison on 20 May 1885, Stephens returned to Northumberland Road where he lived until 1887, dying in July 1914 in Hull. Dudley, however, emigrated to Sydney, Australia, with his family but became a victim of bubonic plague on 22 February 1900. Brooks died of a heart attack in the Parish Infirmary on 22 July 1919, aged 73.

John Haskins, a London engineer, paid for the memorial to Richard on his parents' unmarked grave in Peartree Churchyard, the scripture passage being added at the request of Richard's brother William, showing that the family understood the seamen's predicament.

The final twist in this sad tale lies in the amazing coincidence that a book by Edgar Alan Poe was published in 1838, nearly 50 years before this tragedy. *The Narrative of Arthur Gordon Pym of Nantucket* tells the story of four shipwrecked seamen who spent 16 days at sea, six without food or water apart from a tortoise. They decided that one should die to preserve the others and they drew lots. The seaman who made the suggestion drew the shortest wood splinter was killed and his body was eaten over the next four days. The name of the fictitious seaman: Richard Parker!

Chapter Nine

Tarring the Roads
Tom Webb's Memories

Tom Webb, who was born in a thatched cottage at the (then) top end of Pound Street, in 1910, remembers:

Tarring the roads used to interest me intensely. 'Horlock's Cut' was where the gang commenced their operations with the engine. It was towed to this quiet spot, together with several wooden barrels containing the tar, which had to be emptied into the tank on iron wheels which clanked as it was drawn along the roads by a horse (no motorisation in those days). A fire was lit and contained in a box at the rear of the tank to heat the tar, enabling it to be sprayed onto the roads by a pump, also attached to the vehicle and operated by turning a wheel. One man controlled the horse's movements, another turned the pump wheel, while a third, wearing goggles, directed the fine spray of extremely pungent liquid to and fro over half of the road's surface. I used to be exceedingly disappointed if, for some reason, operations were suspended for several days.

Tom Webb, always a keen cyclist.

Glenfield Memories
Keith Marsh

In 1955, when I was a few months old, my parents bought a house in Glenfield Avenue, built by local firm Cole & Son (who also built Coleson Road, hence its name), so I was brought up in the area. Cars could turn right down Lances Hill then, or turn left, then right up Little Lances Hill. Pocket money was spent at the Monastery Stores on Spangles, sweet cigarettes and gobstoppers, or on caps for the cowboy gun. Saturday mornings were spent at the Broadway cinema at Portswood, watching a selection of children's serials and getting another ABC badge. This entailed a trip on the No. 14 bus. Until the route was extended to Townhill Park it terminated at the bottom of Witts Hill, so we could watch for the bus going past the end of the road one way and leave home knowing we had time to walk around to the stop and catch it when it came back. And if we did miss it, the old 'Guy Arabs' crawled up Mousehole Lane so slowly that we could run and jump on.

The local play area was the wooded slope off Mousehole Lane, parallel with Neva Road; we were off-roading there long before mountain bikes were invented. Deepdene provided the setting for many hours of fun, with its trees, rope swings, air-raid shelters and the orchard over the wall. On the way was a field (Beechwood Gardens now) which usually contained a large white horse which was always pleased to be made a fuss of. We could always find something interesting in Hum Hole, although the mud there was pungent! Football was played on the one-in-five grass slope in Mousehole Lane (much to the annoyance of nearby residents) or in the bottom corner of the St Mary's College playing-field (to the annoyance of the Brothers).

Another memory is of the tradesmen who called, highlighting the fact that few people then had a car. Len the milkman delivered daily from the Brown & Harrison's depot at Benhams Farm (later South Coast Dairies). In the 1950s his horse would pull its cart on to the next gate upon Len's whistle; later he had a battery-assisted hand cart with a curved handle at the front. Then there was the Mother's Pride baker who called twice a week and the fishmonger in his Morris van each Thursday. Another Morris van was driven by Harold Child, the grocer at Bitterne Park, who picked up the order on the way to work and delivered our groceries on the way home to High View Way. His shop was where the launderette is now, and his stockroom was in the cellar, accessed via a trapdoor in the floor; the HSE would not allow that now! Richard Neale, who took over the butchers in Brook Road from Mr Horlock, employed a lad until the late 1970s to deliver by bicycle, which had a huge basket on the front. A delivery we did not use as much as we children would have liked was the Corona lorry, with

A Guy Arab bus of Southampton Corporation being helped up Mousehole Lane after a fall of snow in 1954. The van of Mr Snook the baker is parked on the left. (SOUTHERN EVENING ECHO)

An archetype of the many 1930s houses in the area, this is the Marsh family's home c.1960. Note the Airey prefabricated house in Rossington Avenue behind.

Keith Marsh, a proud member of the 3rd Itchen North (Bitterne) Wolf Cubs. Jen Upton, the young leader at the time, has now given over 40 years of service to the Scout movement for which she was awarded the MBE in 2004.

crates of soft drinks in a multitude of colours and flavours arranged along the side; the glass bottles were refundable for 3d.

Finally there was Mr Witt the greengrocer who called twice a week in his grey Bedford van. He said that Witts Hill was named after his family, but in the 1960s he had a smallholding at Hedge End. When we had a glut of raspberries, Mr Witt was happy to buy them for resale. I have a special fondness for him as he gave me my first Saturday job: I'd meet him at 11 o'clock in Brownlow Avenue, work along that road, then Redlands Drive, calling on customers to collect the order, weighing it up on scales at the back of the van, then delivering back. We'd finish for lunch, then at 2 o'clock I'd meet him to do Glenfield Avenue, Cobden Crescent and Glenfield Crescent. I recall one elderly lady in the latter who always had a dozen brown eggs; trays of eggs were piled on the van's passenger seat and I had to go through them selecting the brownest. I remember the thrill of hanging on to the back of the van as we moved further along the street. Mr Witt was also the 'clearing house' for Brooke Bond tea cards, exchanging swaps for those you didn't have. Having said that, swaps were always useful at school for playing 'flicks'.

Then there were the services that came around: the van from Redcote Convent Laundry, the dustbin men (who emptied our bin into their own, which in turn they emptied into a truck with large up-and-over metal shutters) and John Steward the chimney-sweep who lived in a prefab bungalow on Witts Hill (what excitement when his brush emerged from the chimney pot!). Perhaps the most skilled was the lamp man on his bicycle, who cycled past the street lamps and flicked the on/off switch at the top with a long pole without dismounting! You don't notice the gradual changes until suddenly...

I went to Beechwood Junior School down the other end of our road. The headmaster was Eric Gadd, and we left at the same time, July 1966, he to retire and I to go to comprehensive school. It was not until years later when I developed an interest in local history that I realised what an expert he was on the topic. I have a few recollections of him: receiving handwriting credit slips from him in assembly (he was a staunch advocate of neat writing), a weekly lesson at which he taught our class several poems which we recited at the school concert (including 'There were three sailors from Bristol city...') and his party piece: asking two children to each draw a line on the blackboard, which he would then incorporate into a drawing, whatever the shape. Beechwood at this time had four or five classes per year; the Thornhill estate was being built but not the schools, so a fleet of double-decker buses brought the children to ours. Buses were also used each week to take us to the sports ground in Wynter Road; as one school's bus left from the Wynter Road gate, the next school would be arriving at the one in Hatley Road! At least the toilets there have improved!

A Stroll Round the Park
John Edgar Mann

If you want to upset a native of Bitterne Park try referring to Bitterne Triangle without the vital word 'Park'. Come to think of it, such a reference would probably upset a upset a born 'Bitternite' equally, for Bitterne Park is an entity – and a sizeable one.

Though Bitterne was, and in many ways still is, a village, Bitterne Park is essentially a suburb, and a far-spreading one at that. Yet it has its roots in an imperial past, its serviceable and sometimes modestly elegant homes sitting on land where Romans trod.

The block of flats known as Bitterne Manor House near Northam Bridge pinpoints the site of the Roman settlement of Clausentum. Its very foundations are Roman. The developers of this mini suburb of Bitterne Manor, cut off from Bitterne Park by the rail line to Portsmouth, gave two of their street names Roman reminders (Rampart Road and Vespasian Road after the general in charge of the area who later became Emperor).

Bitterne Manor and Bitterne Park are historically linked. The manor of Bitterne was granted to the bishops of Winchester by Edward I in 1284. Apart from one isolated property deal successive bishops held it until 1868. In the days of the prelates the area really was a park. Cattle and deer roamed over what is now suburbia, and there was hunting with dogs.

Bitterne Park and the manor area ceased to be countryside rather later than many other districts. While admitting that the neighbourhood hasn't the elegance of, say, Highfield, it has its charm. There are still copses here and there, and trees are plentiful on the Park's dips and heights (I've always liked the houses designed in semi-Tudor style by Frank Lowe, uncle of local historian Eric Wyeth Gadd).

Never a village as such (its centre was the Manor House), its focal point is now the Bitterne Park Triangle. And if you wanted to see an ideal suburban shopping centre then this is it.

As a newcomer once remarked, the Triangle lacks few retail essentials, though maybe there might be considered to be one too many takeaways! There's certainly a community feel about the place: witness the doomed fight, mirrored nationwide, to save the branch post office. As elsewhere the powers-that-be failed to recognise its social context.

In its municipal way it's an idyllic spot. Visitors are greatly taken with the clock tower overlooking the river. Previously (until 1934) it graced the junction of Above Bar and New Road.

Traffic problems caused the move, though in any case the working horses it was built to serve had more or less departed. The tower, bequeathed to the town by Mrs Henrietta Sayers in 1889, boasts a reminder of its original animal purpose. A tablet

Standard 1 class at Bitterne Park School pose for the photographer in March 1922.

Left: *An early view of Bitterne Park Triangle, with Lankester & Crook's Bitterne Park Stores and the prominent Bitterne Park Hotel. The clock tower was moved there in 1934.*

The parade of shops at the bottom of Lances Hill, with T.H. Longmore (tailor, outfitter, hosier, hatter) on the corner of Athelstan Road. Note the motorcycle and sidecar in the entrance to MacNaghten Road (far right) and the end of the tramlines down Bullar Road in the foreground. (DOUGLAS HEWITT)

With its ornamental lights, tiling and curved windows, the art nouveau style of the former chemists shop is a gem amongst the shops at Bitterne Park Triangle. It dates from c.1912.

With its towers and castellations this lodge and gateway to Midanbury House had the air of a real castle. It was demolished c.1939 and the Castle Inn built on the site.

quotes Psalm 50:10, 'For every beast of the forest is mine, and the cattle upon a thousand hills'.

Newcomers to the Park often comment on its paucity of pubs. A couple of coaching inns and one or two smaller hostelries, and that's that. Yet Bitterne Park stretches far. Compare it with St Denys over the

river, a real ale-drinker's paradise. The answer to this mystery lies in the origins of the suburb.

In 1882 the National Liberal Land Company bought 317 acres of farmland which would be developed into what we now know as Bitterne Park. These were the days when the electoral register was based on property qualifications. The company had Nonconformist leanings, which accounted for the presence on the board of a temperance representative to see that drinking could be kept within bounds.

The Liberals didn't just provide residential sites. They also made the gift of a free bridge across the Itchen to St Denys. As a result they weren't popular with the owners of nearby Northam Bridge who charged tolls. Cobden Bridge, named after radical reformer Richard Cobden, was reconstructed in 1928.

Thorold Road derives its name from Professor Thorold Rogers, chairman of the National Liberal Land Company. Other champions of the people immortalised in road names on the estate include *Rural Rides* author William Cobbett (Cobbett Road) and Liberal leader Sir William Harcourt (Harcourt Road).

Progress brought social problems, as it often does. Old people used to speak of those terrible days when there were battles on the new bridge between rival gangs of hooligans from Bitterne and St Denys. Many locals dismissed these incidents as mythical. Exaggerated they may have been, but the local press reported them. One reporter seemed particularly upset when a dog was thrown off the bridge.

Bitterne Park's riparian setting means boats. Many of the homes in Whitworth Crescent had their own moorings. So did the Bitterne Park Hotel. Some recent houses in the road, too, are similarly equipped. The Itchen MP, John Denham, lives in one such development. Edwardian postcards show that Bitterne Park had its own Water Carnival. Bring it back, say I!

Anomalies gather round history. Myths cling like barnacles around local history in particular. A friend surfing the internet found the origin of Bitterne attributed to the bird bittern, the word Park being added because of the number of bitterns to be found along the river! No avian connection has yet been proved.

Bitterne probably derives from a word for a storehouse (there was a salt works at Bitterne Manor in medieval times). References to 'Bytterne Parke' go back further than one might suppose.

Passers-by reading the historical plaque of the Station Hotel in Bitterne Park's Bullar Road were met with a string of inaccuracies, now put right by a new plaque.

Several of the gentry who retired to stately Bitterne area piles made their fortunes in India: David Lance (Chessel House), Nathaniel Middleton (Townhill Park House) and a former East India Company surgeon, James Dott (Bitterne Grove).

With more equality of opportunity, men from

'Over the Hill', this distinctive art deco house in Mousehole Lane, was designed for himself by local architect Leslie Kimber c.1935.

Mr and Mrs Rowe (later Mrs Hallet) at Shephard's Cottage c.1916.

humbler backgrounds rose to high positions. Bitterne Park gave us several such men. Stanley Ridges (Hillside Avenue) tap-danced his way from Broadway to Hollywood, settling into middle-aged character parts; Kenneth East (St Catherine's Road) joined the diplomatic corps, retiring as ambassador to Iceland; and His Honour Michael McMullan (Dell Road) became a circuit judge.

Dell Road also produced the thriller novelist Brian Freemantle; MacNaghten Road sired the great Olympic hurdler Donald Finlay; and from Cobbett Road came Roy Chadwick who designed the Lancaster bomber (who later lived in Chessel Avenue).

Some people more than made the grade by staying at home like the Clarks, 'the family that built Midanbury', whose 'Guv'nor', J.W.H. Clark, lived to be a centenarian. At one time the family firm were building 150 houses a year within the parish boundaries.

The developers of the Davis estate off Mousehole Lane and Witts Hill have left behind a reminder of the pre-war architectural style that had its origins in the Bauhaus School of Design. The area's number one example is a fine house near the back entrance of St Mary's College named 'Over the Hill'.

Nevertheless, some of the old houses are disappearing to make way for flats and the Bitterne Park Residents Association has already expressed its concern.

The Shephards of Shephard's Cottage
Keith Marsh

Commonly known as Shephard's Cottage after a family who lived there from the early 1800s, No. 602 Bitterne Road East is unique in that it is the sole surviving example of a cob and thatch cottage in Southampton. Unlike most of the country Southern England has sparse deposits of the stone suitable for building, so cottages were built of locally produced brick, or cob; where stone or slate was used it had to be brought in from afar. Cob was made from mud, straw and often animal dung, built up in layers on a

timber-framed building; a lime-wash was then applied to allow the cob to retain a little moisture whilst deterring rodents, and so giving the distinctive white colour.

In the mid-1800s the Shephard family owned brickworks on both sides of Bitterne Road, in the valley between Bitterne and Thornhill, so the area became known as Shephard's Bottom. The one adjacent to their cottage was Bunkers Hill Brickworks (the road to Thornhill being known as Bunkers Hill) whilst to the north of the road was Redcote Brickworks. In the late 1850–60s these brickyards were supplying 1,000 bricks a day towards the building of the Royal Victoria Hospital, Netley, and Ralph Shephard (as one of the building's six main contractors) was presented with a large coloured print of the hospital by Queen Victoria.

In 1897 'Old' Jim Shephard donated £100 in bricks and cash towards the building of the new Bitterne Infants' School. However, living in Botley Road (as this section of Bitterne Road was once called) overcrowding at the school meant that when his grandson Walter was old enough to attend, he was referred to

Shephard's Cottage undergoing restoration, August 1987.

Sholing Boys' School; that was until Walter's father, 'Young' Jim, reminded Mr Cook the headmaster of the gift!

Good fortune did not last though. A local builder went bankrupt in a building slump, and Shephard's only got 4d. in the pound of the £400 owing for bricks, i.e. about £7. With no houses being built, the brickyards were sold, Bunker Hill (now called Thornhill) Brickworks to Jack Horley, and Redcote to Brazier & Son Ltd. George Cole, who was captain of the Bitterne Rifle Club, was manager of the latter, and the sandpit there became the club's rifle range. Of course the slump eventually came to an end and bricks were wanted again, but the Shephards were now employed elsewhere.

By the 1930s Kathleen Rowe was bringing up her family at the cottage. On one occasion she called the doctor to one of her children and he commented 'It's a wonder you aren't all dead. This place is built of clay!' James Shephard and family lived in an adjacent house, the garden of which they used to full advantage: vegetables were grown (which Granny Shephard sold at the weekly market at Northam), and pigs, chickens, ducks and a cow where kept. When Kathy paid Granny the weekly rent of 10s.6d. (52½p) she received six newly laid eggs as a receipt.

During the 1930s Sunningdale Gardens was built on the Redcote Brickworks, whilst it was planned to build Exleigh Avenue through to Bursledon Road, over the Thornhill Brickworks and the allotments. But the Second World War interrupted plans. Bricks and vegetables were both needed, and Braziers took over the brickfield until Exleigh Close was built in about 1960, the amending of the name reflecting its truncation.

In 1945 Ronald Watts and his wife Queenie moved into Shephard's Cottage and by this time it had a water tap in the yard, making trips to the well a thing of the past. But it still had only bucket lavatories – difficult in icy weather and unpleasant when hot! The tap, though, had not been installed properly, the sump in the yard becoming foul-smelling in wet weather, and the Council inspector ordered Mr Shephard to attend to it.

During the early 1980s, the cottage and the adjacent market garden were sold to Wimpey for housing, and by 1986 Nursery Gardens had been built on the nursery and orchard. At their February 1986 meeting, BLHS members signed a petition to the Council urging the preservation of the cottage, the last cob-and-thatch cottage left in Bitterne. It was suggested that it could become a home for the society's collection of local artefacts, it having already been declared unfit for human habitation. At a meeting with the society and the Council, Wimpey valued the building and its plot at £30,000 and expressed their intent to sell or demolish it. In May came the news that the Council had been able to get the building a Grade II listing with the Department of the Environment, thus delaying demolition. Then in 1987 the cottage was sold to a private buyer. After re-thatching, modernisation, and adding an extension to accommodate the lacked facilities, it was put back on the market the next year for £100,000. It remains an idyllic chocolate-box cottage, though few of the thousands who pass within yards of it each day know of its existence.

Life after the *Titanic*
David Haisman

Halfway up the hill from Millers Pond was our house, 275 Spring Road, the house I was born in, the youngest son of a family of eight boys and two girls. It was 1938, the year the government announced that all Britons would be measured for gas masks, the police recommended that bicycles should have a red rear lamp and the top rate of income tax was 5s.6d.

My mother Edith was a real hero, as her background and upbringing were far removed from the life that she chose when she met and married my father. She had been born in 1896 in one of her father's hotels in Worcester, South Africa. She was the eldest daughter of a wealthy hotelier, Thomas Brown from Blackheath in London. With her convent education and wealthy parents there was little doubt that she would become a respected lady of the community, but, at the age of 15, a voyage on the ill-fated Titanic *was to change that.*

My mother and grandmother were taken to lifeboat 14 after the collision with an iceberg, and as they were being lowered down the ship's side, my grandfather cupped his hands around his mouth and shouted 'I'll see you in New York'. Those were the last words they would ever hear from him and is the title of the biography of my mother

The loss of my grandfather meant that the plan to buy a hotel in Seattle was no longer an option, and eventually my grandmother and mother returned to South Africa, finally settling in Johannesburg. Here my mother met my father, Frederick Haisman also from London, and in 1977 they celebrated their 60th wedding anniversary. My father had been good friends with Robert Hichens, the Titanic's *Quartermaster, who had been at the ship's wheel at the time of the collision with the iceberg. After the birth of my eldest brother, my mother and father moved to Southampton so my father could pursue his career as a draughtsman in the docks, and the engineering and shipbuilding industry. He would become employed on the New Docks scheme.*

Before the war our family lived in Leighton Road and Knighton Road, eventually moving to Spring Road, where the last three sons of the family were born. Millers Pond was a great attraction to all the kids in the neighbourhood and parents had their work cut out trying to keep them all away from the water. My elder

Above: *The Haisman children, c.1939.* Back row, left to right: *Leo, Geoff, Ken with John in front, Joy;* front row: *Donald, David and Brian* (on seat), *Dorothy.*

Yeovil Chase showing Harefield Junior School to the left and Infants' School to the right, nearing completion in 1956. On the left is the Bitterne Sports Ground and top centre, the Glebians Tennis Club. The route of the old drive to Harefield House is still discernable across the playing-field.

(EG PATIENCE / SO'TON CITY ARCHIVES)

David Haisman beside the name plate of the street named after his mother.

brothers would arrive home soaking wet, stinking, and covered in mud. Other favourite haunts were Lord Radstock's estate at Mayfield, Weston Shore, Sholing Brickyard and Wiffens sweetshop in Spring Road. Deciding to give Millers Pond a miss one day, my brother Geoffrey found the railway viaduct of greater interest and asked our mother if she would give him an old sheet. As it was nice weather she gave him one, thinking that he was going to make up a tent in the garden. Half an hour later excited neighbours were at our house shouting that Geoff was going to jump off the viaduct with a home-made parachute! But when he noticed a crowd gathering on the road 50ft below him with Mother waving and shouting frantically, he decided to abort his attempt at sky-diving that no doubt would have made him a candidate for the undertaker.

At the outbreak of the Second World War my three elder brothers, Fred, Ken and Geoff, were serving in the Royal Navy; the fourth, Leo, was in the Merchant Navy as a Bell Boy on the Aquitania. Our mother was more worried about him than the others as she knew that all the Bell Boys on the Titanic had drowned, and repeatedly reminded Leo to make sure that he knew where his lifeboat was! During the war my father was an air-raid warden and was out most nights ensuring the 'blackout' was observed. I remember his blue serge uniform and haversack, and a helmet with 'ARP' on it. He had a white plaited lanyard over his shoulder with a whistle on the end which he tucked into his top pocket. As the war raged on my father became employed by the Admiralty as a draughtsman in Portsmouth Dockyard, before being posted to Simonstown, South Africa in 1941. We followed a year later, six of us remaining children plus Mother, sailing on a troop ship called the Empire Grace. We sailed from Swansea at night, up the Irish Sea to Greenock where our ship embarked 500 troops for St Helena in the South Atlantic. At the start of the four-week voyage we were escorted by a huge convoy of naval warships and supply vessels but these left us one night off Portugal, and headed for Gibraltar, leaving us 'blacked out' and heading into the South Atlantic on our own. For several days we were shadowed by a German U-boat and dropped depth charges intermittently, during which we would get into our bunks with our clothes on or sit up on deck wearing life jackets, waiting for the 'all clear'. The terrible prospect of another ship wreck must have crossed our mother's mind many times over, but she never showed it!

Father's posting to Simonstown ended in 1948 and we returned to Southampton on the maiden voyage of Pretoria Castle. Arriving back we saw just how heavily bombed the town had been, resulting in an acute housing shortage. We were housed in a Nissen hut on a military campsite on Hoglands Park, left by the Americans. Then in 1950 we moved to Yeovil Chase, Harefield, now rapidly developing into a council-housing estate.

I joined Merry Oak School, forming a new group of friends and soon finding ways to pass the days when not at school. Opposite the houses in Yeovil Chase was a cornfield and beyond that towards West End Road was a copse and a disused tennis-court along with the remains of a pavilion and a derelict lodge house. Saturday mornings we attended the Ritz cinema to watch our favourite films, such as Flash Gordon and Roy Rogers with his horse Trigger. At weekends I helped our milkman who worked for Brown & Harrison's Dairies, an elderly man whom I only knew as Mr Austin, with a wonderful old horse called Lofty. Towards the end of the round Lofty would start heading back to the dairy perhaps thinking that it was time to put the nose bag on, so it was my responsibility to ensure that the brake was well applied and the reins kept tight.

I joined the Army Cadets at the drill hall behind the Red Lion, with Captain Lowe in command along with Sergeant Saunders, two very fair men. We learned a great deal about training, discipline and army life, and thoroughly enjoyed spit 'n' polishing boots, shining bugles, pressing tunics, and applying blanco to belts and gaiters. We were proud of our band; blasting away at band practice would rattle the front windows of Walsh's fish and chip shop almost opposite. We all looked forward to Saturday nights when we threw open the doors of the drill hall for the weekly 'Sixpenny Hop'. Our music came from a middle-aged trio, hell-bent on making as much noise as possible, banging the drums, squeezing and stretching the life out of an accordion, and plonking on the ivories; the middle-aged female pianist had a cigarette permanently jutting out of her mouth with the longest fag-ash ever seen refusing to drop off!

Living in Bitterne in the early 1950s were many characters including 'Roly' Rocket with his little horse and cart going up and down Lances Hill. A busy place was Fancy's, the little general store in Pound Street: a front room turned into a shop catering for most requirements, and in those days perhaps the only place in Bitterne open on Sundays.

On retiring from Thornycrofts in 1964, my father and mother moved to Australia but after five years in Brisbane they returned to live in senior citizens' accommodation in Westwood Road, Portswood. By strange coincidence, standing on their little balcony they could look over to Winn Road and see the house where Captain Smith of the Titanic used to live.

In 1984, after 72 years, the wreck of the Titanic was found and I can remember telling my mother and her utter disbelief. She became a bit of a celebrity, everyone wanting autographs and to meet her. Some 11 years later she received an invitation from the American salvage group to go on a short voyage of remembrance to the wreck site. Accompanied by my sister she flew to New York and there boarded the liner Island Breeze and headed into the North Atlantic to a position marked on the chart as 41° 46' N, 50° 14'W. On reaching this, the Island Breeze stopped; 13,000ft below them lay the wreck of the Titanic in total darkness and at peace. A service was held on the open decks for the 1,512 souls that had perished, and a loan piper played a lament. Mother was given a wreath to let fall onto the dark waters below in memory of her father, so her life's wish had been fulfilled.

The Titanic disaster was one of the world's worst shipping disasters, brought about by a complete disregard of the unpredictable forces of nature; no violent storm or heavy sea, no fog, snow or poor visibility, just one huge solitary iceberg, rock solid and threatening, drifting silently into the path of the Titanic. After the sinking that huge iceberg continued to drift silently south, getting smaller each day until eventually becoming part of the sea. As silently as that iceberg had appeared on the scene to cause such tragedy, it would disappear again, leaving no trace.

After Mother had passed away in 1997, Southampton City Council named a street in Freemantle after her, Edith Haisman Close. Just a short distance away is Norman Road where Fred Fleet lived, the lookout man who spotted the iceberg that sank the Titanic. He later took his own life. Today I live in West End, close to the cemetery where Captain Rostron of the Carpathia is buried. If it hadn't been for his actions, professionalism and bravery in rescuing the Titanic's survivors the loss of life would have been far greater.

Hum Hole's Biodiversity
Julian Cremona

I suppose it started with newts. The pond was in a small dip at the end of Glenfield Crescent. Here a turning circle neatly pushed up the soil into a small bank overgrown with gorse, hawthorn and other bushes. At the age of six or seven it seemed like a very steep incline as it descended down to the edge of the pond. Surrounded by trees it was dark and water dripped in from a stream on the upper edge. On the lower part of the valley a dam caused the stream to cascade down a small slope before it continued in a long straight run through the woods below Glenfield School. This dark stagnant pond was good, but not as good as the upper pond. One could jump over the dam and then cut through the woods until you came to the corner of the school copse and then up towards West End Road. I would climb up behind the houses, where the land opened out but to the right there was a steep (and it was steep!) slope down to the 'upper pond'. This was a gem where you were guaranteed a collection of enough newts to annoy Mum for weeks. Once back at home an old glass tank was filled with water and the 20 or so newts went in. You could put a cover over the top but by the next day half would have disappeared. In no time the house had newts turning up in all sorts of places. A quick clipped ear and I would not do it again (well, not for another few weeks or so).

Was Hum Hole the reason I always wanted to be a biologist? No one else in the family had the interest.

Above: Hum Hole today, neglect allowing nature to soften the man-made landscape.

Left: Hum Hole looking towards St Mary's College, before the bypass cut a swathe though it.

But living a few houses down from Hum Hole on Lances Hill, it was a budding ecologist's paradise in the 1950s. It may have started with Palmate Newts (as I later discovered) but the wealth of animal life that called the woodland and open heath home would today make it a listed site of special scientific interest. Dragonflies hunted along the woodland clearings; butterflies collected nectar from the blackberry flowers and weird but colourful flies hovered around the sand outcrops.

I could lose myself completely in Hum Hole. The dense undergrowth dulled the sound of the main road just a few hundred yards away. I became a Victorian expeditionary following the Amazon deep into the darkest depths of West End Road (behind Kitley Electrics). Exploration continues to be my second great love after being a biologist; funny, but no one else in my family likes going further than Bognor. The greater and lesser stag beetles were common in June and occasionally the large wood-boring Tanner Beetle would turn up. I remember White Admirals flying through the woods where the trees thinned out. Once a very rare Camberwell Beauty butterfly landed just yards away. I have never seen one since. The discovery of a small hornets' nest in an old oak tree near the lower pond was especially exciting though no one else thought so when I brought it home! I will never forget the thousands of tiny caterpillars I found in a bush one day. I took them home and kept them in my wardrobe so Mum would not find them. They lived well. One night I was awoken by a dreadful noise; they had all emerged into moths. There were so many that their wings drummed on the inside of the thin utility furniture. On my opening the door they all flew into the room, so I had to open the window and let them out. I identified them as Lackey Moths a little late: they like fruit trees and covered my dad's favourite nectarine tree in the garden with eggs. When it died having been completely defoliated, I blamed Hum Hole for cultivating a plague of locusts but I'm not sure he believed me.

All this was before the building of the Bitterne bypass. It was only in later years that I realised the fantastic biodiversity and richness of the site, all just a stone's throw from the main road to Portsmouth and a busy shopping centre. But it was too late. The Amazon rainforest had become a concrete jungle of channels, water piped underground and paths suitable for shopping trolleys to trundle down from the supermarket and fill up the pond. The cutting back of the shrubs and trees opened Hum Hole up into parkland. The ecosystem was lost forever, along with my childhood.

Merry Oak
Joan Rolfe

A popular walk in about 1920 was along Merry Oak Lane which ran from the junction of Manor and Sholing Roads, curving between tall trees to the Spring Road/Deacon Road junction. There were fields with blackberry bushes but few buildings in the lane, just Gray's white cottage, Sholing Lodge (owned by the Wilshers) and Goodyear's farm before the estate boundary of Merry Oak House was reached. It was then owned by George Errington who also owned Oak Lodge in Freemantle Common Road, which today is used by Southampton Social Services.

Merry Oak House can be traced back to 1800, and an estate survey dated 1815 produced a 'Plan of an estate called Merry Oak, near Southampton. Land owned by George Errington', listing a cluster of outbuildings including 'Greenhouse, wood house, stables, double coach house, bake house, dairy, laundry, granary, hen house, cow house and piggery'. Obviously, many estate workers would have been needed. The plan also depicts an orchard and stable yard, within which is shown an oak tree, captioned 'The Merry Oak'. Was the estate named after the tree or the tree after the estate? Suggestions are that either some merry-making occurred beneath the tree or that Merry Oak is derived from *Maer-ea-ac*, the oak of the boundary stream.

When the family of George Errington vacated Merry Oak House in the 1920s it fell into disrepair and was demolished. By 1928, there was an acute shortage of affordable housing in Southampton so the 51-acre site was compulsorily purchased for the sum of £32,567 for the erection of council-housing and building started almost immediately. Although it was sad to lose beautiful grounds, the planners' skill ensured the retention of areas of fenced grassland and of many lovely trees, even incorporating their names into the new road names: Acacia, Blackthorn, Cypress, Magnolia, etc. One of the original estate wells survived as a feature, with brick surround and oak-framed roof. There was, and I believe still is, a pond at the rear of Blackthorn Road, which, as a child in the 1930s, I often visited during the building works. A large mulberry tree grew nearby. Many of the numerous visible streams at that time are now piped underground.

The new estate, regarded as probably the most attractive of all council-housing, consisted of varied styles of well-designed houses; those in Merry Oak Lane (later renamed Merry Oak Road) were semi-detached with two reception rooms and usually allocated to larger families. Other houses were smaller, but all had indoor bathrooms. Those applying for tenancies had to produce marriage certificates, evidence of a low income and must have children; so, it being realised initially that these children would create an urgent need for a school, land was set aside and in the mid-1930s a co-educational school was opened. Later, when Sholing Girls' School was built, Merry Oak continued as a boys' school until closure in 1985 when it was demolished apart from the hall and reception building which is now used by the Merry Oak Neighbourhood Community Association.

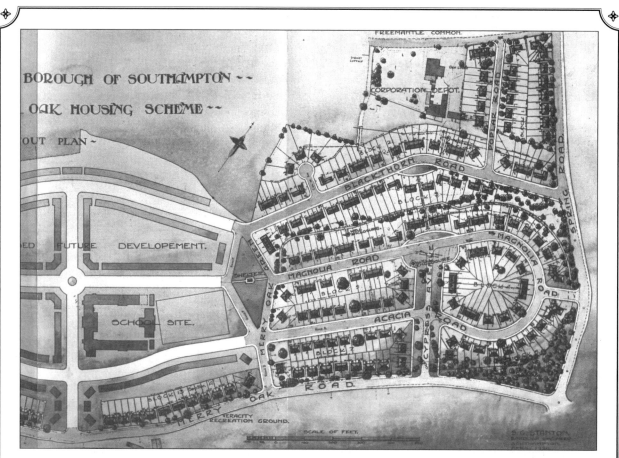

Part of the plan of the Merry Oak Housing Scheme from the book Housing, *c.1930.* (SO'TON CITY ARCHIVES)

Above: *Non-parlour houses in Acacia Road, c.1934.*
(SO'TON CITY ARCHIVES)

Below: *The Merry Oak pub, on the corner of Spring Road and Deacon Road.*

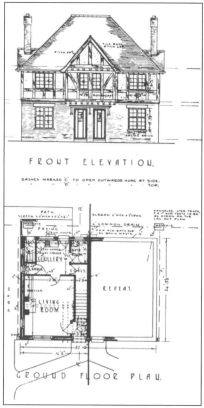

Plans for non-parlour houses to design 21A at Merry Oak.
(SO'TON CITY ARCHIVES)

Elderly people who lived on the estate as children have happy memories of their years at Merry Oak – an attractive and safe place; strictly ruled by park-keepers, the fenced areas were out of bounds, but the Veracity Ground and Freemantle Common provided plenty of space for games.

The estate changed little until some private houses were built in Merry Oak Road and Margam Avenue was developed. Then a Territorial Army drill hall on the corner of Margam Avenue and the Merry Oak public house on the corner of Spring Road were built. In 1939, just before the start of the Second World War, children were evacuated and Merry Oak School stood empty, but, after a while, as civilians had not been subjected to enemy bombing and many children were homesick, a large number returned and the school reopened. Merry Oak and other suburbs were not thought to be targets for bombers, although Thornycrofts and Vickers Supermarine in Woolston – not far away – obviously were.

Spasmodic enemy action throughout the summer of 1940 escalated after the fall of France, with considerable activity over the south of England. Supermarine's aircraft factory was attacked on three separate occasions and almost completely destroyed on Thursday 26 September. Surrounding areas of Woolston were badly hit, bombs were dropped at random in Bitterne but Merry Oak remained unscathed until the night of Saturday 23 November when air-raid sirens sounded just after 6p.m. Hanging flares preceded showers of incendiary bombs, causing many house fires. High-explosive bombs were dropped into this conflagration, which resulted in considerable damage to the little homes of Merry Oak with several families losing their lives; although Anderson shelters had been erected in gardens, many were water-logged and unusable. At midnight, after the raid, the estate was a pitiful sight: smouldering ruins and bomb craters with possessions blown into gardens and trees, water mains shattered and damage to gas supplies all created an air of gloom and sadness everywhere. During the following nights many families trekked into the countryside, sleeping in village halls and barns and returning in the mornings for school or work. Life had to go on.

Some less-sustained air attacks befell Merry Oak during the following years; in June 1941 incendiary bombs on the school destroyed several classrooms by fire, and a large high-explosive bomb made a huge crater in the school field, but, in spite of this, the school continued to function. Damaged houses were demolished, their sites standing empty until after the war; the estate became more unkempt, people were scattered and some original tenants never returned, newcomers taking their place.

When the war ended, rebuilding proceeded slowly owing to shortages of materials and so much needing to be done throughout Southampton, but when the bombed houses of Merry Oak were eventually re-built, they were completely different from those that existed prior to the war. However, the Council later modernised them by interior improvements and adding new windows.

When the government introduced its scheme for sitting tenants to buy their council-houses for a price far less than private house valuations of the time, many tenants seized this opportunity and then upgraded their properties by installing central heating and even building extensions where possible, changing the appearance of the estate yet again. Yet, as the original housing was so well built it still remains attractive to this day. Alas, trees which had been destroyed were not replaced.

No provision was made for car ownership on the Merry Oak estate as this was unheard of for those entitled to become tenants, so at that time the roads were free of parked cars. Today, a vehicle being almost a necessity has resulted in cars, vans, even caravans, standing in and destroying what were once lovely front gardens. These roads have joined almost every road in Southampton by becoming one vast car park; indeed, some roads have now been narrowed to prevent cars speeding through the estate.

In 1961 the only private Community Centre in Southampton was built on the Veracity Ground, financed by a Ministry of Education grant and Woolston Wednesday Football Club. Known as the Festival Hall and run by a Voluntary Management Committee, its present custodian, Mr C. Hannaford, comfitmed that although some activities have been transferred to the Merry Oak Hall, the Festival Hall continues in use as a Senior Citizen's Centre and also provides courses in dressmaking and dog training.

A small group of shops still exists at the top of Merry Oak Road but the older generation will remember Miss Oliver the grocer, the Harrison family at the bakery and Mrs Mills and her daughter at The Dorothea Stores, as well as previous businesses: Florence Trapp and the Uneeda Stores (drapers), John Payne (stationer), Sports Cycles on the corner (now an undertaker), Protheroe the chemist and, of course, Best's fish-and-chip shop where one could buy a pennyworth of chips!

My family were one of the first tenants on the estate, moving to Merry Oak Road in 1930. I remember it well – the attractive houses, friendly neighbours, plenty of playmates and lovely trees to climb, oak trees predominating. The oak was the estate symbol, providing inspiration for the Merry Oak School song, written by Mr Wilkes, a teacher at the school, titled 'Gaudeamus in Robore' (Let us rejoice in the oak). At school assemblies the children shouted out the chorus:

Merry Oak, Merry Oak,
Let us rejoice in the oak –
Gaudeamus in Robore –
MERRY OAK!

The track off West End Road that led to Harefield Farm, by this date (October 1949) demolished. Note the horse-drawn wagon (centre).

(So'TON CITY ARCHIVES)

The same spot in October 1950, the track becoming Beauworth Avenue. *(So'TON CITY ARCHIVES)*

Laying the concrete roads in Harefield in 1950. According to council minutes, concrete was used because of the wet weather. *(So'TON CITY ARCHIVES)*

Type R3 council houses, decorated for the coronation of Queen Elizabeth II, June 1953.

Somerset Gardens Estate Ltd site office and show house, 6 Somerset Avenue, demolished in 2006.

Harefield After the Fire
Keith Marsh

Following the destruction of Harefield House by fire in 1917, the estate, including Newlands Farm, was put up for sale. It was bought by Edwin Jones & Co. Ltd for £14,000. They renewed the farm's lease, and sold off some land at Shales Flats to South Stoneham Rural District Council for building development and a sports field. The Council built some houses in West End Road and Hatley Road, then sold off the remaining plots to local builders such as Haines and H.W. Small. Lloyd & Jenkins homes were in such demand that they could ask for a £50 deposit instead of the usual £25. During the 1920s Edwin Jones joined with several similar stores across the country (including Plummer Roddis) to form the Debenhams consortium, although to keep the family tradition the names weren't changed for another 50 years. Some land and the former indoor riding school were set aside for staff recreational purposes under the control of the Queens Athletic Association, and village functions continued to be held there, whilst produce from the farm stocked the Edwin Jones shops.

In the late 1920s Sidney Kimber, a prominent Southampton alderman, proposed a municipal sports centre for the town. Worried that councillors to the east of the town would not support his plan to buy Red Lodge Farm, he held talks with Edwin Jones about the possible purchase of Harefield as well, but in 1933 the Council approved the purchase of the Bassett site and the Harefield plan was forgotten.

In April 1935 the Newcombe Estate Co. held negotiations over the purchase of all but ten acres of the estate, but Edwin Jones asked £45,000 and the sale fell through. A year later the estate was sold to Charles Cohen of Torquay for £50,000, but he sold the land on to Somerset Garden Estates for £55,000 on 21 December 1936. The retained land was for a smaller recreation-ground and in 1937 plans were submitted for a new wooden pavilion off West End Road, overlooking playing fields. But by June 1939 membership of the QAA was falling, and the club told the Edwin Jones board that it could not pay its way. The company agreed to cancel the club's debts and took possession of the sports ground. In June 1943 Southampton Corporation enquired about purchasing the land for Southern Railway staff, but the sale was not finalised until 1951, and it was instead used for the infant and junior schools. During the war local youths used the old QAA tennis court as a cycle speedway track, and this flat area is still discernable in the far corner of the school playing-field.

Somerset Garden Estates drew up plans to develop Harefield in 1938, with roads being named after towns in that county. They built a show bungalow to use as an estate office (demolished in 2006) whilst building plots were sold off to individual builders, some not being developed until after the Second World War. No. 38 Taunton Drive, built in 1938, was bought new by Mr and Mrs Standen for £600.

During the war undeveloped land was farmed by Mr Best under a contract from the Hampshire Agricultural Executive Committee and he used the first and only tractor on the farm. The war left large areas of Southamptom devastated and many people homeless, so the Corporation acquired several estates, including Harefield, for development. Roads already started retained their Somerset names whilst the layout of the remainder of the estate was changed and the new roads were named after Hampshire villages. Until 1954 Harefield was outside the County Borough so planning permission was needed from Winchester Rural District Council for the houses and flats built by Southampton Council in the early 1950s. Some amenities, such as the church, police houses and nursery schools, did not come to fruition, and because of adverse weather the roads were constructed of concrete as a temporary measure, though some still remain. The neighbourhood centre was built in the 1960s, since when even more homes have been squeezed into Harefield; no doubt this will continue as open spaces (for which Harefield was admired in the 1950s) become scarcer and land prices rise.

Thornhill
Keith Le May

To most Southampton people, Thornhill is synonymous with a large post-1950 council-housing estate, but what preceded it? Along the eastern edge of the map accompanying the 1814 enclosure award for Bitterne is printed 'Thornhill Farm'. This may be the first time that Thornhill appeared in print. The 212-acre farm belonged to William Hallett of Townhill Manor. In 1825 Michael Hoy, a merchant with a Russian company and former sheriff of London, bought the land. It lay within the quadrangle formed by today's Thornhill Park Road, Kanes Hill,

An engraving of Thornhill Park House that accompanied the 1844 sale particulars.
(HANTS RECORD OFFICE, 15M84/P1 FO28)

A view from the BT aerial at Thornhill in 2005, showing Hinkler Road in the mid-foreground, 'bungalow town' and the council estate, and Southampton Water and, finally, the New Forest in the background.

Mon Repos, the home of pioneer aviator Bert Hinkler 1892–1933 (inset) from 1924 to 1933, seen here c.1972. It was dismantled in 1983 and taken to Bundaberg, Australia, where it was rebuilt as a museum to Hinkler.

Bursledon Road and Upper Deacon Road. Hoy died in 1828 with a mansion unfinished.

Hoy's cousin, James Barlow Hoy, a Tory MP for Southampton, inherited and in 1846 his trustees sold it to Henry Dumbleton, a retired judge in the East India Company. Now calling the estate Thornhill Park, he devoted his time to his sheep and cows right up to his death in 1877, aged 94. Colonel Willan, his successor, energetic in public service and a good sportsman, had not only installed a wind-pumped water-supply and steam-generated electricity, but possessed a telephone and a steam car before leaving in 1910. John Campbell, the last owner had, like Hoy and Dumbleton, worked abroad but as a tea and rubber planter in Sri Lanka. His widow, a proficient cellist and pianist and lover of ponies, sold the estate in 1923.

The children living at the mansion remembered with affection some of the employees. Mr and Mrs Busby worked for both the Willans and the Campbells. Mr Busby was head gardener and then bailiff while his wife ran the dairy. Their daughter Mary was a nurse who later lived at Hedge End. Pugsley was a groom who started with Mrs Campbell at the age of 14. Also remembered were Mrs Colbourne the housekeeper and Tarrant the butler who became head carver at Tyrell and Green's restaurant.

From 1926 The Close and some groups of houses on the north side of Thornhill Park Road were built to designs by the highly respected Herbert Collins. On the south side, 'Bungalow Town', in the usual grid fashion, was begun in 1931 and soon afterwards came shops on the same side. Electricity was laid on in 1934. Schoolchildren were bussed to West End, in which parish the area then lay. A church hall was built in Cowper Road in 1938 but not used for worship until after the Second World War.

In these years two local residents in particular became well known. Herbert Hinkler, the pioneering aviator from Australia, came to A.V. Roe's Hamble factory as a test pilot. (Alliot Verdon Roe, incidentally, had been a guest at the Campbell's parties.) On a plot on the southern edge of the estate Hinkler built 'Mon Repos' which much later became 29 Lydgate Road until its dismantling and transhipment for reassembly in Hinkler's home town. This adventurous character made record-breaking long-distance solo flights until his fatal crash in the Alps in 1933.

William Candy, after whom Candy Lane is named, belonged to a large local family. In 1923 he bought Thornhill farmhouse and 57 acres where he grew soft fruit and kept cows and bees. On the latter he was an authority. In 1937 he sold all but two acres but continued to ride a bicycle and drive his Ford 'Tin Lizzie' to do his work as parish councillor, insurance agent and local secretary of the Ancient Order of Foresters. He died in 1952 aged 87.

In which direction did local people look for their needs? The Hoys had strong connections with Southampton and used South Stoneham Church. Henry Dumbleton traded his animals at Botley but was buried at Bitterne. The Willans had their horses shod in Bitterne and their coal brought up from Bitterne Station by farm wagons, but left from Botley Station for their Scottish shooting and fishing holidays and traded with a Botley butcher. Their doctor came from Southampton. The Campbells' doctor also came from Southampton, but they were regular customers of Lankester & Crook at Hedge End and worshipped there at St John's. It was for Botley that Candy was a councillor. It must be remembered, of course, that Botley and Hedge End are nearer Thornhill than Southampton and the road is less hilly.

Estate properties surviving today are the keeper's lodge on the southern edge of Dumbleton's copse, part of the farmhouse, and a pair of cottages opposite it, now Nos 311 and 313 Thornhill Park Road. Along this road outside the estate boundary had been built Thornfield, the home for many years of Lt Col Bucknill but nowadays belonging to the Royal British Legion.

With a pressing need for new council-housing the City Council obtained permission to expand the city boundary in 1954 to include the old estate. Then it bought the undeveloped part. Leon Berger, the City

The church hall at the upper end of Cowper Road, c.1972.

The former Thornhill farmhouse survives near Thornhill roundabout, 2005.

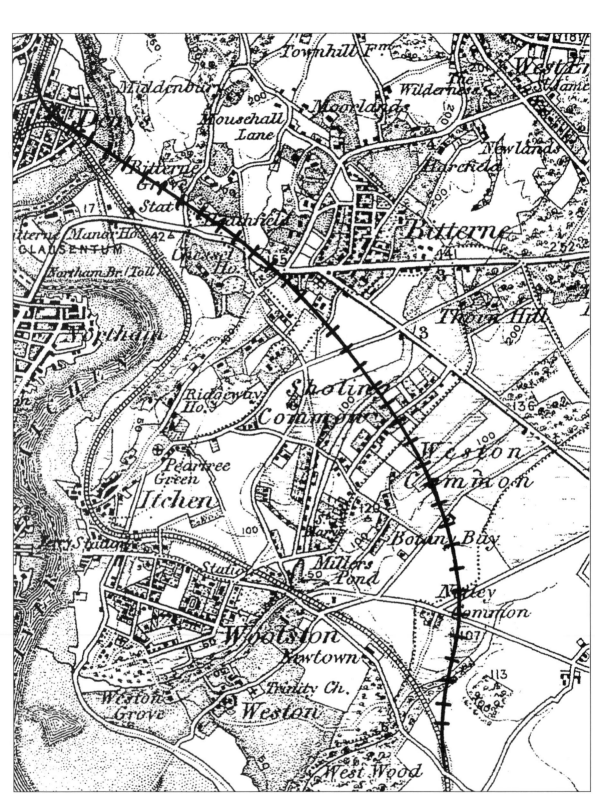

An 1877 map showing the eventual route of the railway through Woolston, on which is shown the proposed route across Sholing and Weston Commons.

(ORDNANCE SURVEY 1-INCH TO 1-MILE MAP, SHEET 315)

Architect, rejected, as he had done previously in Millbrook for instance, the old grid system of building and, using the sloping landscape to good effect, extended the already started Hinkler Road as a spine road, bringing it sweeping down on a curve from the north, across the shallow valley and up and back on itself to Bursledon Road. The stream which it crossed was buried.

By building a mixture of houses and multi-storey blocks a relatively high population density was achieved whilst retaining much open space and valuable tree screens, giving an interesting visual impact. The pre-war practice of naming roads after literary figures was continued. Now within the city, the usual urban facilities have been provided. Ecclesiastically the area has full parish status with a population of about 10,000. It is free from commercial development apart from a small area bordering Bursledon Road.

Some 40 years on, Thornhill is now enjoying a rejuvenation financed by a New Deal for Communities grant of £48.7 million, with the residents' own elected committee deciding how the money is spent.

The Railway and What Might Have Been
Keith Marsh

The railway came to Bitterne in 1866, or rather nearly came! The main line from London to Southampton opened in 1839, forming part of the London & South Western Railway and prompting other schemes. Over several decades many new lines were considered but rejected. One was the 1859 proposal by Southampton & Fareham Railway Company which deposited plans for a line from Fareham, via Warsash and Netley, to a terminus at Woolston, but this was withdrawn in February 1860. By autumn that year other schemes existed including one linking Petersfield, Botley and Woolston, and another from Portswood to Netley. Companies jostled for control of the potential routes to Southampton Docks, the LSWR facing competition from the GWR, LBSCR, and from smaller companies. Initially opposing the Southampton & Netley Railway Company's plan, the LSWR reconsidered when advised to 'adopt' the line, and absorbed the company in 1865.

The Southampton & Netley Railway Company's original route would leave the LSWR line just north of St Denys Road bridge, climb to cross the River Itchen slightly downstream of that built, rise on a 1 in 75 gradient to the north of Bitterne Road, through Hum Hole to the top of Lances Hill then to descend at 1 in 200, crossing Deacon Road, North East Road and Butts Road, to Netley. Despite the engineering work involved (a 140yd bridge and cuttings 56ft deep, on a line only 4.7 miles long) the authorised capital of £64,000 seems low, possibly reflecting the

ease with which the company expected to purchase the land; Thomas Chamberlayne owned much of it and was one of the company's backers. On 1 August 1861 an Act of Parliament authorised construction of the line, based on plans drawn up by the company's engineer, Mr Harkness. However, in the autumn, he was replaced by I.H. Tolme of Galbraith and Tolme (an LSWR associated company) who estimated that £24,000 could be saved by amending the route to approximately that of today, avoiding Bitterne itself. On 22 June 1863 a further Act was passed; one wonders how differently Bitterne would have developed had the route not been changed. Another Act on 14 July 1864 changed the junction at Portswood (renamed St Denys in 1876) so that trains ran from Netley into Southampton, not towards London.

Considerable difficulties were experienced building the viaduct and bridge over the River Itchen, due to the nature of the river bed. The bridge consists of three 115ft openings, with main girders supported by two pairs of iron cylinders sunk into the bed, one to a depth of 60ft, filled with concrete to sea level, then topped with masonry, giving shipping a clearance of 20ft at ordinary high tides, presumably to satisfy the operators of the Winchester barges. Pedestrian use was prohibited by a clause to counter opposition from the Northam Bridge Company, who feared loss of revenue. The *Southampton Times* gave details of the bridge:

About 270 tons of cast iron was used on constructing the cylinders for the piers and about 300 tons of wrought iron in the girders, the entire cost of the viaduct being about £15,000. At either end of the viaduct and over each pier are the Southampton arms and the bridge at night is illuminated by gas for which four ornamental columns have been erected.

The line was constructed as single-track, with a passing loop on the down side at Bitterne, so necessitating two platforms. Positioning the loop here seems strange, Woolston being nearer the line's mid-point, but it may have assisted in train working at Portswood, which then only had two platforms. An iron station building was planned for Bitterne, but instead one of red brick (modest compared with Woolston and Netley) was constructed on the down platform, with a wooden shelter on the up. Initially called Northam Road for Bitterne, the station was named Bitterne Road when the line opened; the LSWR had a policy of suffixing 'Road' to the name of stations away from the area they served: Beaulieu Road, Lyndhurst Road, etc. The change to Bitterne was made in November 1896 when residential development increased in the vicinity. Close to the station, the main Bitterne Road had to be raised by 14ft, being carried over the railway by a girder

Bitterne Stationmaster Henry Gaiger (centre) *with his four-man staff, c.1925.*

An idyllic rural scene as a train passes between the Chessel estate and Chessel Bay, and approaches Bitterne Station, c.1920.

Bitterne Station c.1906, looking towards St Denys.

bridge, to which alterations were made in 1910 and in 1931/32. Until 1903, when the present footbridge was built, passengers crossed the track via a foot crossing. Also on the down platform was a signal-box, built low enough to give the signalman visibility under the bridge; it was closed on 10 October 1966 and demolished in 1969. Just to the south of the road bridge is another bridge, built to give the farmer at Little Chessel access to the fields across the line. The line then climbs gradually as it follows the east bank of the river towards Woolston.

When the line was examined by the Board of Trade Inspector on 22 February 1866 he reported several items incomplete, so it was not opened until 5 March. The service that year consisted of eight trips each way, Monday to Saturday, with three on Sunday, the journey taking nine minutes from Southampton Docks Station (later Southampton Terminus) to

The railway was an obvious target for the Luftwaffe's bombers and its course alongside the river made locating it simple. Workman are here repairing the tracks in June 1942.

147

Bitterne Road and another 14 to Netley; a typical train consisted of six four-wheeled coaches and a brake van hauled by a tank engine, the timetable enabling the service to be operated by a single train. Fares from Bitterne Road to Southampton Docks were 4d. (first class), 3d. (second) and 2d. (third); double that to Netley.

The line from Netley to Fareham opened on 2 September 1889 and until April 1911 it remained single track, with passing loops at Bitterne, Netley and Swanwick. At Bitterne, the north end of the loop led into a head shunt giving access to two sidings. In 1899, St Denys was extensively altered by adding two new platforms serving the Fareham line; the service then consisted of a dozen trains each way, five starting at Southampton West (now Southampton Central), and most running through to Portsmouth.

In 1902 Bitterne Station building was enlarged, and, to improve the small goods yard, land was acquired including a house that became 117 MacNaghten Road. The stationhouse was let to station staff whilst 117 became the stationmaster's home. Until 1895, when Bitterne Park became part of Southampton, MacNaghten Road was called Station Road. Donald Finlay, the Olympic 110m hurdler who won a bronze medal at the 1932 Los Angeles Olympics and silver in 1936 at Berlin, was brought up at No. 115.

The line was doubled through to Bitterne on 27 February 1910, then from Bitterne to Woolston on 10 April, the original line becoming the up line and the passing loop forming part of the down. Cross-overs provided access to the goods yard, and an additional siding was laid behind the down platform, giving yard capacity of 18 wagons. Whereas from many stations the railway provided a delivery service, here it was contracted for many years to Mr Rockett of Pound Street, who collected goods from the station, delivering them by horse and cart. For a while there was a short private siding to serve the British Petroleum Company and the Colliery Supply Company Ltd which had a small wooden office at the station yard entrance. The goods yard closed on 13 July 1959, the tracks being removed three years later.

During the Second World War the Luftwaffe found the railway line around Chessel Bay an easy target, with the line's proximity to the Woolston factories, shown by damage suffered in June 1942.

In the 1950s the civil engineer for the railway negotiated with Southampton Corporation to use an area adjacent to Peartree Green as a tip for waste materials. Sidings were installed, the tip being used from December 1954 until August 1955 and from June 1956 to June 1976, after which the sidings were removed. The waste is now buried and the area landscaped.

In 1957 steam engines on local lines were replaced by Hampshire diesel electric multiple units with improved services in timings and frequency, but to some people the excitement of rail travel was lost. Gas lamps on the station produced a mellow light, welcoming, on a February night in the 1960s a group of party-goers in costume, who decided to shelter from the cold before going up Lances Hill in the heavy snow. The gas lighting was replaced by electric in 1968.

Colour-light signalling was introduced on 9 March 1980, replacing the old semaphore signals, and in 1989 the third-rail was laid ready for electric trains in May 1990. Coincident with electrification, the station became unstaffed, the station building boarded up and the wooden hut on the up platform demolished. Passengers are now protected from the weather by two bus-stop-type shelters and get information via a two-way radio link, if working.

In 1923 the LSWR became part of Southern Railways, one of the 'Big Four' railway companies that were nationalised to form British Railways in 1948. In 1972 a 'leak' in the *Sunday Times* revealed plans to abandon the line, which at the time was reliant on a government subsidy, but it survived. In 1993 privatisation of the railways began, and the infrastructure is now in the hands of Network Rail, whilst train services through Bitterne are currently provided by operating companies South West Trains, Wessex Trains and Southern.

Chapter Ten

The BLHS Story

Although the BLHS was constituted in 1981, its seeds were sown during the previous decade. A teenager by the name of Ian Abrahams began to amass a collection, not just of pictures and documents relating to Bitterne, but of objects too, such as old cash registers, kitchen utensils, signs and sweet machines, much of it collected on a tradesman's hand-cart. This was a time of great change: wartime austerity was now a memory and every conceivable item was changing. Wood, bakelite, glass, rubber and leather were giving way to the lighter, cheaper plastics and alloys.

In 1977 Ian moved into the old Manse in Dean Road and set up a museum in the front room displaying the many artifacts that he had accrued. He held several exhibitions in the United Reformed Church hall and began giving illustrated talks about Bitterne. These seemed to strike a chord with local people who attended in their hundreds, bringing with them more items for Ian's collection and their memories of the past.

One of the most supportive people was Irene Pilson (née Randall-Coles). Born in 1910 at Ailsa Villas, Brook Road, she married and moved to a newly built bungalow in Hatley Road; even after moving to Curdridge in 1961, Irene never lost her love of Bitterne, and corresponded regularly with her many friends. It was her letter published in the *Southern Evening Echo* in 1969 which led her to write her books, as she had replies from former Bitterne people all over the world, keen to rekindle memories.

Interest in Bitterne was further stimulated in the *Echo* by excellent articles penned by John Edgar Mann and Peter Carne, and following several meetings, the BLHS was formed in June 1981, under the chairmanship of Ian Abrahams.

In 1982 the Manse had to be vacated to make way for the bypass, and an appeal was launched to raise money for a permanent home for the rapidly growing collection: the bypass was cutting a swathe

Doreen Snaith and Jeanne Nicol staff the book stall and display at the 1997 Southampton Balloon Festival.

Above: *Members of the BLHS before their annual summer fete in 1986. Standing, left to right: 'Happy' Thwaites, Esme Cremona, Norman Planken, Irene Pilson, Joan Holt, Nick Cuffley (the lion), Vera and Bert Instone, Jack Hasler, George Brennan, Violet O'Rourke, Bill Hulbert, Dorrie Williams, Bob Payne, Marjorie O'Halloran, June Ellwood (who stitched the banners), Cis Hallett, Keith Ellwood, Barbara Wright, Kit Watson, Alice Brennan, Phil Tonry, Jean Abrahams, Lily Gurman;* sitting: *Mark and Simon Morris, Mildred Russell, Daphne Toogood, Dorothy Purver, Janet Planken.*

Below: *The BLHS Heritage Centre and Charity Shop at 225 Peartree Avenue opened in 1993.*

Founder member Jack Hasler in the Heritage Centre where he helped numerous visitors with their research until his passing in 2003.

through the village and items such as foundation-stones and shop fittings were desperately retrieved. Vice-chairman of the society was Bob Payne of R.C. Payne & Son, and for several years he allowed the BLHS to use his shop as a base. It was here that Irene Pilson launched her first book *Memories of Bitterne* in 1984; at the time she said 'I have had to leave out much more than I could put in' and so *More Memories…* was published a few years later. There can be few other areas which have had so much of their past faithfully recorded by one person and we owe a great debt of gratitude to her.

Another activist was local historian John Holt who had written an account of the area's 2,000 year history, *A Bend in the River,* for the festival which Bitterne Parish Church held in October 1973. In April 1982 he led the first of many walkabouts around Bitterne, pointing out features of historical relevance. That year also saw the first 'roadshow', with Bill Hulbert, Irene Pilson, George Brennan and Mildred Russell taking a display to Moorhill School.

In 1983 the BLHS were invited to put a permanent exhibition and research centre in the study room of Bitterne (then Eastern) Library, which remained for

several years. Another achievement that year was the publication of the society's first book *Bitterne: A Village Remembered*, and this has been followed by several more books plus a series of over 30 local papers.

The 1980s was a busy decade for the society as members ran many 'village' events to raise funds such as Ye Olde Bitterne Fayres and Christmas markets, in costume of course. And the society was an eager supporter of the revived Bitterne carnival. The pinnacle of 1987 must surely have been the society's success in saving Bitterne's last thatched cottage.

By the early 1990s the collection was immense and, with no likelihood of a permanent home, the suggestion was made that a shop be rented, and in 1993 No. 225 Peartree Avenue was opened as a charity shop and heritage centre, the latter part being subsidised by the former. The opening was performed by Irene under the direction of the Peartree village crier, Mike Isaacs. Three years later, when 231 Peartree Avenue became vacant and with space ever short, it was decided to expand by moving the shop (which is half local history books, etc., half second-hand goods) to 231, leaving 225 as a heritage and study centre. But a large proportion of our collection remains in storage.

Above: *Woodlands School students Kerry Hodgson and Matt Romo, with Culture Secretary Chris Smith and TV personality Tony Robinson, borrowed an ARP helmet and pump for the launch of the Local History Initiative in London, February 2000.*

Below: *More storage required! Lloyd & Jenkins were much respected builders for over 75 years. In October 2006 Mrs Mary Jenkins decided to dispose of the firm's workshops in Commercial Street, but first invited the BLHS to rescue any worthy items: what a task! Here Mr Gordon Jacobs, the firm's last employee (who had worked for them since leaving school) surveys the articles selected. Sadly Mrs Jenkins passed away a month later.*

Tom Misselbrook, BLHS President since 1981, with daughter Diane and granddaughter Jemma, cutting the BLHS Christmas cake in 1999. For five decades Misselbrook's Car Sales provided local people with their 'set of wheels'.

A trip to the National Tramway Museum at Crich, April 2006. Southampton Corporation tram 45 was bought by the LRTL for £10 in 1948 and became the first tram to be preserved at Crich. Admired here by Bill and June Monk, Ray Marsh, Dorothy Smith and Peter Shorter amongst others, it was run specially for the society.

We have made several attempts at securing a permanent home, the attempt to acquire 11 Dean Road being the most significant, but with property prices soaring, the dream of a museum for Bitterne remains just a dream.

For 26 years the BLHS has been raising awareness of the history of Bitterne by regular meetings, giving talks, helping with research, coach trips, loaning items and giving talks to schools, and publications (including a quarterly magazine). With over 250 members, it is now one of the largest and most respected of local history societies.

Epilogue

On 15 October 2006 there was a special service to mark the 200th anniversary of Methodism in Bitterne. Among the invited guests was a former minister of Bitterne Methodist Church, Revd Mike Walling, who ended his prayers in the service with these words:

Today we pray especially for this local community of Bitterne, that its rich history may continue into the future, bearing the fruits of neighbourliness, justice and compassion.

A photograph, recently donated by the Jenkins family, that perfectly illustrates the transformation of Bitterne from rural landscape to residential townscape. Taken c.1935, from the hill below Mousehole Copse, the view is looking east towards Cobden Crescent where houses are being built. Glenfield Avenue is just visible to the right, centre background is the flat-roof of 'Over the Hill' in Mousehole Lane, and the outhouses (left background) are at St Mary's College. (Jenkins family)

Subscribers

Chris and Mary Abraham, Bitterne

Frank Abraham, Bitterne, Southampton

Mr and Mrs J. R. Abraham, Mona Vale, NSW, Australia

Jean Abrahams (née Brown), Bitterne

In Memory of Bob Axford, Fair Oak (Formerly Bitterne)

Mrs Muriel Barfoot, Bitterne, Southampton

Julie D. Barker, Southampton, Hampshire

Martyn Basford, Bitterne

Marilyn Bechter (née Chalk), Woodfalls, Wiltshire

Ella G. Beer, Sholing, Southampton

Chris J. Beezley, Bath, Somerset

Mr Tom Raymond Bemister, Bitterne, Southampton

Gordon Birch and Family

Doreen C. Bloodworth, Warsash, Hampshire

Peter and Jan Boyd-Smith, Bitterne

Edward Bridle, West End

Hazel M. Brooks, Rownhams, Southampton

Ted Broomfield, Sholing, Southampton

Jim Brown, Sholing

Mrs Ena L. Butler, Bitterne, Southampton

Janice Butler, Itchen

Janet Caplen, Braintree, Essex

Jean Carey (née Holley), Rownhams, Southampton

John C. Carter, Bitterne

Mr and Mrs A.M. Chalk, Tattenhall, Cheshire

C.M. Christison, Bitterne Manor House

Pauline Churcher, Harefield, Southampton

Carol Churcher, Harefield, Southampton

Mary and Peter Clifford, Bitterne, Sholing

Mr Martin Charles Clift & Mr Jai John William Mitchell, Midanbury, Southampton

Joan V. Collis, Bitterne, Hants

Ian Cooper, Bitterne, Hampshire

Dawn I.V. Cooper

Keith Cooper, Hawley, Hampshire

Malcolm S. Corbidge, Eynham Avenue, Bitterne

Beryl Cordell, St Elizabeths, Bitterne

Patrick and Sheila Corkery, Hedge End

R. Cornwall, Bitterne, Hampshire

Laurence and Marie Crawley

Bob Crease, Bitterne Park

Margaret Crous (née Long), South Africa

Teresa M. Cruickshank (née Mist), Woolston, Southampton

Laura and Jenny Davis, Bitterne

Rose and Bill Dawson, Bitterne, Southampton

Dawson Family

Elsie De'ath, Romford, Essex

Kathleen Dixon (née Cross), Maidstone

Margaret R. Donaldson, Bognor Regis, West Sussex

Norman W. Doughty, Bitterne, Southampton

Ronald J. Downer

Peter and Jill Dreyer

Alan. R. Drysdall, Bitterne

George and Joyce Dymott

Marie Edmunds (née Whitlock), Hedge End

Mrs Ena M. Etall, Bitterne, Southampton

Louise Evans, Blaengarw, S. Wales

John and Margaret Farley, Durley,
    Southampton

Mr Reginald Stanley Forder and Mrs Sylvia
    Marjorie Forder, Bitterne, Hampshire

Ronald Fry, Bitterne, Hampshire

Vic and Carol Funnell, Bitterne Road East

Bert Gatehouse (In memory of 'Bitterne Bert'),
    Bitterne, Southampton

Graham Andrew Gentry, Bitterne, Hampshire

Renee George Gentry, Woolston, Hampshire

Rennie Gentry, Itchen

Mrs Mollie Giles, Bitterne

Daisy Golding

Martin Gulliver, Abingdon, Oxfordshire

Doreen and Jim Gulliver, Bitterne

Douglas and Dorothy Hague, Bitterne,
    Southampton

Mrs Joan Haizelden, Bitterne, Hampshire

Mrs Keren Haizelden, Bitterne, Hampshire

Mrs Doreen Hall (née Thorn), Whites Road

Colin Hamerton, Bitterne, Hants

Mr D.R. Hankins and Lady H.M. Hankins

Joan and Ted Hannaford (née Elphinstone),
    Wimborne

Sara-Jane Harris, Bitterne Manor, Hampshire

Janet S. Hart (née Butler), Bitterne

Lorna (Bovey) Henderson, Fair Oak

Mr David Hewitt, Bitterne Park

Douglas Hewitt, Bitterne Park, Southampton

Derek A.G. Hindle

Darren Hinson, Bitterne

Eric E. Holley, Bitterne, Southampton

Sue Hollis, Bitterne, Hampshire

Laura E. Holloway, Bitterne, Hampshire

Barbara Jennifer House, Bitterne, Southampton

Mr Nigel Hunter, Bitterne, Southampton,
    Hampshire

D. Jacobs, Bitterne, Hampshire

Miss Marion James, Bitterne

Professor Michael Jones, Trondheim, Norway

Janet and Bryan King

Michael Hamilton and Vivienne Lamb,
    Bitterne, Hampshire

Mrs G Lamb, formerly of Bitterne, Hampshire

Michael J. Lambert, Bitterne, Hampshire

Brian Lamerton, Bitterne

Alison Large (née Long), Bitterne

Bob Lavington

Keith Le May, Bitterne, Southampton

Ken Lockyer, Bitterne, Southampton

Patrick R.A. Lonnon, Bitterne, Hants

Chris Lyons, Thornhill, Southampton

Dorothy and Ray Marsh, Bitterne

Julie, Keith, Vickie and Suzie Marsh, Harefield

Kate Martin, Dean Road, Bitterne

Alan and Christine Matthews, Sholing,
    Southampton

Celia and John Mayo, Bitterne

McCaffery Girls, Bitterne

Christine M. McWilliams, Bitterne, Hampshire

Doreen Medley, Southampton, Hampshire

John W.J. Mist, Portswood, Southampton

James (Jim) B. Mist, Southampton

Lucy V. Mist, Bitterne, Southampton

Benjamin (Ben) N.J. Mist, Bitterne Park,
    Southampton

Denis Mitchell, Weston, Southampton

Denise Mutton, Mevagissey

Mrs Sandra Naish, Bitterne, Southampton

Jeanne Nicol, West End

Sandra Noice, Southampton, Hants

Andrew James O'Brien, Bitterne, Hants

Madge E. K. Oldfield

Osment Family

Mrs Margaret Peppitt

Chris de la Perrelle, Bedchester, Dorset

Rose-Marie Ann Petty

Mrs G. Price (née Cox), Yatton, Bristol

Ken Prior, Bitterne, Hampshire

Miss Catriona Ratcliff, Swaythling,
  Southampton

Roy and Monica Reardon, Sholing,
  Southampton

Eric and Liz Reed, Thornhill

Alec A. Remsbery, Bitterne

Norman. H.C. Rendell, Bitterne

Joan M. Rickards, Bitterne, Hampshire

Araminta (Minty) Beth Ringshaw Dowle,
  Bitterne

Mrs Sylvia Roberts, Bitterne

Paul C. Roberts, Microsoft, Seattle

Brian Robertson, Bitterne

Andrew Robertson, Bitterne

Aubrey Robertson, Bitterne, Southampton

Christopher Robertson, Faversham, Kent

Joan H. Robinson, Bitterne, Hants

Howard and Peter Robinson, Bitterne, Hants

Mrs Thelma Robinson, Fair Oak, Hampshire

Howard Rogers and Family, Butchers, Bitterne

Jim and Lin Rose

Henry Ross-Osborne, Bitterne, Hants

Elizabeth Rothery, Bursledon

P.R. Russell, Bitterne 1918-1989

Percy Russell, Bitterne, Southampton

Ron Sandells

Barbara R. Scott, Caxton Ave, Bitterne

John and Sharman Sheaf, Hampton, Middx

Miriam and John, Sholing Reupholstery Service

Mary and Pete Shorter, Bitterne

Raymond Simpson

Rita and Charles Sivier, Midanbury

John Sly, Godson of Bitterne Brewery proprietor

Robert and Jean Smith, Bitterne, Hants

Maureen A. Smith, Merryoak

Southampton Society of Model Engineers Ltd

John M. Stockley, Bitterne

Mr L. Stockley, Ironside Court, Hamton Street,
  Southampton

Liz and Fred Storey, Bitterne

Fanny Sweetland, Bitterne Park, Hampshire

Mr R. Tarry, Bitterne, Hampshire

Valerie Telford, Bitterne

Nick and Linda Tuck, Bitterne, Southampton

Mrs A. Turtle, Eastleigh, Hampshire

Mrs Mary Tyrrell (née McLean), Bitterne

Arthur Vail, Bitterne, Hampshire

Pamela V. Walker, Bitterne, Hampshire

John F.W. Walling, Newton Abbot, Devon

Ian and Sue Ward

Lesley Watson, Sydney, Australia

Mrs Gillian Watson, Bitterne, Hants

Dorothy Watters (née Grant), Cornwall

George West, Southampton

Joyce Mary White, Bitterne Village

Charles John White, Lee on the Solent,
  Hampshire

Rosaleen Wilkinson, Shirley, Southampton

W.F. Willsher, Bitterne Park, Hampshire

A. F. J. Wilson

Heather Wood, Southampton

Melissa Claire Woods,

The Yardley Family, Bitterne

June Young, Bitterne, Southampton

Further Titles

For information regarding up-to-date availability,
please check our website at www.halsgrove.com

The Book of Addiscombe • Canning and Clyde Road
Residents Association and Friends

The Book of Addiscombe, Vol. II • Canning and Clyde Road
Residents Association and Friends

The Book of Ashburton • Stuart Hands and Pete Webb

The Book of Axminster with Kilmington • Les Berry
and Gerald Gosling

The Book of Axmouth & the Undercliff •
Ted Gosling and Mike Clement

The Book of Bakewell • Trevor Brighton

The Book of Bampton • Caroline Seward

The Book of Barnstaple • Avril Stone

The Book of Barnstaple, Vol. II • Avril Stone

The Book of Beaminster • Beaminster Museum

The Book of The Bedwyns • Bedwyn History Society

The Book of Bere Regis • Rodney Legg and John Pitfield

The Book of Bergh Apton • Geoffrey I. Kelly

The Book of Bickington • Stuart Hands

The Book of Bideford • Peter Christie and Alison Grant

Blandford Forum: A Millennium Portrait • Blandford Forum
Town Council

The Book of Bitterne • Bitterne Local Historical Society

The Book of Blofield • Barbara Pilch

The Book of Boscastle • Rod and Anne Knight

The Book of Bourton-on-the-Hill, Batsford and Sezincote •
Allen Firth

The Book of Bramford • Bramford Local History Group

The Book of Breage & Germoe • Stephen Polglase

The Book of Bridestowe • D. Richard Cann

The Book of Bridgwater • Roger Evans

The Book of Bridport • Rodney Legg

The Book of Brixham • Frank Pearce

The Book of Brundall • Barbara Ayers and Group

The Book of Buckfastleigh • Sandra Coleman

The Book of Buckland Monachorum & Yelverton •
Pauline Hamilton-Leggett

The Book of Budleigh Salterton • D. Richard Cann

The Book of Carharrack • Carharrack Old
Cornwall Society

The Book of Carshalton • Stella Wilks and Gordon
Rookledge

The Book of Carhampton • Hilary Binding

The Parish Book of Cerne Abbas • Vivian and
Patricia Vale

The Book of Chagford • Iain Rice

The Book of Chapel-en-le-Frith • Mike Smith

*The Book of Chittlehamholt with
Warkleigh & Satterleigh* • Richard Lethbridge

The Book of Chittlehampton • Various

The Book of Codford • Romy Wyeth

The Book of Colney Heath • Bryan Lilley

The Book of Constantine • Moore and Trethowan

The Book of Cornwood and Lutton • Compiled by
the People of the Parish

The Book of Crediton • John Heal

The Book of Creech St Michael • June Small

The Book of Crowcombe, Bicknoller and Sampford Brett •
Maurice and Joyce Chidgey

The Book of Crudwell • Tony Pain

The Book of Cullompton • Compiled by the People
of the Parish

The Second Book of Cullompton • Compiled by the People
of the Parish

The Book of Dawlish • Frank Pearce

*The Book of Dulverton, Brushford,
Bury & Exebridge* • Dulverton and District Civic Society

The Book of Dunster • Hilary Binding

The Book of Easton • Easton Village History Project

The Book of Edale • Gordon Miller

The Ellacombe Book • Sydney R. Langmead

The Book of Elmsett • Elmsett Local History Group

The Book of Exmouth • W.H. Pascoe

✦ FURTHER TITLES ✦

The Book of Fareham • Lesley Burton and Brian Musselwhite

The Book of Grampound with Creed • Bane and Oliver

The Book of Gosport • Lesley Burton and Brian Musselwhite

The Book of Haughley • Howard Stephens

The Book of Hayle • Harry Pascoe

The Book of Hayling Island & Langstone • Peter Rogers

The Book of Helston • Jenkin with Carter

The Book of Hemyock • Clist and Dracott

The Book of Herne Hill • Patricia Jenkyns

The Book of Hethersett • Hethersett Society Research Group

The Book of High Bickington • Avril Stone

The Book of Homersfield • Ken Palmer

The Book of Honiton • Gerald Gosling

The Book of Ilsington • Dick Wills

The Book of Kessingland • Maureen and Eric Long

The Book of Kingskerswell • Carsewella Local History Group

The Book of Lamerton • Ann Cole and Friends

Lanner, A Cornish Mining Parish • Sharron Schwartz and Roger Parker

The Book of Leigh & Bransford • Malcolm Scott

The Second Book of Leigh & Bransford • Malcolm Scott

The Book of Litcham with Lexham & Mileham • Litcham Historical and Amenity Society

The Book of Llangain • Haydn Williams

The Book of Loddiswell • Loddiswell Parish History Group

The Book of Looe • Mark Camp

The New Book of Lostwithiel • Barbara Fraser

The Book of Lulworth • Rodney Legg

The Book of Lustleigh • Joe Crowdy

The Book of Lydford • Compiled by Barbara Weeks

The Book of Lyme Regis • Rodney Legg

The Book of Manaton • Compiled by the People of the Parish

The Book of Markyate • Markyate Local History Society

The Book of Mawnan • Mawnan Local History Group

The Book of Meavy • Pauline Hemery

The Book of Mere • Dr David Longbourne

The Book of Minehead with Alcombe • Binding and Stevens

The Book of Monks Orchard and Eden Park • Ian Muir and Pat Manning

The Book of Morchard Bishop • Jeff Kingaby

Mount Batten – The Flying Boats of Plymouth • Gerald Wasley

The Book of Mulbarton • Jill and David Wright

The Book of Mylor • Mylor Local History Group

The Book of Narborough • Narborough Local History Society

The Book of Newdigate • John Callcut

The Book of Newtown • Keir Foss

The Book of Nidderdale • Nidderdale Museum Society

The Book of Northlew with Ashbury • Northlew History Group

The Book of North Newton • J.C. and K.C. Robins

The Book of North Tawton • Baker, Hoare and Shields

The Book of Notting Hill • Melvin Wilkinson

The Book of Nynehead • Nynehead & District History Society

The Book of Okehampton • Roy and Ursula Radford

The Book of Ottery St Mary • Gerald Gosling and Peter Harris

The Book of Paignton • Frank Pearce

The Book of Penge, Anerley & Crystal Palace • Peter Abbott

The Book of Peter Tavy with Cudlipptown • Peter Tavy Heritage Group

The Book of Pimperne • Jean Coull

The Book of Plymtree • Tony Eames

The Book of Poole • Rodney Legg

The Book of Porchfield & Locks Green • Keir Foss

The Book of Porlock • Dennis Corner

The Book of Portland • Rodney Legg

Postbridge – The Heart of Dartmoor • Reg Bellamy

The Book of Priddy • Albert Thompson

The Book of Princetown • Dr Gardner-Thorpe

The Book of Probus • Alan Kent and Danny Merrifield

The Book of Rattery • By the People of the Parish

The Book of Roadwater, Leighland and Treborough • Clare and Glyn Court

The Book of St Audries • Duncan Stafford